PRAISE FOR *The*

T0115990

"Jenkins is one of America's to
—*Forbes*

". . . persuasively and cogently argued . . . marvelously accessible for the lay reader and replete with fascinating details to help personalize the ambitious sweep of global history Jenkins undertakes. This is an important counterweight to previous histories that have focused almost exclusively on Christianity in the West."
—*Publishers Weekly,* starred review

"Philip Jenkins's marvelous new book . . . tells the largely forgotten story of Nisibis, and thousands of sites like it, which stretch from Morocco to Kenya to India to China, and which were, deep into the second millennium, the heart of the church. While Christians will be particularly concerned with this story, it will be of interest to, and significant for, far more than they.
—*The Weekly Standard*

"In leaner, clearer prose than ever before, Jenkins outlines and analyzes this history, which few present-day Christians have even heard of."
—*Booklist*

"Beyond its useful correctives to standard church histories, the book also probes the meaning of Middle Eastern Christianity's long history. Jenkins shows, for example, that much can be learned about inter-religious strife in the twenty-first century by heeding the history of Christian communities that lived intermingled among Muslims for centuries."
—*Books & Culture* (Favorite Books of 2008)

"*The Lost History of Christianity* is a fascinating study of the first thousand-plus years of the church—a church rooted in the Middle East, Africa, and Asia. We have much to learn from the tale of its reach, its particular way of being Christian, and its eventual decomposition "
—*Beliefnet.com* (One of the Best Religious Books of 2008)

"Jenkins's well-crafted new volume, filled as one has come to expect from the author with a good number of provocative insights, is not only a welcome addition to the literature on Christianity as a truly global religion, to which he has already made substantial contributions, but also an invitation to retrieve a forgotten chapter of history that has not inconsiderable relevance to current events."

—*Religion & Ethics Newsweekly*

"Philip Jenkins' book is a tour de force in historical retrieval and reconstruction, a work of scholarly restoration that strikes an overdue balance in the story of Christianity. Based on the neglected and overlooked record of developments east of the Roman Empire, the book explores significant continuities in Christian history. It is studded with insight, with the story presented in a lively and lucid style."

—Lamin Sanneh, professor of world Christianity and
professor of history, Yale University

"Philip Jenkins always writes well on very interesting topics. This time his topic is more than interesting—it is essential reading for anyone with any interest in the history of Christianity."

—Rodney Stark, author of *The Rise of Christianity*

"Once again Philip Jenkins has expanded and enriched our understanding of Christianity by stretching his venturesome scholarship over time and space. In this highly readable and sobering exploration of how religions—including our own—grow, falter, and sometimes die, he adds a unique dimension to present day religious studies in a voice and style that non-specialists can also appreciate."

—Harvey Cox, Hollis Professor of Divinity,
Harvard University

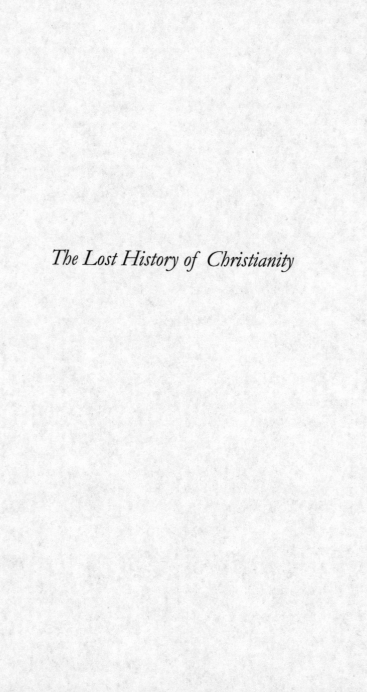

The Lost History of Christianity

The Lost History of Christianity

The Thousand-Year Golden Age
of the Church in the Middle East, Africa, and
Asia—and How It Died

—

Philip Jenkins

HarperOne
An Imprint of HarperCollinsPublishers

HarperOne

Cover map and Map 1.3 courtesy of the Osher Map Library, University of Southern Maine. Heinrich Bunting; German, 1545–1606; Die gantze Welt in ein Kleberblat; From: Itinerarium Sacrae Scripturae; Magdeburg, Germany, 1581; Woodcut; Osher Collection; OS 1580-01Bunting/HMW 376. Maps 1.1, 2.1, and 2.2 by Topaz Inc.

HarperCollins books may be purchased for educational, business, or sales promotional use. For information, please e-mail the Special Markets Department at SPsales@harpercollins.com.

HarperCollins Web site: http://www.harpercollins.com
HarperCollins®, 🏭®, and HarperOne™ are
trademarks of HarperCollins Publishers.

FIRST EDITION

Designed by Level C

Library of Congress Cataloging-in-Publication Data is available upon request.

ISBN 978–0–06–147281–7

23 24 25 26 27 LBC 19 18 17 16 15

Contents

Illustrations

Maps

Tables

A Note on Names and -isms

Throughout this book, I refer to the Eastern Christian churches that are commonly known as *Jacobite* and *Nestorian*. Both names raise problems, and some historical explanation is useful at the outset. At the risk of ignoring subtle theological distinctions, though, a reader would not go far wrong by understanding both terms as meaning simply "ancient Christian denominations mainly active outside Europe."

Christianity originated in the Near East, and during the first few centuries it had its greatest centers, its most prestigious churches and monasteries, in Syria, Palestine, and Mesopotamia. Early Eastern Christians wrote and thought in Syriac, a language closely related to the Aramaic of Jesus and his apostles. These churches became involved in passionate debates that divided Christians into several leading schools or factions, which often fought each other with distinctly un-Christian violence. One great divide happened in the fourth century, when the Council of Nicea (325) reasserted the doctrine of Christ's divinity. But over the coming decades, the mainstream Christians who accepted that doctrine were divided over additional issues, especially concerning the Person of Christ. Yes, Christ was in some sense both human and divine, but what was the exact relationship between the two elements? How could someone say that Jesus was both man and God?

According to the Catholic or Orthodox, who eventually triumphed within the Roman Empire, Christ had two natures, which were conjoined and commingled. Many Easterners followed the Patriarch Nestorius, who accepted the two natures but held that these were not absolutely united in the mystical sense taught by the Orthodox. This meant that the Virgin Mary could not rightly be called the Mother of God. Following bitter struggles, these *Nestorians* were cast out of the fold at Ephesus in 431. Most Egyptians and Easterners, however, held that Christ had only one nature, so that the divine overwhelmed the human. They thus became known as Monophysites, believers in "one nature." In 451, the ecumenical council at Chalcedon defeated the Monophysites and declared them heretical. I am oversimplifying the differences between the various teachings, which in fact were much less stark than is suggested here: modern historians stress that the different schools had much more in common than their enemies suggested.

The Council of Chalcedon left the Orthodox in command of the empire and the mainstream church apparatus, and over the next two centuries they excluded and persecuted the newly defined heretics, although these probably formed majorities in many of the empire's eastern regions. In Egypt and Syria, Monophysites were so commonplace that they were known simply as Egyptians (Copts) and Syrians (*Suriani*), respectively. In the sixth century, a Syrian leader named Jacobus Baradaeus organized the Monophysites into an underground parallel church that became known as the *Jacobites*. By the time of the Arab conquests in the seventh century, the Jacobites probably held the loyalty of most Christians in greater Syria, while the Nestorians dominated the eastern lands, in what we now call Iraq and Iran. The West Syrian church was Jacobite; East Syrians were Nestorian.

Using these sectarian labels is misleading if it paints these churches as anything less than authentically Christian. Not surprisingly, modern adherents resent the names, just as much as a Roman Catholic would hate to be described as a papist or a Romanist. *Jacobite* was a dismissive name devised by their foes; while to themselves, the Nestorians were simply, and properly, "the Church of the East." Both faithfully accepted the Council of Nicea, both clung to a faith that had been handed down to them from the apostles via the Great Church, and indeed both had an even more conservative approach to the canon of scripture than did the European-based churches. Around 800, the great Nestorian patriarch Timothy listed the fundamental doctrines that were shared by all the different groups—Nestorian, Monophysite, and Orthodox: all shared a faith in the Trinity, the Incarnation, baptism, adoration of the Cross, the holy Eucharist, the two Testaments; all believed in the resurrection of the dead, eternal life, the return of Christ in glory, and the last judgment.[1] We must never think of these churches as fringe sects rather than the Christian mainstream in large portions of the world. Among African and Asian Christians, these two strands of Christianity would certainly have outnumbered the Orthodox.

Having said this, the bodies in question are so central to the story that they must be described somehow, even if the terms used were originally negative. Any history of Christianity that fails to pay due attention to these Jacobites and Nestorians is missing a very large part of the story. Nor are the official names used by the heirs of these churches themselves any less controversial. Technically, the modern heirs to the Jacobites are "Syrian Orthodox," which is confusing if we apply the Orthodox name retroactively to medieval conditions. The Nestorian church evolved into the Assyrian Church of the East, with a questionable emphasis on the Assyrian racial heritage. Some scholars prefer "West Syrian" for *Jacobite* and "East Syrian" for *Nestorian,* but neither term has entered common usage. While recognizing the limitations, then, I will use the older labels.

Other issues arise with names drawn from African and Asian languages, which are transliterated in various ways. The Mongol ruler whom I call Hulegu has in various sources been referred to as Hulagu, Holaaku, and Hülâgû, while Genghis Khan is more correctly called Chinggis. Older sources refer to the Uygur people as Uighurs, and to the Ongguds as Onguts. I have tried to achieve consistency, but in doing so I may not always have fulfilled the most precise linguistic standards, which change quite rapidly.

The Lost History of Christianity

1

The End of Global Christianity

Religions die when they are proved to be true. Science is the record of dead religions.

—Oscar Wilde

Religions die. Over the course of history, some religions vanish altogether, while others are reduced from great world faiths to a handful of adherents. Manichaeanism, a religion that once claimed adherents from France to China, no longer exists in any organized or functional form; nor do the faiths that dominated Mexico and Central America half a millennium ago. In some cases, religions may survive in some parts of the world but are extinguished in territories that they once regarded as entirely their own. For a thousand years, India was mainly Buddhist, a faith that now enjoys only marginal status in that land. Once Persia was Zoroastrian; most of Spain, Muslim. It is not difficult to find countries or even continents, once viewed as natural homelands of a particular faith, where that creed is now extinct, and such disasters are not confined to primal or "primitive" beliefs. The systems that we think of as great world religions are as vulnerable to destruction as was the faith of the Aztecs or Mayans in their particular gods.[1]

Christianity, too, has on several occasions been destroyed in regions where it once flourished. In most cases, the elimination has been so thorough as to obliterate any memory that Christians were ever there, so that today any Christian presence whatsoever in these parts is regarded as a kind of invasive species derived from the West. Yet such a comment about the destruction of churches runs contrary to the story of Christianity as it features in the popular consciousness.

Usually, this history is presented as a tale of steady expansion, from the Middle East to Europe and ultimately onto the global stage. Christianity appears to have spread freely and inexorably, so that we rarely think of major reverses or setbacks. When we do hear of disasters or persecutions, they are usually mentioned as the prelude to still greater advances, an opportunity for heroic resistance to oppression. Protestants know how their faith survived all the persecutions and slaughter of the wars of religion; Catholics recall how the worst atrocities inflicted by Protestant and atheist regimes could not silence true belief. Modern observers witness the survival of the churches under Communism, and the ultimate triumph symbolized by Pope John Paul II. As the hymn teaches, truth will endure, in spite of dungeon, fire, and sword.[2]

Anyone familiar with Christian history has read of the planting, rise, and development of churches, but how many know accounts of the decline or extinction of Christian communities or institutions? Most Christians would find the very concept unsettling. Yet such events have certainly occurred, and much more often than many realize. During the later Middle Ages, mass defections and persecutions across Asia and the Middle East uprooted what were then some of the world's most numerous Christian communities, churches that possessed a vibrant lineal and cultural connection to the earliest Jesus movement of Syria and Palestine. Seventeenth-century Japan thoroughly eliminated a Christian presence that had come close to becoming a real force in the country, possibly even to achieving a national conversion. Repeatedly through its history, the church's tree has been pruned and cut back, often savagely.[3]

These episodes of removal or mass destruction have profoundly shaped the character of the Christian faith. In modern times, we are accustomed to thinking of Christianity as traditionally based in Europe and North America, and only gradually do we learn the strange concept of the religion spreading to the global stage as Christian numbers swell in Africa, Asia, and Latin America. So grounded is Christianity in the Western inheritance that it seems almost revolutionary to contemplate this kind of globalization, with all its potential impact on theology, art, and liturgy. A faith primarily associated with Europe somehow has to adapt to this wider world, adjusting many assumptions drawn from European culture. Some even ask whether this new global or world Christianity will remain fully authentic, as European norms seem to represent a kind of gold standard.[4]

But such questions are ironic when we realize how unnatural the Euro-American emphasis is when seen against the broader background of Christian history. The particular shape of Christianity with which we are familiar is a radical departure from what was for well over a millennium the historical norm: another, earlier global Christianity once existed. For most of its history, Christianity was a tricontinental religion, with powerful representation in Europe, Africa, and Asia, and this was true into the fourteenth century. Christianity became predominantly European not because this continent had any obvious affinity for that faith, but by default: Europe was the continent where it was not destroyed. Matters could easily have developed very differently.

In describing the fall of the non-European churches, I am not offering a lament for a worldwide Christian hegemony that never was, still less for a failure to resist rival religions such as Islam. We should rather regret the destruction of a once-flourishing culture, much as we mourn the passing of Muslim Spain, Buddhist India, or the

Jewish worlds of eastern Europe. With the possible exception of a few particularly bloody or violent creeds, the destruction of any significant faith tradition is an irreplaceable loss to human experience and culture. Furthermore, the Christian experience offers lessons that can be applied more generally to the fate of other religions that have suffered persecution or elimination. If a faith as vigorous and pervasive as Middle Eastern or Asian Christianity could have fallen into such total oblivion, no religion is safe. And the means by which such an astonishing fall occurred should be of keen interest to anyone contemplating the future of any creed or denomination.

Above all, rediscovering the lost Christian worlds of Africa and Asia raises sobering questions about the nature of historical memory. How can we possibly have forgotten such a vast story? In terms of the story of Christianity, which we usually associate so centrally with the making of "the West," much of what we think we know is inaccurate, in terms of the places and times at which things happened and how religious change occurred. Moreover, many aspects of Christianity that we conceive as thoroughly modern were in fact the norm in the distant past: globalization, the encounter with other faiths, and the dilemmas of living under hostile regimes. How can our mental maps of the past be so radically distorted?

A Third Christian World

Much of what we today call the Islamic world was once Christian. The faith originated and took shape in Syria-Palestine and in Egypt, and these areas continued to have major Christian communities long after the Arab conquests. As late as the eleventh century, Asia was still home to at least a third of the world's Christians, and perhaps a tenth of all Christians still lived in Africa—a figure that the continent would not reach again until the 1960s. Even in 1250, it still made sense to think of a Christian world stretching east from Constantinople to Samarkand (at least) and south from Alexandria to the desert of the Ogaden, almost to the equator.[5]

When we move our focus away from Europe, everything we think we know about Christianity shifts kaleidoscopically, even alarmingly. Let us, for example, take one legendary turning point in the history of Western Christianity. By the year 800, the Frankish king Charles—Charlemagne—had drawn most of western Europe under a single united Christian rule. On Christmas Day of that year, in Rome, the pope crowned him emperor, consecrating the long association of church and state in the medieval West. For many modern observers, this coronation symbolizes much that is distasteful about the story of Christianity: its alliance with state power, its thoroughly European nature, and its arrogant isolation from other faiths and cultures. Today, the word *Christendom* implies for many a theocratic regime in which the most stringent moral and doctrinal codes were enforced through law, while Jews and other outsiders were excluded or subjected to violence and insult. And all too often, Christian states were associated with ignorance, in a world that remembered only vestiges of classical learning and science. Although Charlemagne presided over a "renaissance" of sorts, it was a pallid affair compared with the ancient world, to say nothing of the true Renaissance of the fifteenth century.

Historians can argue over the realities of Charlemagne's Christendom, but this was only one part of a much larger Christian story, and one that is massively more diverse, and more impressive, than the common stereotype suggests. When we speak of the medieval church, we are usually referring to conditions in western Europe, and not to the much wealthier and more sophisticated Eastern world centered in Constantinople. But there was, in addition, a third Christian world, a vast and complex realm that stretched deep into Asia.

To appreciate just how radically different this lost Eastern Christianity was, consider one individual who was closely contemporary with Charlemagne. About 780, the bishop Timothy became patriarch, or catholicos, of the Church of the East, which was then based at the ancient Mesopotamian city of Seleucia. He was then aged about fifty-two, well past the average life expectancy for people of this era. Nevertheless, he lived on well into his nineties, dying in 823, and in that long life, Timothy devoted himself to spiritual conquests as enthusiastically as Charlemagne did to building his worldly empire. At every stage, Timothy's career violates everything we think we know about the history of Christianity—about its geographical spread, its relationship with political state power, its cultural breadth, and its interaction with other religions. In terms of his prestige, and the geographical extent of his authority, Timothy was arguably the most significant Christian spiritual leader of his day, much more influential than the Western pope, in Rome, and on a par with the Orthodox patriarch in Constantinople. Perhaps a quarter of the world's Christians looked to Timothy as both spiritual and political head. At least as much as the Western pope, he could claim to head the successor of the ancient apostolic church.[6]

When they think about Christian history, most modern Westerners follow the book of Acts in concentrating on the church's expansion west, through Greece and the Mediterranean world, and on to Rome. But while some early Christians were indeed moving west, many other believers—probably in greater numbers—journeyed east along the land routes, through what we today call Iraq and Iran, where they built great and enduring churches. Because of its location—close to the Roman frontier, but just far enough beyond it to avoid heavy-handed interference—Mesopotamia or Iraq retained a powerful Christian culture at least through the thirteenth century. In terms of the number and splendor of its churches and monasteries, its vast scholarship and dazzling spirituality, Iraq was through the late Middle Ages at least as much a cultural and spiritual heartland of Christianity as was France or Germany, or indeed Ireland.

Iraq and Syria were the bases for two great transnational churches deemed heretical by the Catholic and Orthodox—namely, the Nestorians and Jacobites. Well into the Middle Ages, the Christian strongholds of the Middle East included such currently newsworthy Iraqi cities as Basra, Mosul, and Kirkuk, while Tikrit—hometown of Saddam Hussein—was a thriving Christian center several centuries after the coming of Islam. Nisibis and Jundishapur were legendary centers of learning that kept alive the culture and science of the ancient world, both of the Greco-Romans and of the Persians. In their scholarship, their access to classical learning and science, the Eastern churches in 800 were at a level that Latin Europe would not reach at least until the thirteenth century.

Focusing on the Asian, Eastern story of Christianity forces us to jettison our customary images of the so-called Dark Ages. From Timothy's point of view, the culture and learning of the ancient world had never been lost; nor, critically, had the connection with the primitive church. We easily contrast the Latin, feudal world of the Middle Ages with the ancient church rooted in the Semitic languages of the Middle East, but in Timothy's time, the Church of the East still thought and spoke in Syriac, and its adherents continued to do so for several centuries afterward. As late as the thirteenth century, they still called themselves *Nasraye,* "Nazarenes," a form that preserves the Aramaic term used by the apostles; and they knew Jesus as Yeshua. Monks and priests bore the title *rabban,* teacher or master, which is of course related to the familiar *rabbi.* Church thinkers used literary approaches that have as much to do with the Talmud as with the theologies of Latin Europe. Through such bodies, we can trace a natural religious and cultural evolution from the apostolic world through the Middle Ages. If we are ever tempted to speculate on what the early church might have looked like if it had developed independently, avoiding the mixed blessing of its alliance with Roman state power, we have but to look east.

Repeatedly, we find Timothy's churches using texts that, according to most Western accounts, should have been forgotten long since. Eastern scholars had access to abundant alternative scriptures and readings, some of them truly ancient—scarcely surprising when we remember how close they were physically to the setting of so much Jewish and early Christian history. One stunning hint of just what was available to them comes from one of Timothy's letters, written around the year 800, when a Jew in the process of converting to Christianity told him of the recent finding of a large hoard of ancient manuscripts, biblical and apocryphal, in a cave near Jericho. The documents had since been acquired by Jerusalem's Jewish community. Modern readers naturally draw parallels with the discovery of the Dead Sea Scrolls, and, then as now, scholars were thrilled. Timothy responded with all the appropriate learned questions, seeking to track down "several passages which are cited in our New Testament as from the Old, but of which there is no mention in the Old Testament itself." How did the newly found texts compare with the known Hebrew versions? With the Greek Septuagint? He was delighted to hear "that these passages exist, and are found in the books discovered there." His questions are all the more impressive when we think what scholars in the Latin West would have made of such a find at this time. The Westerners had no inkling of such distinctions, nor knew the relevant languages in any but the most rudimentary form, even in the spiritual powerhouse of Ireland. Literally, only a very few Western Christian scholars at the time would have known how to hold the manuscripts: which way was up?[7]

Timothy found rich treasures in the scrolls. "My Hebrew informant told me that they had found among these books more than two hundred Psalms of David," he wrote, and Nestorian writers preserve readings of noncanonical Psalms that also appear in the Qumran scrolls. Syriac writers also knew a host of lesser and later Jewish postbiblical texts, and Old Testament apocryphal writings, the pseudepigrapha. Like its ancient predecessors, Timothy's church remained thoroughly in dialogue with Semitic and Jewish traditions. Our accepted chronology of the ancient church is wrong: ancient Semitic Christianity dies out not in the fourth century, but in the fourteenth.[8]

Over the past thirty years, scholars have rediscovered the many spiritual currents that characterized the earliest church, the various lost or forgotten Christianities that were remembered, if at all, as heretical byways of the faith. For scholars like Elaine Pagels, Bart

Ehrman, and Karen King, these mystical and speculative ideas flourished—together with their distinctive lost Gospels—until they were largely suppressed during the fourth century, following the Council of Nicea. Yet Eastern Christians also continued to pursue mystical quests in ways that were familiar in the early church, and they did so long after the fourth century. In contrast to the rigid homogeneity that is so often associated with the Western Middle Ages, Eastern prelates had to confront real diversity of thought, with daring mystical and theological speculations.

One continuing influence was the third-century Father Origen, who had proposed that the soul was preexistent and that salvation and damnation might be temporary states leading ultimately to a grand restoration of all things, the *apokatastasis*. At this climax beyond history, even the Devil would be redeemed, and all would share the divine nature. Origenism long continued to agitate the Nestorian church. Some mystics taught that, as true salvation was spiritual, bodily resurrection was irrelevant, and there would be neither judgment nor punishment. Visionaries sought contemplative ecstasy in which verbal prayer would no longer be relevant, and some rejected sacraments and offices, in their quest for the pristine simplicity of a restored Garden of Eden. Above all, such mystics taught silence and solitude, together with strict asceticism, using language highly reminiscent of the ancient Gnostics. These theories were still circulating widely enough to force Timothy to confront them in the 780s. We have to ask ourselves: at what point can we speak of the death of the ancient church, the primitive church, the patristic church? Intellectually and spiritually, it was assuredly alive in Timothy's day, and for centuries afterward.[9] The Syriac churches represent the ultimate lost Christianity.

The Countries of the Sunrise

But Timothy's church was anything but a mere fossil, as centuries of missionary fervor had projected the faith of Yeshua into an incomprehensibly vaster world. Although largely forgotten today, these Eastern ventures mirrored, and exceeded, the much more celebrated missionary successes in Europe. Thomas Hobbes famously described the papacy as "the ghost of the deceased Roman Empire, sitting crowned upon the grave thereof." The Church of the East likewise built upon the ruins of older empires—in this case, the great Persian realm, and before that, archaic states like Assyria, Babylonia, and Elam.

To appreciate the scale of the Church of the East, we can look at a list of the church's metropolitans—that is, of those senior clergy who oversaw inferior hierarchies of bishops grouped in provinces. In England, to give a comparison, the medieval church had two metropolitans: respectively, at York and Canterbury. Timothy himself presided over nineteen metropolitans and eighty-five bishops. Though the exact locations of metropolitan seats changed over time, map 1.1 on page 12 identifies some of the leading centers. Just in Timothy's lifetime, new metropolitan sees were created at Rai near Tehran, and in Syria, Turkestan, Armenia, and Dailumaye on the Caspian Sea.

The presence of metropolitan seats in Turkestan and central Asia is amazing enough, but the list of bishoprics and lesser churches includes just as many shocks: Arabia had at least four sees, and Timothy created a new one in Yemen. And the church was growing in southern India, where believers claimed a direct inheritance from the missions of the apostle Thomas. One ninth-century copper plate records the grant of land to one of Thomas's Indian churches, by a means that would have staggered contemporary Europeans: the boundaries were marked by walking a she-elephant around the grounds.[10]

Timothy himself was committed to the church's further expansion, and he commissioned monks to carry the faith to the shores of the Caspian Sea, even into China. He reported the conversion of the Turkish great king, the *khagan,* who then ruled over much of central Asia. In a magnificent throwaway line, Timothy described, about 780, how "[i]n these days the Holy Spirit has anointed a metropolitan for the Turks, and we are preparing to consecrate another one for the Tibetans." Timothy was deeply conscious of the church's universality. When debating a technical liturgical question, he drew support from the practice of the wider churches of the sprawling Christian world he knew: the Persians and Assyrians don't do this, he argued, and nor do the churches of "the countries of the sunrise—that is to say, among the Indians, the Chinese, the Tibetans, the Turks." The church operated in multiple languages: in Syriac, Persian, Turkish, Soghdian, and Chinese, but not Latin, which scarcely mattered outside western Europe.[11]

To put this geographical achievement in context, we might think of what was happening in contemporary Europe. Before Saint Benedict formed his first monastery, before the probable date of the British king Arthur, Nestorian sees existed at Nishapur and Tus in Khurasan, in northeastern Persia, and at Rai. Before England had its first archbishop of Canterbury—possibly before Canterbury had a Christian church—the Nestorian church already had metropolitans at Merv and Herat, in the modern nations of (respectively) Turkmenistan and Afghanistan, and churches were operating in Sri Lanka and Malabar. Before Good King Wenceslas ruled a Christian Bohemia, before Poland was Catholic, the Nestorian sees of Bukhara, Samarkand, and Patna all achieved metropolitan status. Our common mental maps of Christian history omit a thousand years of that story, and several million square miles of territory. No reasonable historian of modern Christianity would leave Europe out of the story; and omitting Asia from the medieval record is just as unconscionable. We can't understand Christian history without Asia—or, indeed, Asian history without Christianity.

Neither the Nestorian nor the Jacobite churches apparently knew or cared much about European developments. Timothy would certainly have known about Charlemagne, if only because the Frankish ruler exchanged diplomatic missions with the caliphate, and Timothy was aware that Rome had its own patriarchate. Even so, he felt that

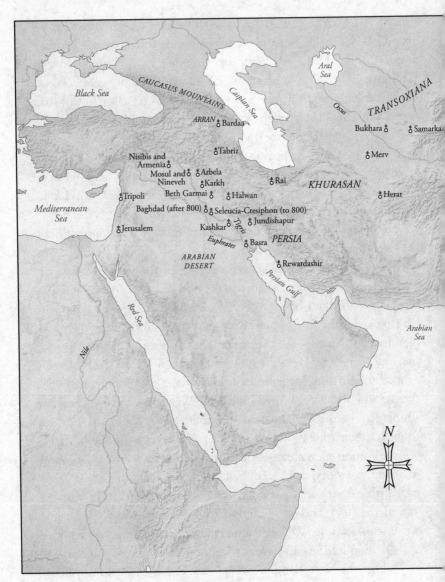

MAP 1.1. NESTORIAN METROPOLITANS

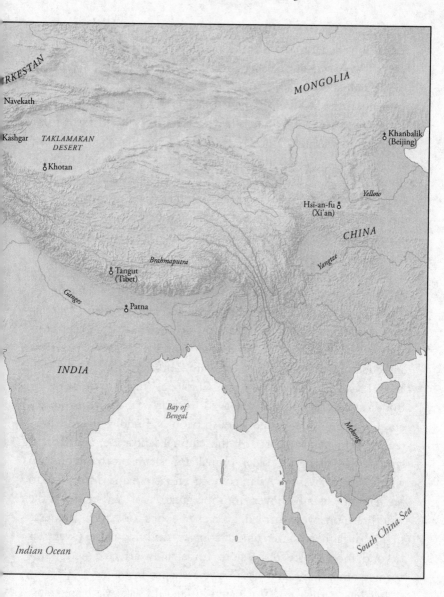

many reasons gave natural primacy of honor to his own Seleucia. If Rome drew its authority from Peter, Mesopotamia looked to Christ himself, a descendant of that ancient Sumerian Abraham. Was not Mesopotamia the original source of monarchy and civilization, not to mention the location of the Garden of Eden? Just as the rivers flowed out of Eden, so the other patriarchates flowed forth from Mesopotamia. And obviously it was the East, rather than the West, that had first embraced the Christian message. The natural home of Christianity was in Mesopotamia and points east. According to the geographical wisdom of the time, Seleucia stood at the center of the world's routes of trade and communication, equally placed between the civilizations that looked respectively to the Atlantic and the Pacific.[12]

In modern terminology, the Eastern churches were thoroughly enculturated, presenting their faith in the languages of the cultures they encountered, sharing their artistic and literary forms. Operating as it did on a global scale, Timothy's church had no choice but to engage in dialogue with several other world religions—with Islam and Judaism, of course, but also with Zoroastrianism, Buddhism, and Taoism. In central Asia, the Christians' main rivals were the Buddhists, who were then engaged in their own great missionary era. For many Mongol and Turkish peoples, Buddhism and Christianity were familiar parts of the cultural landscape, and existed comfortably alongside older primal and shamanic traditions. So widespread were these Asian contacts, in fact, that it is tempting to see Timothy as a holdover from the great Axial Age in which the world religions were formed, even as he looks forward to later eras of global faith and intercultural contact. And the process went far beyond mere polite discussion: Christianity affected and transformed other faiths, and was in turn reshaped by them.

In China particularly, Christianity in Timothy's age was being transformed by local religious traditions. The Church of the East was anything but a newcomer in China, and Christianity first established itself in that land about 600, roughly at the same time that Tibet first welcomed Buddhism. About 780, a Nestorian community erected a monument that recounted the Christian message in Buddhist and Taoist terms, just as European Christians were trying to make the faith acceptable to peoples of western and northern Europe:

> The illustrious and honorable Messiah, veiling his true dignity, appeared in the world as a man; . . . he fixed the extent of the eight boundaries, thus completing the truth and freeing it from dross; he opened the gate of the three constant principles, introducing life and destroying death; he suspended the bright sun to invade the chambers of darkness, and the falsehoods of the devil were thereupon defeated; he set in motion the vessel of mercy by which to ascend to the bright mansions, whereupon rational beings were then released; having thus completed the manifestation of his power, in clear day he ascended to his true station.[13]

The intellectual categories used here would have baffled a first-century Jew, but no more so than the Latin formulations of Anselm or Thomas Aquinas. Both in China and in southern India, some Nestorians used a distinctive symbol in which the cross is joined to the lotus, symbol of Buddhist enlightenment.

Around the time this memorial was erected, in 782, the Indian Buddhist missionary Prajna arrived in the Chinese imperial capital of Chang'an, but was unable to translate the Sanskrit sutras he had brought with him into either Chinese or any other familiar tongue. In such a plight, what could the hapless missionary do but seek Christian help? He duly consulted the bishop named Adam, whose name headed the list on the Nestorian monument. Adam had already translated parts of the Bible into Chinese, and the two probably shared a knowledge of Persian. Together, Buddhist and Nestorian scholars worked amiably together for some years to translate seven copious volumes of Buddhist wisdom. Probably, Adam did this as much from intellectual curiosity as from ecumenical goodwill, and we can only guess about the conversations that would have ensued: *So, what exactly is this "bodhisattva" we hear so much about? Do you really care more about relieving suffering than atoning for sin? And your monks meditate like ours do?* Scholars still speculate whether Adam infiltrated Christian concepts into the translated sutras, consciously or otherwise.[14]

Adam's efforts bore fruit far beyond China. Other residents of Chang'an at this time included Japanese monks, who took these very translations back with them to their homeland. In Japan, these works became the founding texts of the two great Buddhist schools—respectively, Shingon and Tendai; and all the famous Buddhist movements of later Japanese history, including Zen and Pure Land, can be traced to one of those two schools. To appreciate the full diversity of the Christian experience, it is eye-opening to think what was happening in western Europe at this exact time. The year 782 marked one of the worst horrors of Charlemagne's reign, the reputed beheading of forty-five hundred Saxons who resisted the Frankish campaign of forced conversion to Catholic Christianity.

Faith Speaks to Faith

Timothy's church also had critical interactions with Islam, inevitably because for the past century and a half most Eastern Christians had lived under Muslim political power. Christians largely flourished under that authority, although subject to legal disadvantages. Timothy lived in a universe that was culturally and spiritually Christian but politically Muslim, and he coped quite comfortably with that situation. As faithful subjects, the patriarch and his clergy prayed for the caliph and his family. The catholicos was a key figure at the court of the Muslim caliph, and when the city of Seleucia itself went the way of ancient Babylon, fading into ruin in its turn, the caliphate moved its capital to Baghdad; and Timothy naturally followed. Most of his patriarchate coincided with the legendary caliphate of Harun al-Rashid, the era of the Arabian Nights.[15]

As in the case of Buddhism, Christians had to engage intellectually with Islam, and the interactions were impressive, even moving. Timothy's famous dialogue with the caliph al-Mahdi survives as a precious monument of civilized, intelligent religious exchange. The caliph spoke "not in a harsh and haughty tone . . . but in a sweet and benevolent way." Given the setting, of course Timothy had to acknowledge the virtues of the Prophet Muhammad, who (he agreed) must have "walked in the path of the prophets." But the patriarch took every opportunity to explain and defend the Christian position. He concluded with a statement that would have appalled contemporary Europeans, secure in the dogmas they knew. Timothy, in contrast, ruled a church that knew many civilizations and faiths, each equally confident of its own rightness. He asked the king to imagine that

we are all of us as in a dark house in the middle of the night. If at night and in a dark house, a precious pearl happens to fall in the midst of people, and all become aware of its existence, every one would strive to pick up the pearl, which will not fall to the lot of all but to the lot of one only, while one will get hold of the pearl itself, another one of a piece of glass, a third one of a stone or of a bit of earth, but every one will be happy and proud that he is the real possessor of the pearl. When, however, night and darkness disappear, and light and day arise, then every one of those people who had believed that they had the pearl, would extend and stretch their hand towards the light, which alone can show what everyone has in hand. The one who possesses the pearl will rejoice and be happy and pleased with it, while those who had in hand pieces of glass and bits of stone only will weep and be sad, and will sigh and shed tears.[16]

In the same way, Timothy said, the pearl of true faith had fallen into the transient mortal world, and each faith naively believed that it alone possessed it. All he could claim—and all the caliph could assert in response—was that some faiths could see enough evidence that theirs was the real pearl, although the final truth would not be known in this world.

Timothy could speak so freely because Eastern Christians played such a critical role in building Muslim politics and culture, and they still had a near stranglehold over the ranks of administration. Their wide linguistic background made the Eastern churches invaluable resources for rising empires in search of diplomats, advisers, and scholars. Eastern Christians dominated the cultural and intellectual life of what was only slowly becoming the "Muslim world," and this cultural strength starkly challenges standard assumptions about the relationship between the two faiths. It is common knowledge that medieval Arab societies were far ahead of those of Europe in terms of science, philosophy, and medicine, and that Europeans derived much of their scholarship from the Arab world; yet in the early centuries, this cultural achievement was usually Christian and Jewish rather than Muslim. It was Christians—Nestorian, Jacobite, Orthodox, and others—who preserved and translated the cultural inheritance of the ancient world—the science, philosophy, and medicine—and who transmitted it to centers like Baghdad and Damascus. Much of what we call Arab scholarship was in reality Syriac, Persian, and Coptic, and it was not necessarily Muslim. Syriac-speaking Christian scholars brought the works of Aristotle to the Muslim world: Timothy himself translated Aristotle's *Topics* from Syriac into Arabic, at the behest of the caliph. Syriac Christians even make the first reference to the efficient Indian numbering system that we know today as "Arabic," and long before this technique gained currency among Muslim thinkers.[17]

It was during Timothy's time that Baghdad became a legendary intellectual center, with the caliph's creation of the famous House of Wisdom, the fountainhead of later Islamic scholarship. But this was the direct successor of the Christian "university" of Jundishapur, and it borrowed many Nestorian scholars. One early head of the House of Wisdom was the Christian Arab Hunayn, who began the massive project of translating the Greek classics into Arabic: the works of Plato, Aristotle, and the Neoplatonists, as well as medical authorities like Hippocrates and Galen. Reputedly, the caliph paid Hunayn for these books by quite literally giving him their weight in gold. Such were the Christian roots of the Arabic golden age.[18]

Making a Christian East

When Timothy died in 823, he had every reason to hope for his church's future. The new caliph was friendly to Christian clergy and scholars, and although some ordinary Christians were drifting toward the new faith, there were few signs of any ruinous defections. Even if conditions under Islamic rule ever did become difficult, the Church of the East had plenty of opportunities to grow outside that realm, with all the new conversions in central Asia and China, and the continuing presence in India. Even more than today, South and East Asia were by far the most heavily populated parts of the world. An ever-expanding Church of the East should be more than able to hold its own against the Orthodox Church in Constantinople, the obvious rival for leadership in the Christian world.

Any reasonable projection of the Christian future would have foreseen a bipolar world, divided between multiethnic churches centered respectively in Constantinople and Baghdad. Timothy would probably have felt little hope for the future of Christianity in western Europe. Already in Timothy's last days, Charlemagne's vaunted empire was fragmenting, and falling prey to the combined assaults of pagan Northmen and Muslim Saracens. In the century after 790, ruin and massacre overtook virtually all the British and Irish monasteries that had kept learning alive over the previous two centuries, and from which missionaries had gone out to evangelize northern Europe. Spain was already under Muslim rule, and southern Italy and southern France seemed set to follow. In 846, Saracens raided papal Rome, plundering the Basilica of Saint Peter and the tomb of the Fisherman. Latin Europe's low point came soon after 900 when, within the space of a couple of years, areas of central France were ravaged in quick succession by pagan Vikings from the north, Muslim Moors from the south, and pagan Magyars from the east: Christians had nowhere left to hide. Perhaps history would ultimately write off the Christian venture into western Europe as rash overreach, a diversion from Christianity's natural destiny, which evidently lay in Asia. Europe might have been a continent too far.

Later events often seemed to be following those hopes and fears. Many would agree with the Victorian scholar who declared: "It may be doubted whether Innocent III [pope, 1198–1215] possessed more spiritual power than the patriarch in the city of the Caliphs."[19] Innocent was the most powerful pope of the Western Middle Ages. Later in the thirteenth century, Nestorian influence was so strong among the Mongols who conquered the Middle East that for a few years, Christian leaders dreamed that Baghdad itself might be the capital of a new Christian empire that would consign Islam to the catalog of forgotten heresies.

The enduring power of Christianity in Asia and Africa must raise doubts about many of the statements that scholars conventionally make about the history of that religion, when conditions in Europe are taken to be the norm for the whole church. While most Christians in Europe certainly lived in a kind of "Christendom," in which church and state could be seen as broadly identical, that was far from the reality facing the millions of Christians who lived under other and possibly hostile faiths, under Persian, Muslim, Hindu, or Chinese rule. These believers were well accustomed to a modern idea of Christianity as a minority faith operating far from centers of power, usually suffering official discrimination, and facing the recurrent danger of persecution. About 1420, an Italian traveler observed that "[t]hese Nestorians are scattered all over India, in like manner as are the Jews among us."[20] He found it hard to grasp the idea of Christians as a scattered group living among many other creeds, probably as a small minority. Yet, viewed over the whole span of Christian history, such an experience was no less typical than the dominant status enjoyed by members of nominally Christian societies.

Remapping the World

In visualizing this older Christian world, we need to reconstruct our sense of geography no less than of history. Though maps rarely lie, in the sense of cartographers presenting data they know to be false, the way we choose to visualize information can give a radically distorted impression of reality. When we think about the spread of Christianity, we commonly use maps focused on Europe and the Mediterranean, as we know intuitively that this was the scene of the most intense and important activity.

MAP 1.2. CHRISTIAN EXPANSION

The Christian world, it appears, had always been what it was when map 1.2 appeared in 1915, a largely European reality: indeed, this particular map suggests that the geographical center of historic Christianity was located somewhere in Austria. And this presentation was more inclusive than many, in stretching as far east as Syria and Armenia. The message offered is that beyond the colored margins, Christianity never existed, or at least never mattered. Our maps don't include South America, because it is irrelevant to the story before 1492; by the same token, why should we include Asia or Africa?

As a useful alternative image, we can turn to the symbolic world maps that Christians commonly used through the Middle Ages and the early modern period, which depicted the three continents as lobes joined together in Jerusalem (map 1.3).[21]

Depicting the world in such simple geometric forms did not mean that early cartographers were ignorant or incompetent, as they were quite capable of drawing up highly accurate charts for practical navigation. Rather, these maps carried a higher truth: Jerusalem was the center of the world, the natural site for Christ's act of self-sacrifice and redemption. (Timothy, of course, would have pushed the center of gravity still farther east!) These images also reflected a world in which Christianity had a strong presence across Asia and much of northern Africa. Criticizing traditional visual concepts of Christian history, Andrew Walls has suggested that, instead of placing a vital early Syrian center like Edessa on the distant eastern fringes of Europe, it makes at least as much sense to locate it at the far west of an Asian map, in the lower left-hand corner.[22] Walls was not of course suggesting that such an Asian-focused interpretation would be complete or comprehensive, but that it would be no less accurate than the Eurocentric vision.

The End of a World

And yet this older Christian world perished, destroyed so comprehensively that its memory is forgotten by all except academic

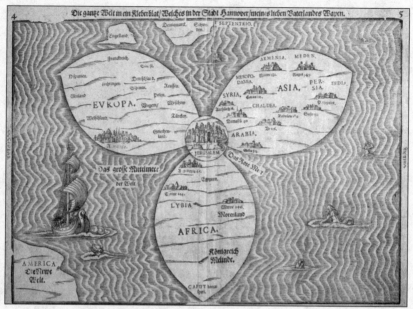

MAP 1.3. THE THREE-FOLD WORLD

specialists. During the Middle Ages, and especially during the four-teenth century, church hierarchies were destroyed, priests and monks were killed, enslaved, or expelled, and monasteries and cathedrals fell silent. As church institutions fell, so Christian communities shrank, the result of persecution or ethnic and religious cleansing. Survivors found it all but impossible to practice their faith without priests or churches, especially when rival religions offered such powerful attractions.

The statistics of decline are sobering. Look, for instance, at Asia Minor, the region that is so often mentioned throughout the New Testament: it is here that we find such historic names as Iconium and Ephesus, Galatia and Bithynia, the seven cities of the book of Revelation. Still in 1050, the region had 373 bishoprics, and the inhabitants were virtually all Christian, overwhelmingly members of the Orthodox Church. Four hundred years later, that Christian proportion had fallen to 10 or 15 percent of the population, and we can find just three bishops. According to one estimate, the number of Asian Christians fell, between 1200 and 1500, from 21 million to 3.4 million. In the same years, the proportion of the world's Christians living in Africa and Asia combined fell from 34 percent to just 6 percent. Actually, the contraction outside Europe was probably more dramatic than even these figures suggest, but the basic point is accurate.[23]

And what of the Nestorians, the great Church of the East? In southern India, several million Christians today represent the remnants of those missions, although most are affiliated with Catholic or Orthodox churches, which have become the "mainstream" of world Christianity. But elsewhere, the Church of the East largely ceased to exist, and virtually all its once-famous cities and centers now stand in territories that are largely or exclusively Muslim. By the 1920s, the survivors of this once-vast Nestorian Church, which once attracted the loyalty of Tibetans and Mongols, were reduced to "a miserable community of about forty thousand refugees"[24] in northern Iraq. But even then, their sufferings were not at an end. Some years later, they were subjected to massacres so severe as to force legal thinkers to construct a new vocabulary of human savagery. The concept of genocide evolved from discussions of their plight. Timothy's distant successor today—the catholicos patriarch of the Holy Apostolic Catholic Assyrian Church of the East—is based not in Baghdad, but in Chicago.

A brutal purge of Christianity, most spectacularly in Asia, left Europe as the geographical heart of the Christian faith, and as the only possible base for later expansion. The destruction was not total, but whole areas were swept clean of Christian communities, and believers elsewhere were reduced to a tiny fraction of the population. To borrow the image of the medieval maps, the three lobes became just one. If we look at the whole Middle East, broadly defined, from Egypt to Persia, from Turkey to Arabia, then by 1900 this region had about 5 million Christians in total. This made up a pathetic 0.9 percent of the world's Christian population, which was then overwhelmingly concentrated in Europe and its overseas settlements. In absolute numbers, there were fewer Christians in the Middle East than in Oceania—that is, mainly, the fairly new colonies of Australia and New Zealand.[25]

Cut Off from the Roots

The disasters of the late Middle Ages tore Christianity from its roots—cultural, geographical, and linguistic. This "uprooting" created the Christianity that we commonly think of today as the true historical norm, but which in reality was the product of the elimination of alternative realities. Christianity did indeed become "European," but about a millennium later than most people think. As Andrew Walls remarks, "[I]t was not until comparatively recent times—around the year 1500—that the ragged conversion of the last pagan peoples of Europe, the overthrow of Muslim power in Spain, and the final eclipse of Christianity in central Asia and Nubia combined to produce a Europe that was essentially Christian and a Christianity that was essentially European."[26]

The geographical shift away from Asia has cultural and political implications, in that no region, no church, can claim special authenticity or authority on the basis of representing the historic core of the Christian tradition. In this geographical sense, Christianity has no heart, no natural core. Medieval Christians spent two hundred years in bloody efforts to reclaim the home of their faith, in the Holy Land, but their struggle proved fruitless. This lack of a heartland is in stark contrast to the history of Islam, which originated in Arabia and neighboring lands, and has always continued to find its heart there. From that solid base, Islam has spread over large sections of Asia and Africa, occasionally losing some territories, such as Spain and the Balkans, but always retaining its heartland and speaking its Arabic language.

The Christian center of gravity, on the other hand, has shifted over time. For long centuries, the faith found its most active centers in the Near East, but in later eras, the cultural and demographic heart of the church moved to Europe and the Atlantic world, and in our time appears to be shifting to the global South. But unlike Islam, Christianity has not retained its original foundation, in that its original homeland—the region where it enjoyed its greatest triumphs over its first millennium—is now overwhelmingly Muslim. To offer a parallel example to understand how radical the uprooting of Christianity was, we would have to imagine a counterfactual world in which Islam was extinguished in Arabia and the Middle East, and survived chiefly in Southeast Asia, using scriptures translated into Malay and Bengali. Christianity is just as severed from its original context.

Throughout the history of the faith, Christians have used the primitive church as an idealized standard by which to judge their own days, and have tried as far as possible to construct their own faith and practice according to the tenets of New Testament Christianity. Yet the better we understand the authentic worlds of the Christian East, the harder it becomes to contemplate any such vision of a "return to basics." Timothy and his contemporaries genuinely did live in a world that had a recognizable continuity from the earliest church, a pattern of organic development in terms of social and economic arrangements, of language, culture, and geography. We can debate how far that world represented authentic primitive Christianity, but it is quite certain that no later ages could possibly replicate the apostolic world anything like as faithfully. The loss of continuity—the loss of the core—makes moot later efforts to enforce the culture-specific regulations of the earliest Christian communities.

Looking for the Mainstream

The throttling of the great Eastern churches raises other theological questions for modern-day Christians. Most fundamentally, if Christianity has no historic core, how can we speak of a "mainstream," a historic norm or standard against which later movements or positions can be judged? When we trace the history of Christianity, we emphasize the kinds of Christian belief that characterized the churches of the old Roman Empire, the Catholic and Orthodox, but they achieved their absolute hegemony only as a consequence of the (relatively late) fall of the older rival churches. Many mainstreams once flowed.

In theology, for instance, the Catholic/Orthodox taught one particular approach to understanding the Incarnation, a fundamental belief from which thinkers strayed at peril to their lives, and later Protestants largely inherited this theology. A thousand years ago, though, orthodoxy (with a small *o*) represented one theological position among several, and very different opinions prevailed in large and populous sections of the Christian world. Neither Jacobites nor Nestorians were anything like as floridly heretical as the Gnostics, who have attracted so much attention in recent years. Yet even on an issue as basic as the Person of Christ, what we today call mainstream historical orthodoxy looks more like the view that happened to gain power in Europe, and which therefore survived. And what was true of such weighty doctrines applied even more forcefully to lesser matters, to questions of liturgy and devotion. European churches, especially the Roman Catholic Church, became the mainstream of belief by dint of being, so to speak, the last men standing.

The Eastern experience must make us reconsider our view of Christian history. When a movement or church fails or vanishes, hindsight can make us assume that it was doomed to failure from the outset, and that it was never going to play a serious role in history. Yet movements that ultimately became marginal were not always so. The perception that alternative Christianities seem to perish so rapidly after separating from the parent stem just reflects the tendency of later scholars to ignore their existence. In reality, Nestorians and Jacobites remained very influential for over eight hundred years after the great church councils expelled them from the imperial fold, and they attracted believers over a huge geographical area. To put that achievement in context, that time span is far longer than the entire history of Protestantism to date. If such endurance does not mark a variant of Christianity as a thoroughly legitimate expression of the faith, what does?

When modern observers look at the course of Christianity, they often apply a kind of Darwinian perspective, assuming that some versions of the religion succeeded because they were better adapted to their circumstances than were others. From a theological standpoint, this would mean that some kinds of Christianity survived and flourished because they were more faithful, and truer to the divine plan. And the fact of survival in turn validates the present-day beliefs of Christians who follow those particular forms of the faith: faith interprets history, which supports faith. Yet such a model meshes poorly with the actual history of those other churches, which perished not through their own theological failures or contradictions, their own loss of faith, but through secular politics. In no sense were they less authentically Christian than the churches of Rome and Constantinople. If matters had developed differently, perhaps Christianity today would be thoroughly and "naturally" Asian and Nestorian, just as obviously and traditionally as we think of it as Euro-American. Neither faith, nor piety, nor scholarship, nor ancient tradition served to keep the churches alive across most of their ancient homelands, a great extinction that should offer a sobering message to modern-day believers. The success of a particular religion or faith tradition in gaining numbers and influence neither proves nor disproves its validity.

How Religions Die

Theologians seldom address the troubling questions raised by the destruction of churches and of Christian communities. Most important, we need to realize that such incidents of decline and disappearance are quite frequent, however little they are studied or discussed. Dechristianization is one of the least studied aspects of Christian history.[27]

Partly, the lack of interest in vanishing churches is a matter of practicality, in that dying organizations tend not to produce records of their extinction. A rising movement or congregation produces historians who lovingly seek out records of the foundation and trace whatever they can find about the early days. The founding text of Christian history is the *Church History* by Eusebius, who pieced together every snippet of information, legend, and gossip he could find about the origins of the burgeoning Christian movement of the fourth century. John Foxe, in the sixteenth century, was no less dedicated to collecting details about all the heroes and martyrs whose sacrifices laid the foundations for the new Protestant churches.[28]

But in contrast, imagine a church in the process of dissolution. The churches are ruined or deserted, no successors can be found for the bishoprics, while despairing ordinary believers are drifting away to other faiths. Perhaps priests and monks are being hunted, in fear of their lives. At some point, it becomes possible to identify the last Christian priest or pastor in a city or a region, perhaps even the very last believer. In such desperate conditions, few have the will or capacity to write their histories of decline and fall, and fewer still to preserve them for posterity. When one faith succeeds another, its members will devote little care to the fading writings of a rival religion they may well regard as wrong, or even diabolical. Some enthusiasts might even regard the destruction of these older records as praiseworthy: such pious book burning is the reason so few written records survive of the Aztec and Mayan religions. And at least before the coming of modern forms of media and communication, fellow believers in other lands knew or cared little about such distant events. The reason we know so much about the fall of the Japanese church was that the fate of its European priests was of immense concern to literate fellow Catholics in Manila and Macao, who preserved every detail of their sufferings. Once the European priests were gone, no one bothered to record the fate of the remaining tens of thousands of humble native Christians.

For many reasons, then, later historians have few materials to work with in order to understand examples of eclipse or extinction. As one Victorian scholar wrote of North Africa after the Muslim conquest, "[T]his church has perished so completely that the very causes of its ruin have disappeared."[29] The fact that we know so much more about the European churches than their non-European counterparts does not necessarily reflect their greater importance at the time: rather, they survived long enough for scholars to preserve and study their records. The Cathar Church of thirteenth-century France, the Albigensians, left no historian to write an inspiring work about the blood of martyrs being the seed of the church, or to claim that one could never really kill an idea.

The Triumph of Persecution

Given that the destruction of Christianity has not been much studied, we can make certain general observations, stressing above all the role of states. Though churches may lose political influence under Christian states or in predominantly Christian societies, though they might be secularized, they do not vanish anything like as thoroughly as in the African and Asian examples mentioned. In most of these cases, churches collapsed or vanished because they were unable to cope with the pressures placed upon them by hostile regimes, mainly Muslim. While religions might sicken and fade, they do not die of their own accord: they must be killed.

In stressing the role of conflict with Islam, we should not exaggerate the intolerant or militaristic nature of that religion. Some egregious examples of church extinction were perpetrated by other faiths, by Buddhists or followers of Shinto, or by Christians themselves, most thoroughly in the case of the Cathars. Nor did the spread of Islam chiefly result from force and compulsion at the hands of Muslim soldiers who supposedly offered a crude choice between the Quran and the sword. For several centuries after the original conquests, the great majority of those who accepted Islam converted quite voluntarily, for the usual range of reasons that explain such a transformation: some changed their religions for convenience or advantage, but most because they accepted the claims of the new religion to provide a definitive revelation of God's will. Many ordinary people probably accepted Islam for the same reason that their ancestors had become Christian—namely, that they followed the lead of local lords or other notables. Conversion was all the easier because, in these early centuries, Islam bore a much closer resemblance to Christianity than it would in later eras, making the transition less radical. From the tenth century onward, many prospective converts were attracted by the example of Muslim saints and sages, whose charismatic powers recalled those of earlier Christian saints. Nothing in Muslim scriptures makes the faith of Islam any more or less likely to engage in persecution or forcible conversion than any other world religion.

Islam also grew later on because Muslim regimes encouraged the immigration of fellow believers from other lands, who quickly outnumbered the older, native populations. Although religious change is commonly discussed in terms of conversion, it is often a matter of population transfer rather than of the transformation of personal convictions. As in the Americas following the Spanish and Portuguese conquest, converting an area to a new faith does not necessarily mean securing the allegiance of the whole people. Rather, the older inhabitants can be expelled, or are outnumbered and diluted by newer population stocks. In the Middle Eastern context, too, immigrants benefited from their different economic background. Anthropologists commonly find that pastoral peoples outbreed their sedentary peasant neighbors, and eventually end up owning most of their land. As the Middle East became progressively Arabized in language and culture, so the ground was prepared for the newly dominant religion. Gradually, after three or four centuries, Muslims came to constitute majorities, usually through peaceful means.

But just as undeniably, many Christians and others (Jews and Zoroastrians) were driven to accept the new faith, whether by outright persecution or systematic discrimination, exercised over centuries. Most of the lands conquered by Islam during the initial expansion of that faith were at the time heavily Christian, and large sections of the population retained that loyalty until intolerable pressures drove them to accept conversion. Nor did Christianity simply fade away of its own accord, following a centuries-long downward slope to oblivion. Across the Christian worlds of Africa and Asia, the twelfth and thirteenth centuries marked a widespread cultural renaissance in many lands and many tongues, movements that produced some of the greatest thinkers and authors of the Christian Middle Ages. Only around 1300 did the axe fall, and quite suddenly.

This stress on coercion is striking in light of the modern belief in the essentially tolerant nature of Islam through most of its history, an image that is often associated with idealized pictures of the friendly coexistence that supposedly prevailed in medieval Spain, the *convivencia*. But coexistence in some times and places does not preclude persecution in others. Much as Christian Europe treated its Jewish population, good social relationships between Muslims and Christians could endure for decades or even centuries. But in the world of Islam as in Europe, persecution when it did arise could be savage, devastating the minority community, and in both cases, the fourteenth century witnessed a crescendo of violence and discrimination. Muslims attacked Christians as subversives and traitors, even accusing them of plotting mega–terror attacks on beloved mosques and public monuments. Such theories became plausible with the introduction of the new superweapon of gunpowder.[30]

Around the world, in fact, the years around 1300 produced an appalling trend toward religious and ethnic intolerance, a movement that must be explained in terms of global factors, rather than merely local. The aftereffects of the Mongol invasions certainly played their part, by terrifying Muslims and others with the prospect of a direct threat to their social and religious power. Climatic factors were also critical, as the world entered a period of rapid cooling, precipitating bad harvests and shrinking trade routes: a frightened and impoverished world looks for scapegoats. For whatever reasons, Muslim regimes and mobs now delivered near-fatal blows to weakened Christian churches. Even today, jihadi extremists look back to the hard-line Muslim scholars of this very era as their role models in challenging the infidel world.

African and Asian Christians have often throughout their history faced the reality of armed religious warfare. Islam was not uniquely prone to persecution, and Muslim regimes generally behaved no worse than others: Christian states have little to boast of in their own treatment of religious minorities. For lengthy periods of Muslim history, in fact, acts of religious violence were rare and sporadic. Even when we look at incidents in which Muslim forces destroyed Christian communities, we must ask whether these groups were acting in the name of religion, or if Islam happened to be the faith of invading nations or tribes, who applied the extraordinarily destructive standards of nomad warfare. On other occasions, however, we can speak without hesitation of religiously motivated jihad. All religious traditions have their military theologies—Hindus, Christians, and Buddhists; and we should not exempt Islam from this category. Anyone who believes that boundless aggression and ruthless tyranny over minorities are built into the DNA of Islam needs to explain the quite benevolent nature of Muslim rule during its first six centuries; but advocates of Islamic tolerance must work just as hard to account for the later years of the religion's historical experience.

So extensive, indeed, were persecutions and reductions of minority groups, from the Middle Ages through the twentieth century, that it is astonishing how little they have registered in popular consciousness, or how readily the myth of Muslim tolerance has been accepted. One factor distorting memory has been the total oblivion into which the non-European Christian communities have fallen, and the assumption that the familiar realities of the present day must always have existed. For those accustomed to a near–solidly Muslim Middle East, it seems incredible that a different situation might ever have existed, or if it did, that it could ever have experienced a different outcome.

The Remnant

The difference in Christian responses to occupation or persecution also demands explanation. Faced with such challenges, some churches evaporated quickly, and Christianity scarcely lingered in the wider community. This is what happened to the once-influential churches of ancient Africa, the area that we would today think of as Algeria and Tunisia. As one Catholic scholar observed, "In this overwhelming disaster of the Arab invasion the churches of Africa were blotted out. Not that all was destroyed, but that remnant of Christian life was so small as to be matter for erudition rather than for history."[31] In the sixth century, some five hundred bishops operated in this region; by the eighth century, it is hard to find any. Ironically, one of the paladins of North African Christianity in the third century had been the prophetic church father Tertullian, who wrote the famous line about the blood of martyrs being the seed of the church; yet some centuries later, this very church all but vanished before the Muslim invaders. In this case, seemingly, the seed had fallen on stony ground.

In Egypt, by contrast, which has been under Muslim rule since 640, not only does native Christianity survive to this day, but the Coptic Church has often exercised social and political influence. Even in the twentieth century, it probably still retained the loyalty of 10 percent of Egyptians. Possibly, such radical differences reflect different official policies, differing degrees of persecution, though nothing suggests that the conquerors of North Africa were dedicated to a kind of religious genocide. The differing outcomes chiefly arose from variations in the churches themselves, and that remark applies also to other parts of the old Christian world.

The question of how some churches survived demands at least as much attention as does that of why others died. To some extent, decisions taken by churches themselves determined whether they died or lived, whether they went the way of Africa or Egypt, or took some intermediate course. Some commonsense explanations come to mind, though none work very well for explaining this distinction. In theory at least, church structures should play some role, in that highly centralized and hierarchical organizations are more vulnerable to destruction than more decentralized groupings. So are churches whose operations depend entirely on ordained clergy as opposed to grassroots activism. And churches centered on monasteries, with large landed estates, are of course singularly vulnerable. Yet by all these criteria, the Egyptian church—hierarchical, clerical, and monastic—should have been an early candidate for extinction.

The key difference making for survival is rather how deep a church planted its roots in a particular community, and how far the religion became part of the air that ordinary people breathed. The Egyptian church succeeded wonderfully in this regard, while the Africans failed to make much impact beyond the towns. While the Egyptians put the Christian faith in the language of the ordinary people, from city dwellers through peasants, the Africans concentrated only on certain categories, certain races. Egyptian Christianity became native; its African counterpart was colonial. This difference became crucial when a faith that was formed in one set of social and political arrangements had to adapt to a new world. When society changed, when cities crumbled, when persecution came, the faith would continue in one region but not another.[32]

Ghosts

Religions die, but they leave ghosts. Religious persecutions drive believers to take refuge in more congenial areas, creating influential diasporas that spread ideas and cultural trends. This pattern, so familiar in Jewish history, is also found frequently in a Christian context, where exiles from crumbling communities have so often invigorated new societies and their churches.

A religion that dies in one area, in the sense of having no known active followers, may have many covert or clandestine believers, and—rather like the collapse of churches—crypto-Christianity is a thoroughly understudied phenomenon. In theory, true hidden believers should be immune to study, as they never break cover, and the people who can be studied are only the less discreet. But we often do hear of crypto-Christians, and the stories are startling, all the more so for Westerners accustomed to thinking of Christianity as the established faith of states.

Even after the overwhelming persecution that uprooted the Japanese church, thousands of "hidden Christians," *kakure kirishitan,* somehow maintained their clandestine traditions in remote fishing villages and island communities. This catacomb church strayed far from mainstream Catholicism, and many of its practices make it look almost like a Shinto sect: their Eucharistic elements are rice, fish, and sake. They knew nothing of the wider church, believing themselves to be the world's only true Christians. Yet the story still amazes. One moving documentary from the 1990s, *Otaiya,* actually allows us to hear very old believers reciting Catholic prayers that first came to the region over four hundred years ago, some in Church Latin and sixteenth-century Portuguese. They pray *"Ame Maria karassa binno domisu terikobintsu,"* a recollection of "Ave Maria gratia plena, dominus tecum, benedicta . . ." And they lovingly display a fragment of a silk robe once worn by one of the martyred Fathers. The film shows us the last two members of the indigenous hereditary priesthood, both frail men in their nineties, the distant successors of Saint Francis Xavier and the Jesuit pioneers.[33]

And crypto-Christians are startlingly abundant. The *World Christian Encyclopedia* suggests that in the year 2000, 120 million believers fell into this crypto-Christian category, some 6 percent of the world's Christians, mainly concentrated in Asian nations like India and China. If we were to separate them out from the main body of believers, those crypto-Christians alone would today constitute the world's fifth largest religion.[34] This is also, largely, a distinctively Christian phenomenon: while other religions, including Judaism and Islam, possess their secret believers, the absolute numbers are tiny beside those of crypto-Christians. Those figures may well be inflated or overoptimistic, but secret Christian communities have survived for centuries under hostile regimes, Muslim and other.

Ghosts also haunt the new religions that succeed the old. Destroying the organized worship of Mexico's old gods did not prevent ordinary believers from practicing familiar rituals and customs. Indeed, they integrated them into the new faith of Catholic Christianity, in the process reshaping the practice of that new religion. Across large sections of Africa and Asia, also, Islam and other religions built upon the ruins of older Christian communities, and incorporated many of the older ideas. The Christian impact on Islam was profound, and can be traced at the deepest roots of that faith. Mosques look as they do because their appearance derives from that of Eastern Christian churches in the early days of Islam. Likewise, most of the religious practices of the believers within those mosques stem from the example of Eastern Christians, including the prostrations that appear so alien to modern Westerners. The severe self-denial of Ramadan was originally based on the Eastern practice of Lent. The Quran itself often shows startling parallels with Eastern Christian scriptures, devotional texts, and hymns, and some scholars have even argued that much of the text originated in Syriac lectionaries, collections of readings for church use. The countless mosques built on the foundations of older churches—in many cases, using large portions of the older architecture—serve as a visual symbol of a lengthy and transforming process. Only by understanding the lost Eastern Christianities can we understand where Islam comes from, and how very close it is to Christianity.

Such incorporation of older faiths continued long after the initial spread of Islam. Asia Minor, for instance, had been Christian for twelve hundred years by the time the Muslim Turks secured political dominance, and many old Christian families survived, albeit as social inferiors. Women particularly tended to keep old beliefs alive, as they had neither the duty nor the opportunity to operate in the public sphere, where they would have been forced to reveal their religious loyalties on a daily basis. Christian women could pass on older ideas within the household, among the serving classes, and even to the children of Muslim masters. As late as the nineteenth century, many rural Turks who considered themselves faithful Muslims insisted on getting their children baptized, to safeguard their physical and spiritual health.[35] In much popular Muslim practice, we hear the echoes of older voices.

On occasion, the remnants of old religions transform their victors. No worthwhile history of Islam could omit the history of the Sufi orders, whose practices so often recall the bygone world of the Christian monks. It was the Christian monastics who had sought ecstasy and unity with the divine by the ceaseless repetition of prayers, a practice that would become central to the Sufi tradition. Once dead, Sufi adepts continued to attract devotees to their tombs, so that venerated sheikhs fulfilled exactly the same role for Muslims that the Christian saints had in their day. Christianity and Islam have far more in common than many rigorous believers of either faith would care to admit. The ruin of Middle Eastern and Asian Christianity had complex consequences for other faiths as well.

The connection between Islam and older Eastern forms of Christianity is so intimate, in fact, as to raise unsettling questions for modern-day members of both faiths. Often, when faithful Christians complain about aspects of that alien religion, they are in fact denouncing customs or beliefs that are deeply rooted within the most ancient forms of their own Christian faith. And while Muslims praise the prophet Jesus, few are aware of just how extensive a heritage they draw from the churches of the *Nasraye*, the Nazarenes. Christianity and Islam haunt each other beyond the skills of the world's greatest exorcists to expel. One would like to think that a recognition of these closely intertwined roots would provide a foundation for closer dialogue between the sister faiths.

Past and Present

Understanding the fallen churches tells us a great deal about the history of Christianity and its interaction with other faiths. But this story also has many implications for the present day, especially as modern churches confront the implications of globalization. In 2006, for instance, Pope Benedict's speech at Regensburg aroused the anger of Muslims who felt he had portrayed their faith as based on force and persecution. If nothing else, this affair demonstrated the enduring power of history, and specifically regarding the means by which the Middle East became Muslim. Who would have thought that quoting a fourteenth-century Byzantine emperor could have generated street demonstrations in the twenty-first century?[36]

Less noticed at the time, however, was a perhaps still more controversial theme, as Benedict insisted that authentic Christianity *had* to be based on the Greek philosophical tradition, establishing the European intellectual model as the inevitable norm for all future ages. This would be a far-reaching principle in an age when African and Asian Christians are trying to define their relationships with their surrounding cultures. Yet an awareness of the Christian past reminds us that through much of history, leading churches have successfully framed the Christian message in the context of non-Greek and non-European intellectual traditions, of Buddhism, Taoism, and Confucianism. That precedent is encouraging for modern intercultural encounters. Far from being a daring innovation, the globalized character of modern Christianity is better seen as a resumption of an ancient reality.

Also from a modern perspective, the issue of dechristianization is more troubling for many than it might have been even twenty or thirty years ago. Such a trend seems to be happening quite rapidly in contemporary Europe, where increased secularization has coincided with the mushrooming of immigrant Muslim communities. Many Europeans worry that a decline of Christian loyalties will be followed not by a nonjudgmental secular utopia, but by a society increasingly dominated by harsh forms of Islam, reinforced by threats of armed terror and mob violence. Conservative Americans have been happy to reinforce fears of an emerging Eurabia, suggesting that the inevitable fate of non-Muslims in such an order would be the degrading subject status of *dhimmitude*.[37] Suddenly, the destruction of bygone Christian societies seems highly relevant: hence, perhaps, Pope Benedict's rediscovery of the Byzantine past.

In this case, the historical examples of failed churches actually give some grounds for optimism, at least in pointing to the contrasts with the present situation. Little on Europe's horizon recalls the circumstances of the historic Middle East. There is no plausible prospect of a Muslim regime anywhere in western Europe, or of the re-creation of the social order on the lines of Muslim law. Realistically, people of Muslim background will constitute a substantial minority of the European population rather than a majority, and it is far from clear that most will define themselves primarily according to strict religious loyalties. European Christianity may be in anything but a healthy state, but Islam need not be its greatest cause for concern.

Matters are of course very different in other parts of the world, above all in Africa, which is currently home to 20 percent of the world's Christians, and that proportion should grow steeply in coming decades. *Should* grow—but there are concerns. The books in which African church leaders read the proud history of ancient Christianity on that continent also tell a story of ultimate ruin.

Hence the alarm about the spread of Islamic regimes and sharia law in various parts of the continent, in populous nations like Nigeria, where Muslims make no secret of their desire to reshape society in ways they find congenial. When we also recall that regions close to the equator will suffer the harshest and most immediate effects from global climate change, the prospects for social tension and religious violence are serious. While African Christians have enough momentum to survive all but the most serious challenges, hostile regimes could pose a danger. Growing Christian populations in South and East Asia might face similar long-term pressures.

Yet even for the West, the collapse of bygone churches, the destruction of Christian communities, still has a powerful contemporary relevance. Above all, this historic experience should teach a powerful lesson about the vulnerability of this faith—of any faith—and how transient it might be in any particular setting. Christians might point with confidence to the closing passage of the Gospel of Matthew, in which Jesus promises his disciples that he will be with them always, even until the end of the world. Yet that verse says nothing about the form of that continued presence, whether it would be represented within one particular church tradition, or even within an organized community. We can usefully recall the words of Saint Vincent de Paul, writing about 1640, at one of the most catastrophic moments of European history, in the depths of internecine slaughter during the Thirty Years' War. Watching Christians of various shades murdering and persecuting each other daily, Saint Vincent recalled that Jesus promised that his church would last until the end of time, but that he never mentioned the words *in Europe.* The church had flourished in different regions of the world in the past, and would in the future. Perhaps, he considered, the church of the future would continue in its full glory, but in Africa, Asia, or South America. At least as far as particular regions or continents are concerned, Christianity does not come with a warranty.

Viewed over the two-thousand-year span of Christian history, this was a profound observation, which has been validated time and again. Once, the prospect of a non- or post-Christian Syria or Mesopotamia would have seemed inconceivable, as the Christians of these lands knew incontrovertibly that they stood at the heart of the faith. That knowledge was part of their consciousness, as assuredly as twentieth-century citizens of France or Britain knew that their nations were fundamentally Christian. A thousand years ago, the Christians of Asia Minor held just the same assurance; yet that region today bears the name of Turkey, a country that notionally claims 99 percent Muslim loyalty.

A society that today considers itself Christian might in a century or two have equal confidence in its complete identification with Islam, or radical secularism, or Buddhism, or some other religion not yet born. That caveat also applies to specific denominations. If Christianity itself does not bear a warranty, still less do specific denominations or forms of the faith, and this point is not lost on Latin American Catholics, or Orthodox believers in Eastern Europe. Even if Christianity still flourishes in those parts of the world in a century or so, it might well be in forms that present-day majorities would find puzzling and uncongenial. Such an acknowledgment of transience and frailty should make Christians cautious about trying to associate their faith inextricably with any particular tradition or cultural form, still less any given political order.

We can certainly draw lessons from the mistakes churches make that hasten their demise, but other lessons also present themselves. Indeed, rather than asking why churches die, we should rather seek to know how they endure for so long, in seemingly impossible circumstances. The fate of Middle Eastern Christians is particularly impressive in this respect: as late as 1900, after all the coercion and disdain, they still made up some 10 percent of the region's population. We have much to learn about their adaptability in the face of dominant languages and cultures, their ability to learn the new languages of power, without abandoning their core beliefs. Christians around the world have vast accumulated experience about dealing with minority status, and with exclusion from power and influence on a scale vastly greater than that faced by any modern church in the West.

A Terrible History

The best reason for the serious study of history is that virtually everyone uses the past in everyday discourse. But the historical record on which they draw is abundantly littered with myths, half-truths, and folk history; historians can, or should, provide a corrective for this. This remark applies particularly to the history of Christianity and of the Christian church, which represents a familiar component of popular knowledge, part of "what everybody knows." Whatever the religious beliefs of a given audience, a majority of people, whether in private or public life, feels comfortable referring to aspects of that history, and particularly to great institutions or events, like the Crusades, the Inquisition, or the persecution of witches. Media accounts regularly draw on a standard body of assumptions and beliefs about Christian history, which is seen as a barely relieved saga of intolerance and obscurantism. Kathleen Jefferts Schori, presiding bishop of the U.S. Episcopal Church, neatly summarized this approach when she challenged Pope Benedict's claim that "Muslims have a history of violence. So do Christians! They have a terrible history. Look at history in the Dark Ages. Charlemagne converted whole tribes by the sword." James Carroll, author of the sweeping polemic *Constantine's Sword,* argues that "[e]ven in its foundation, the church was getting it wrong. That's why Christians go to church, as much to be forgiven as to be fed."[38]

The conventionally negative account of Christian history includes much that is true, in some places and at some times: we need not look far to find religious hatred and anti-Semitism, militarism and corruption. But the story is much more diverse than is commonly believed, much less a catalog of rigid orthodoxies enforced from above by the repressive mechanisms of church and (Christian) state. The familiar image of a western Europe hagridden by popes and clergy is only a tiny part of a much wider global canvas in which many different shades and varieties of Christianity coexisted, often suffering oppression: some coped; some succumbed altogether. So vast is this story in its geographical scope, so critical for later religious developments worldwide, that it is astonishing that it has been all but lost. We have forgotten a world.

2

Churches of the East

No one has been sent to us Orientals by the Pope. The holy apostles aforesaid taught us and we still hold today what they handed down to us.
—Rabban Bar Sauma, c. 1290

Merv (Merw) is the ancient name of one of the world's most evocative dead cities, located in the south of what is now Turkmenistan. In ancient times, it was Alexandria Margiana, one of the many cities named for the Macedonian conqueror, and through the Middle Ages this oasis community prospered on the strength of its location on the Silk Road. From the eighth century, it was a base for Muslim military expansion into central Asia. Its population swelled to two hundred thousand in the mid–twelfth century, making it (briefly) one of the largest cities on the planet.[1]

For several centuries, it was also one of the world's greatest Christian centers. Merv had a bishop by the 420s, and in 544 it became a metropolitan see of the Eastern (Nestorian) church. It was an ideal base for mission ventures to the east, among the Turkic tribes of central Asia, and beyond that, into China. Around 500, the school of Merv was translating essential works from Greek and Syriac into the languages of central and eastern Asia. The city had a rich history of Christian intellectual and spiritual life from the sixth century through the thirteenth, and Merv could compete in vigor with any

European center, certainly before the universities emerged in western Europe during the twelfth century. Merv's scholars had access to Syriac versions of Aristotle at a time when these texts were quite forgotten in western Europe. Several of the greatest Syriac scholars, including the brilliant Isho'dad, bear the title "of Merv."

Christians needed to maintain the highest intellectual standards because of the constant competition they faced from other faiths. From the seventh century, Merv was under Muslim rule, but Christians coexisted with Buddhists, Zoroastrians, and Manichaeans. The city was notorious for producing idiosyncratic blends of different faiths, old and new. Eighth-century Merv was the home of *al-Muqanna,* the Veiled Prophet, who claimed to be God incarnate.[2]

Although well known to specialists, Merv's story fits poorly with conventional assumptions about the development of Christianity. In a sense, the tale is both too ancient for our expectations, and too modern. It is too "ancient" in that it involves the survival of a Semitic Christianity into the second millennium. It is too "modern" in its portrayal of Christians living not as the intimate allies of a Christian king but as tolerated minorities; of a church in a multifaith society; and above all, of Asian Christians in a wholly non-European context.

For most nonexperts, Christian history after the earliest centuries usually conjures images of Europe. We think of the world of Charlemagne and the Venerable Bede, of Thomas Aquinas and Francis of Assisi, a landscape of Gothic cathedrals and romantic abbeys. We think of a church thoroughly complicit in state power— popes excommunicating emperors, and inspiring Crusades. Of course, such a picture neglects the ancient Christianity of the Eastern empire, based in Constantinople, but it also ignores the critical story of the religion beyond the old Roman borders, in Africa and Asia. We suffer perhaps from using unfamiliar terms like *Nestorian,* so that the Eastern religious story seems to involve some obscure sect or alien religion rather than an extraordinarily vigorous branch of the Christian tradition. Only by stressing the fully Christian credentials of these Asian-based movements can we appreciate the abundant fullness and diversity of the global church during the millennium after the Council of Nicea—and the depth of the catastrophe when those movements fell into ruin. Anyone who knows the Christian story only as it developed in Europe has little inkling of the acute impoverishment the religion suffered when it lost these thriving, long-established communities.

Christianity and Empire

The Roman Empire in which Christianity emerged extended far beyond the boundaries of Europe, and its richest provinces were in the Near East and North Africa. By the fifth century, Christianity had five great patriarchates, and only one, Rome, was to be found in Europe. Of the others, Alexandria stood on the African continent, and three (Constantinople, Antioch, and Jerusalem) were in Asia. After the fall of the Roman Empire in the West, Christianity maintained its cultural and intellectual traditions in the Eastern empire, in Asia Minor, Syria, and Egypt.[3]

Western historians are most familiar with the churches of the Roman Empire, which ultimately split between the Catholic and Orthodox, but for centuries these churches were at their most dynamic in the Middle East. Eastern cities like Antioch, Edessa, and Nisibis were the glories of the Christian world. Still in the eighth century, Rome itself was a remote outpost of an empire based in Constantinople, and the popes operated within a Byzantine political framework. The papacy was as thoroughly Eastern in language and culture as anywhere in Asia Minor, with the dominance of Greek (which was by now known as the "Roman" language) and Syriac. Between 640 and 740, no fewer than six popes derived from Syria, in addition to several Greek natives. When the Roman church in the 660s decided to bolster the emerging church in England, it sent as the new archbishop of Canterbury Theodore of Tarsus, from Cilicia, supported by the African abbot Hadrian. The last of the

"Greek" Fathers acknowledged by the church was the Syrian John of Damascus, who was Greek only in language. John (originally named Mansur) lived and worked in eighth-century Syria, and he held high office in the court of the Muslim caliph. Christianity in his age still looked like a Syrian spiritual empire.[4]

Repeatedly, we find that what we think of as the customs or practices of the Western churches were rooted in Syria or Mesopotamia. Eastern churches, for instance, had a special devotion to the Virgin Mary, derived partly from popular apocryphal Gospels. This enthusiasm gave rise to a number of new feasts such as the Purification and the Annunciation, as well as the commemorations of Mary's birth and passing, or Dormition. At the end of the seventh century, all these feasts were popularized in Rome by Pope Sergius, whose family was from Antioch. From there, the new Marian devotion spread across western Europe.[5]

Eastern churches also produced the musical traditions that are such a glory of Catholic culture. Syria, after all, has a strong claim to be the source of Christian music. No later than the second century, Syria (Edessa?) produced the *Odes of Solomon*—what has been termed "the earliest Christian hymnbook." The earliest known pioneer of Christian music and chant was the Gnostic Bardaisan of Edessa, who around 200 composed hymns and songs that won a wide audience. Seeking to counter his heretical influence, Syrian church leaders like Ephrem of Edessa kept the older melodies and rhythms but added their own orthodox lyrics. Syrian music profoundly influenced later composers both East and West. It also shaped the various musical forms in the Western Latin world, and the Ambrosian chant of Milan was ordered "to be sung in the Syrian manner."[6]

The sequence of Eastern popes in Rome naturally imported customs and music familiar to them. When modern Catholics and Episcopalians sing the Agnus Dei in their liturgy, when they invoke the "Lamb of God, who takes away the sins of the world," they are following the Syrian custom imported to the Western church by Pope Sergius. Describing the arrival of Theodore and Hadrian from the Mediterranean, Bede records that "[f]rom that time also, they began in all the churches of the English to learn Church music." What we call Gregorian chant is a later synthesis of these local musical traditions, which ultimately stemmed from Syria.[7]

This Asian dominance continued for centuries. By the tenth century, the Byzantine Empire still had fifty-one metropolitans, supervising a hierarchy of 515 bishops, and of these, thirty-two metropolitans and 373 bishops were still to be found in Asia Minor. Some of the metropolitan sees here, based in cities with associations dating back to the earliest Christian era, ruled over whole subordinate hierarchies as numerous as those of some Western nations. The metropolitan see of Ephesus had 34 subordinate bishops; Myra had 33; Laodicea and Seleucia, 22 each; Sardis and Antioch-in-Pisidia, 21 each.[8] Easterners could afford to scorn the pretensions of Rome and the upstart churches of the West. One Byzantine Emperor mocked Latin as "a barbarian and Scythian language," unworthy to be spoken in the civilized ambience of Greek and Syriac: it was scarcely fit for Christian use.

Moving East

Let me present a story that is radically unfamiliar to most Western readers.

From its earliest days, Christianity spread throughout the empire, despite severe persecutions at the hands of imperial officials, who feared it as alien and subversive. Yet despite long sufferings and many martyrdoms, the new faith slowly won grudging toleration. Christians established influential churches and schools in the great cities and communication hubs. Benefiting from the empire's peace and stability, Christians spread along the protected trade routes, and used the familiar languages of the ruling elites. The ecclesiastical hierarchy closely mirrored the old imperial structure of cities and provinces, and when that empire faded away, the Christian church survived on its ruins.

Now, it may sound ludicrous to describe such a story as unfamiliar, as I am apparently describing the well-known course of Christian expansion into the Roman world. But in fact, this was also the story of the *Persian* Empire, where Christians won some of their most enduring successes. The Eastern expansion faithfully mirrors that in the West.

So central is the Roman world to the traditional story that for centuries, Christian historians have given a providential interpretation to the spread of Roman power. Rome built the roads and defended the sea routes along which traveled the missionaries, who spoke to their audiences in the widely familiar tongues of Greek and Latin. Obviously, it seems, Christianity's destiny lay to the west, in Europe. In fact, though, choosing a different map would give a completely different perspective on the worldview of the earliest Christians, and the opportunities available to them. The most important corrective for traditional visions of religious change involves the borders of the Roman Empire, which seem to demarcate the limits of Christian expansion. Yet these borders, which changed dramatically over time, placed few real limits on trade, whether in goods or ideas.[9]

Once we remove the symbolic constraint of the borders, we get a better sense of the opportunities available to early Christians. The Mediterranean world had its very familiar routes, but so did the lands east and northeast of Jerusalem, through Syria, Mesopotamia, and beyond. Still in early Christian times, travelers could follow sections of the ancient Persian Royal Road, which ran from southwestern Iran through Babylon and into northern Mesopotamia. These were the Asian worlds subjected by Alexander the Great, and they were littered with place-names commemorating him and his generals—all the Alexandrias, Antiochs and Seleucias that stretch as far east as Afghanistan: Kandahar takes its name from Alexander. Through the late Middle Ages, Eastern Christians even continued to use a calendar based on the Seleucid Era. Instead of dating events

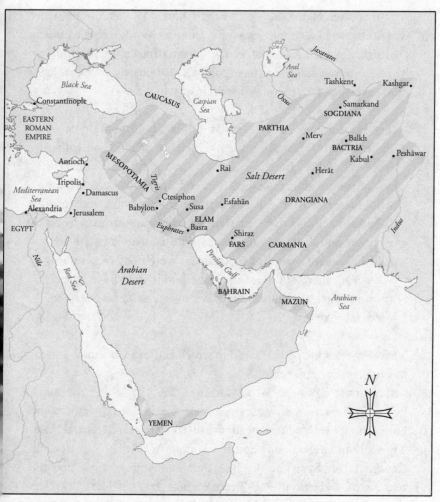

MAP 2.1. THE SASSANIAN PERSIAN EMPIRE

from the birth of Christ, their point of reference was still the establishment of Seleucid rule in Syria/Palestine in 312/311 B.C.[10]

In the sixth century, the geographer Cosmas Indicopleustes described this Eastern world in terms that, although not always accurate, show how clearly contemporaries recognized the scale of an

Asia that stretched as far as *Tzinitza,* China. Cosmas himself, who was probably a Nestorian, owed his name to having sailed to India. He calculated the breadth of Eurasia, from China to the Atlantic, to be roughly four hundred stages, or twelve thousand miles, using a crude average of thirty miles for each stage:

> The measurement is to be made in this way: from Tzinitza to the borders of Persia, between which are included all Iouvia [the land of the Huns?], India, and the country of the Bactri-ans, there are about one hundred and fifty stages at least; the whole country of the Persians has eighty stations; and from Nisibis to Seleucia there are thirteen stages; and from Seleucia to Rome and the Gauls and Iberia, whose inhabitants are now called Spaniards, onward to Gadeira, which lies out towards the ocean, there are more than one hundred and fifty stages; thus making altogether the number of stages to be four hun-dred, more or less.[11]

That was the scale of the world in which Eastern Christians sought to proclaim their message.

The great Antioch on the Orontes, the city where the name "Christian" first arose, was a terminus for an ancient trade route connecting the Mediterranean world to Persia and central Asia. Throughout late antiquity and the Middle Ages, the legendary Silk Road ran from Syria into northern Persia and into what are now the nations of Uzbekistan and Turkmenistan. Beyond Merv, travelers crossed the Oxus River (the Amu Darya) to enter central Asia proper, and reached Bukhara and Samarkand. The route ultimately took them over forty-five hundred miles, into the heart of China. As Cosmas knew, "He then who comes by land from Tzinitza to Persia shortens very considerably the length of the journey." From Bukhara, one could follow the branching roads and tracks that linked central Asia to the Indian subcontinent.[12]

Focusing as we do on the Roman dimensions of early Christianity, we can forget just how accessible these Asian lands were for Middle Eastern believers, for Christians in Antioch or Edessa. We are scarcely surprised to learn that by 200 A.D. there were Christians in Gaul and Britain, in Carthage and Northwest Africa, but Christians had traveled far to reach these western lands. From Jerusalem to Athens is eight hundred miles as the crow flies: it is fourteen hundred miles to Rome, fifteen hundred to Carthage, and over two thousand to Paris or London. But just imagine traveling similar distances in the opposite direction, by land rather than sea. Going east from Jerusalem, the distance to Baghdad is just six hundred miles. From Jerusalem to Tehran is less than a thousand miles, while it is fourteen hundred to Merv and eighteen hundred fifty to Samarkand. Just in terms of mileage, Jerusalem is equidistant from Merv and Rome. Jerusalem is actually closer to the seemingly exotic territories of central Asia than it is to France. And if going west meant relying on Roman stability, eastward travelers depended on Persian power. As in Europe, early followers of Jesus spread into a world already extensively colonized by Jews, who had made Mesopotamia an intellectual center of their faith. Between the fourth and sixth centuries, thriving Jewish academies created the Babylonian Talmud.[13]

Alternatively, ancient sea routes connected the Mediterranean and Indian worlds, and abundant discoveries of Roman goods in southern India remind us of the sea traffic from Egypt. Between the fourth century and the ninth, Christian communities became widespread around the littoral of the Indian Ocean, the Red Sea, and the Persian Gulf. Major settlements and churches existed throughout Arabia and Yemen, Persia and southern India. If early Christians could reach Ireland, there was no logical reason why they should not find their way to Sri Lanka.[14]

Lost Kingdoms

Not surprisingly, then, we must look beyond the borders of Rome to find the world's earliest Christian states. The world's first Christian kingdom was Osrhoene, beyond the eastern borders of the Roman Empire, with its capital at Edessa: its king accepted Christianity around 200.[15] That regime did not last long, but neighboring Armenia made this the official religion around the year 300 and retains the faith until the present day. The Christian kingdom reached its height under the Bagratid rulers of the early Middle Ages, when the royal capital of Ani became one of the great cities of the Eastern Christian world. Although Ani has been a ghost town for centuries, enough ruins of cathedrals, churches, basilicas, and monasteries survive to give some impression of "the city of 1,001 churches." If the site stood in western Europe, it would be as cherished as Chartres or York Minster. The conversion of Armenia also led to the creation of an Armenian alphabet by the fifth century, and soon, a substantial written literature. Christianity became inextricably bound up with Armenian culture, identity, and nationhood.[16]

Georgia was converted shortly after Armenia, and both lands have left a splendid heritage in the form of ancient churches and monasteries, not to mention Christian manuscript art. Georgia, too, acquired its alphabet from Christian missionaries. To the east of Osrhoene was the small border kingdom of Adiabene, with its capital at Arbela. Whether or not the kingdom formally accepted Christianity, as legend claims, Arbela was undoubtedly an early Christian center. (It also had a strong Jewish presence.)[17]

The strength of Christianity in Egypt made it very likely that the faith would expand up the Nile, deep into Africa, and Syrian missionaries led the way. Nubia survived as a Christian kingdom from the sixth century through the fifteenth, dominating the Nile between Khartoum and Aswan, and straddling the modern-day border of Egypt and Sudan. Nubia's churches and cathedrals were decorated with rich murals in the best Byzantine style, showing their dark-skinned kings in royal robes. Its main cathedral at Faras was adorned with hundreds of paintings of kings and bishops, saints and biblical figures—images that lay forgotten under the sands until rediscovered in the 1960s. This Christian state became a major player in African politics. In 745 its king invaded Egypt, with the goal of defending the patriarch of Alexandria:

> And there were under the supremacy of Cyriacus, king of the Nubians, thirteen kings, ruling the kingdom and the country. He was the orthodox Ethiopian king of Al-Mukurrah; and he was entitled the Great King, upon whom the crown descended from Heaven; and he governed as far as the southern extremities of the earth.

By the 830s, the patriarch of Alexandria "appointed many bishops, and sent them to all places under the see of Saint Mark the evangelist, which include Africa and the Five Cities and Al-Kairuwân and Tripoli and the land of Egypt and Abyssinia and Nubia."[18]

Ethiopia, or Abyssinia, was still more powerful than Nubia, and its Christianity longer lasting. It was in fact converted even before Constantine accepted the faith. The kingdom's ancient center was Aksum, which had historically been a key point of contact with pharaonic Egypt, and by 340 this was the kingdom's main Christian see. Over the next three centuries, the Bible and liturgy were translated into the local language of Ge'ez. From the late fifth century, Syriac Christians were credited with introducing monasticism, which led to the foundation of many houses across northern Ethiopia.[19] When Europeans discovered the country in the seventeenth century, they were astounded by the degree of Christian devotion. Even an author from Counter-Reformation Portugal, where religious houses were far from scarce, asserted that

> [n]o country in the world is so full of churches, monasteries and ecclesiastics as Abyssinia; it is not possible to sing in one

church without being heard by another, and perhaps by several. . . . this people has a natural disposition to goodness; they
are very liberal of their alms, they much frequent their
churches, and are very studious to adorn them; they practice
fasting and other mortifications . . . [they] retain in a great
measure the devout fervor of the primitive Christians.[20]

So rich is Ethiopia's Christian heritage, as it now enters its eighteenth century of existence, that it is impossible to describe it in any
detail, but we should stress how absolutely Christian tradition has
become established within the East African landscape. When Ethiopians read or hear the Bible, they do not need to imagine that the
events are at all distant in time or space. Aksum is, after all, the reputed home of the Ark of the Covenant. The sacred landscape is
no less apparent at Lalibela, New Jerusalem, the setting for the clus-
ter of awe-inspiring rock-hewn churches built in the thirteenth century that are among the miracles of medieval architecture. The
medieval ruling dynasty claimed descent from Solomon and the
queen of Sheba, and this history was elaborated in the fourteenth-
century chronicle the *Kebra Nagast*. With so much evidence to hand,
who could doubt that Ethiopia was the true Israel?[21]

Ethiopian Christianity was also a thoroughly African affair, in
which the church depended on the patriarchs or popes of Alexandria, who ruled through their representatives, the *abunas*. Struggling
for control with them were the local monastic leaderships: Africans
argued with Africans. The nation was on occasion a potent ally for
Egypt's Christians, when they fell under Muslim rule: as late as the
fourteenth century, Ethiopia tried to prevent the ongoing persecution in Egypt by threatening to dam the Nile.[22]

Nestorians and Jacobites

When Christians traveled beyond the Roman frontier, they had to
leave the protection of the empire, but the very fact of imperial

power could be a mixed blessing. Already by the third century, Persia had a substantial Christian presence, concentrated in the south of the country, along the Gulf. Once Rome became Christian, the link with that foreign government made life difficult for Christians living under the rule of the rival superpower of the time. (From the third century through the seventh, Persia was ruled by the powerful Sassanian dynasty.) The Persians responded by executing hundreds of bishops and clergy in a persecution at least as murderous as anything ever inflicted by pagan Rome: in the fourth century, the Persians killed sixteen thousand Christian believers in a forty-year period.[23]

Yet operating beyond the reach of Roman power had advantages for religious groups who now found themselves condemned or persecuted by imperial authorities—for Jews, and also for those Christian sects that the established Catholic/Orthodox deemed heretical. As the church-state alliance became ever more firmly entrenched in Rome and Constantinople, so ever more Christian believers were forced to flee beyond the frontier, especially into those weakly controlled borderlands that became such fertile territory for religious innovation and interaction.[24] The number and importance of such religious dissidents grew steadily with the fifth-century splits over the relationship between Christ's human and divine natures. Monophysite teachings dominated in Syria and Egypt, and also prevailed in the Christian states of Armenia and Ethiopia. Orthodox supporters of the Council of Chalcedon were so massively outnumbered that they were dismissively known as Melkites—"the emperor's men"—suggesting that only their desire to please government could account for their wrongheaded opinions.[25]

Once free of Roman oversight, Christian leaders were free to establish their own churches, following the doctrines they believed to be correct. Within the Persian Empire, the main Christian church was based in the twin cities of Seleucia-Ctesiphon, the imperial capital that was the successor to ancient Babylon, and the most populous city in the world at that time. This church followed the teachings of Nestorius after 431, detaching itself from the authority of Antioch: in 498 its head, the catholicos, took the title of patriarch of Babylon, the patriarch of the East. In the sixth century, Asian Monophysites also developed their own church apparatus, through the organizing ability of Jacobus Baradaeus. From his base in Edessa, Jacobus created a whole clandestine church, in which he ordained two patriarchs and eighty-nine bishops. These two alternative churches, the Nestorians and the Jacobites, represented powerful rivals for the Orthodoxy that held power in Constantinople.[26]

The Persians, meanwhile, were delighted to discover that so many Roman subjects were disaffected from Roman rule, and they protected these potential enemies of Roman power.[27] By 550, Cosmas the India-Sailor reported:

> And so likewise among the Bactrians and Huns and Persians, and the rest of the Indians, Persarmenians, and Medes and Elamites, and throughout the whole land of Persia there is no limit to the number of churches with bishops and very large communities of Christian people, as well as many martyrs, and monks also living as hermits.[28]

The Nestorians and other non-Orthodox churches initially coped well with the Muslim regime that supplanted the Persians, and who accepted their Christian subjects as tributaries and taxpayers if not as full equals.

Landscapes

Eastern Christianity had many spiritual and cultural centers, and the map of these religious powerhouses remained little changed between about 500 and 1200—that is, across the seemingly irrevocable change caused by the Arab conquests. Outside Constantinople, great monastic houses included Mar Saba in Palestine and Deir Mar Musa in Syria, each a fortified complex surrounded by the settle-

MAP 2.2. THE HEART OF THE CHRISTIAN MIDDLE EAST

ments of hundreds of hermits. (*Mor* or *Mar* is the Syriac word for "master" or "lord," and it serves the same function as *saint* in the Western churches.[29]) Legendary Egyptian centers included Saint Catherine's monastery in Sinai and Saint Antony's near the Red Sea, while "the holy desert" of Wadi el-Natrun was an extensive landscape of perhaps a hundred religious houses and hermitages, some very ancient. When the Armenian traveler Abû Sâlih offered a travel guide to Egypt's churches and monasteries around 1200, he was still describing a flourishing network of active monastic houses and pilgrimage shrines that was as extensive as anything in contemporary western Europe.[30]

The Christian continuity at such centers is astonishing. When the legendary icons of Saint Catherine's were displayed in the United States in 2006–7, the greatest treasure was a painting of Saint Peter that was apparently commissioned at or shortly after the opening of the house, in the sixth century. Over time, too, these houses acquired some of the greatest libraries that existed after the end of classical antiquity: Saint Catherine's has over three thousand manuscripts, in Greek, Arabic, Syriac, Georgian, and Slavonic. Another fine collection existed at Deir es-Souriani, the Monastery of the Syrians, in Egypt's Wadi el-Natrun. This library was the life's project of the tenth-century abbot Moses of Nisibis, who made it his business to gather all the works of Syriac learning he could find, some 250 manuscripts.[31]

Between the Rivers

Syriac-speaking Christianity found a stronghold in Mesopotamia, around the northern reaches of the rivers Euphrates and Tigris. Northern Mesopotamia was an ancient land, one of the original hearths of civilization, and it was the core of ancient Assyria. Today, though, these older names have vanished and bear no relationship to modern state divisions: in terms of modern nations, we are speaking of the area where Iraq, Turkey, and Syria come together, and where activists now struggle to create a new Kurdistan. The region includes many names that are much in the news as centers of political violence and instability. Southeastern Turkey, centered on Diyarbakir, is the heart of militant Kurdish resistance to the Turkish state. Yet for centuries, the major churches and religious houses here were as famous as any in Christian Europe.

To understand the region's importance for the history of Christianity, we have to imagine the completely different ethnic, political, and religious landscape between, say, the fourth century and the fourteenth. Northern Mesopotamia lay close to the most significant early powerhouses of Christian expansion, such as Edessa, and it is not surprising to find so many thriving Christian communities in the region. Diyarbakir was once Amida, a thriving monastic center and a patriarchal seat, while nearby Malatya was once the Christian metropolis of Melitene. Northwest of Mosul lies the Tur Abdin Plateau, the Mountain of the Servants of God. In this area we find the cities of Nisibis and Mardin, as well as a group of perhaps a hundred monasteries that have been described as the Mount Athos of the East.[32]

This region was critically important for both Nestorians and Jacobites. When the Romans closed the Nestorian university at Edessa, its leaders took up residence farther east at Nisibis, under Persian protection. As a chronicler boasted, "Edessa darkened and Nisibis brightened."[33] Even so, Edessa remained "the Blessed" for all denominations well into the Muslim period. By the seventh century, the Nestorian church alone had six provinces in Mesopotamia, ruling over a substantial hierarchy. Nisibis itself was a metropolitan see with six lesser bishoprics under its control.[34]

At different times, Jacobite leaders were based in Amida and in Tikrit, a city that in modern times gained notoriety as the home of Saddam Hussein and his Sunni Muslim al-Tikriti clan, which dominated Iraq under the Baathist regime. Once, though, Tikrit served as the seat of the Maphrianus (Mapheryan, or Consecrator), who headed the Jacobite church throughout Persia and the East. As late as the eleventh century, Melitene still counted fifty-six churches, and seven Jacobite dioceses looked to Melitene.[35]

Monasteries proliferated, and although most have left no physical trace, religious houses must once have been as thick on the ground as anywhere in the Christian world, including Ireland. Even today, a handful of ancient monasteries survive to suggest what they must have been like when they were the holiest shrines in an overwhelmingly Christian landscape. From the Jacobite tradition, we find the network of houses around Tur Abdin in what is now southeastern Turkey, each marked by the huge water cisterns needed for survival in this arid land. The house of Mor Gabriel, founded in the late fourth century, is today the oldest functioning monastery of the Jacobite Church (known in modern times as "Syrian Orthodox"). The building itself dates from around 510 but contains older fragments.[36] Nearby stands Mor Hananyo, Saint Ananias. Its yellow brick construction has also given this structure the name of Deir ez-Za'feran, the Saffron Monastery, and its history dates back to the 490s. From the eleventh century, these houses would also be the centers of the ecclesiastical hierarchy. Jacobite patriarchs lived at Antioch until 1034, when they moved to Mar Barsauma, near Melitene, which was home to several hundred brothers. In 1293, the patriarchs took up residence at Deir ez-Za'feran, where their successors remained until 1924.[37]

Nestorians, too, had their venerated monasteries, especially the house of Beth 'Abhe, near Mosul, which had some three hundred brothers. Just how commonplace smaller monasteries and hermitages must have been across northern Mesopotamia is obvious from the ninth-century work the *Book of Governors,* by the bishop Thomas of Marga. Thomas's stories often involve abbots and churchmen visiting religious houses, many of which have dropped out of the historical record. Today, they survive only as fragmentary remains under Iraqi village mosques.[38]

To the Ends of the Earth

By the seventh century, the Nestorians had an elaborate network of provinces and dioceses in Persia and neighboring lands, and they were naturally looking north and east. After all, the Persian Empire then stretched deep into central Asia, into the far western territories of what is now China. Already by the sixth century, Christian missionaries were reaching into the heart of Asia, and from the very beginning they recognized the need for vernacular scriptures, inventing alphabets where necessary. Some bold spirits even translated holy books into the language of the Huns. In 591, the Byzantines were puzzled to find that Turkish envoys from Kyrgyzstan had crosses tattooed on their foreheads: "They had been assigned this by their mothers; for when a fierce plague was endemic among them, some Christians advised them that the foreheads of the young be tattooed with that sign."[39]

Christian missionaries spread among the peoples of central Asia—the Turks, Uygurs, and Soghdians, and later the Mongols and Tatars. In 644, a chronicle tells how "Elias Metropolitan of Merv, converted a large number of Turks." Traveling beyond the Oxus, the metropolitan met a king on his way to war, and the king promised he would be converted if Elias showed him a sign. The metropolitan

> was then moved by divine power, and he made the sign of the heavenly cross, and rebuked the unreal thing that the rebellious demons had set up and it forthwith disappeared completely. When the king saw what Saint Elijah [Elias] did ... he was converted with all his army. The saint took them to a stream, baptized all of them, ordained for them priests and deacons, and returned to his country.

By 650, the Church of the East had two metropolitans beyond the Oxus, probably based at Kashgar and Samarkand, besides twenty bishops. At the end of the eighth century, the patriarch Timothy renewed the church's eastward drive, to the lands of the Turks and Tibetans, in a golden age of missionary expansion.[40]

Apart from the efforts of monks and clergy, widely traveled Soghdian merchants spread the faith across central Asia. Indeed, Syriac Christian writers used the word *merchant* as a metaphor for those who spread the gospel. One hymn urges:

Travel well girt like merchants,
That we may gain the world.
Convert men to me,
Fill creation with teaching.

Such merchants also brought the Syriac language. Even the Mongol word for "religious law" or "Buddhism"—*nom*—probably comes from the Greek *nomos,* via Syriac. We see the product of Soghdian labors at a site like Suyab in Kyrgyzstan, where the Nestorian church stands near a Buddhist monastery and a Zoroastrian fire temple. Spectacular religious diversity is also obvious in the scriptures from the Uygur center in the Turfan oasis, in what would later become Chinese Turkestan. Although Turfan is best known for its Manichaean texts, it also produced Christian documents, in Syriac, Soghdian, and Turkish, as well as Buddhist writings.[41] At a Christian cemetery in Kyrgyzstan, inscriptions in Syriac and Turkish commemorate Terim the Chinese, Sazik the Indian, Banus the Uygur, Kiamata of Kashgar, and Tatt the Mongol.[42]

China and India

The Chinese missions naturally attracted special attention. China, after all, was already more populous than the whole of Europe. We are not sure when Nestorians reached China—just when did the first Christian see the Pacific?—but already in 550, some monks smuggled silkworms from Serinda (China) to the Byzantine Empire. In creating the Western silk industry, this act was of revolutionary economic significance, but the religious implications are harder to assess. Already in 550, these monks had lived "a long time" in Serinda, and were used to traveling back and forth to Byzantine lands.[43]

The earliest formal mission can be dated to 635, when missionaries reached the Chinese imperial capital of Ch'ang-an, establishing a mission that endured for over two hundred years. Either fortunately or through acute judgment, they arrived in the early days of the new Tang dynasty, when entrenched interests were not as determined to exclude outside faiths as they might have been either before or afterward. In fact, the reigning emperor, Taizong, proved startlingly open to all kinds of foreign influences, including Buddhism. His regime granted toleration to a Christianity that was described as "mysterious, wonderful, spontaneous, producing perception, establishing essentials, for the salvation of creatures and the benefit of man." This was *Jingjiao,* the "luminous teaching" from the distant land of Daqin (Tachin), or Syria. Monasteries spread across the country, using local building styles: the remains of one can still be seen in Shaanxi Province, in the seventh-century Daqin pagoda. By the end of the eighth century, the Chinese church was led by Bishop Adam, whom we have already met as an ally of Buddhism, but who also promoted his own cause. The appointment of a metropolitan in the early ninth century proves the existence of multiple bishoprics.[44]

In this case, the Nestorian mission proved to have shallow roots, and apparently failed to develop a mass local following: virtually all the names on the famous Nestorian monument of the late eighth century are Syriac. Indeed, this mission would be destroyed in the mid–ninth century when the Taoist emperor Wuzong condemned and expelled foreign religions and closed monasteries. As the imperial edict commanded,

As for the Tai-Ch'in (Syrian Christian) and Muh-hu (Zoroastrian) forms of worship, since Buddhism has already been cast out, these heresies alone must not be allowed to survive. People belonging to these also are to be compelled to return to the world, belong again to their own districts, and become taxpayers. As for foreigners, let them be returned to their own countries, there to suffer restraint.[45]

The ease with which Nestorians were expelled suggests the limitations of their mission, and particularly their failure to spread beyond a particular ethnic group.

Between the tenth century and the thirteenth, Christianity has no recorded history in China, which does not mean that it did not maintain a subterranean existence. But Nestorians returned in force when the Mongols conquered the nation and established the Yuan dynasty (1271–1368). Mongol rulers like Kublai Khan were happy to tolerate the Christian and Buddhist religions, and Marco Polo often reports finding Christian communities. Not surprisingly, Nestorians were firmly established in those areas that had the best trading contacts with the outside world, along the Silk Road, and on the southeastern coast, in cities such as Zhenjiang (Chinkiang), with its seven monasteries, and Hangzhou. Building on Nestorian efforts, Roman Catholic missionaries arrived at the end of the thirteenth century, with the goal of establishing a whole Chinese hierarchy, with bishops at Beijing, Zaitun (Quanzhou), and elsewhere.[46]

Another scene of Nestorian successes was in India, where Christian communities claimed a succession dating back to Saint Thomas the apostle. Christianity appeared in southern India no later than the second century, and other missions and monasteries followed. Around 425, we hear of an Indian priest translating the Epistle to the Romans from Greek into Syriac. In 550, Cosmas reported, from firsthand observation, that

[e]ven in Taprobanê [Sri Lanka], an island in Further India, where the Indian Sea is, there is a church of Christians, with clergy and a body of believers, but I know not whether there be any Christians in the parts beyond it. In the country called Malê [Malabar], where the pepper grows, there is also a church, and at another place called Calliana there is moreover a bishop, who is appointed from Persia.[47]

India by this time had an indigenous church with its own hierarchy. Through the Middle Ages, churches operated on India's Malabar coast, in modern Kerala. As faithful members of the Church of the East, they used a Syriac liturgy and looked to the patriarch of Babylon as their spiritual head. Major churches existed at Mylapore (near Chennai), the alleged site of Thomas's martyrdom, and Nestorian crosses survive at Kottayam.[48]

Unlike other churches, which so often feature in the record of martyrdoms and persecutions, the Thomas Christians were blessed with having very little history to report. In 1500, a Nestorian reported that, in India, "there are here about thirty thousand families of Christians, our co-religionists. . . . They have begun to build new churches, are prosperous in every respect and living in peace and security." These churches also continued Christian expansion long after it had ceased elsewhere. In 1503, we hear of the ordination of "three pious monks" as bishops: the patriarch "sent them to the country of India, to the islands of the sea which are inside Java, and to China." Java was then closely tied to Indian trade routes. We have no idea how much earlier Christians had exploited those connections, or just how far they might have penetrated into Indonesia and Southeast Asia. Scholars have speculated on possible Nestorian ventures into Burma, Vietnam, the Philippines, and Korea.[49]

Although the Nestorian church was the most widespread, other Christian groups also had a broad Asian presence. In 1280, the Jacobite patriarch still "oversaw twenty metropolitans and about a hundred bishops from Anatolia and Syria to lower Mesopotamia and Persia."[50] By way of comparison, the English church at the same time had just twenty-five bishops.

No less impressive is the expansion of the Manichaean movement, which by this stage had evolved outside any recognizable form of Christianity, but which followed a geographical and political trajectory very much like those of the Syriac-speaking churches. Mani himself was a Mesopotamian, born in Babylon, and he spent his early years among the Elchesaites, a Jewish-Christian Gnostic sect. Mani's own movement became a separate religion that taught an absolute struggle between the irreconcilable forces of light and darkness. However, Manichaeans still believed that Jesus, like Buddha, was one of the great prophets who came to enlighten believers. After the newly Christian Roman Empire brutally suppressed Manichaean monks and teachers, the faith survived beyond the borders, and it spread along the Silk Road. In 762 the Manichaeans acquired state backing when the leader of the Uygur nation accepted the faith. This was potentially epoch making, as the Uygur Empire at that time covered a vast territory north of China.[51]

Converting Asia?

Calculating the numerical strength of these mission churches is all but impossible, not least because demographers differ so widely on the figures for organized and settled regions such as Egypt, and are even vaguer when dealing with remote nomadic communities. We can say confidently, though, that populations in the early Middle Ages were far smaller than might be expected in comparable regions today, so that the whole caliphate might have amounted to only 30 or 40 million people. That small scale of population was significant because establishing Christianity among a relatively small community might be a very valuable investment in the long term, if that group rose to political power. Conversely, a religion that existed among small compact populations was relatively easy to destroy by massacre or ethnic cleansing.

For all missionaries in that era, the ultimate dream was to convert a king or a ruling class, who would then bring the whole state into the church. This is what happened, briefly, when the Manichaeans won over the Uygurs. The Nestorians repeatedly came close to winning over whole peoples, most impressively the Mongol conquerors of the thirteenth century, but they rarely succeeded in creating a Christian state. The church did, however, achieve a real foothold among several important peoples, including the Uygurs and the Onggud Turks. Their greatest triumph came about 1000, when the king of the Kerait Turks (on the shores of Lake Baikal) accepted the faith that had originally been imported into his realm by Christian traders, probably from Merv. Reportedly, he brought over two hundred thousand of his subjects, and the Keraits retained a Christian presence for some four hundred years. The Keraits would not found a lasting state, but such a conversion might well have had great effects. Other, similar tribes would, after all, create great empires—the Seljuk Turks, who conquered much of the Byzantine Empire, and the Sons of Othman, who founded the vast Ottoman realm. Who was to say that the Keraits might not someday build their own Christian empire? In the event, Kerait women extended Christian influence through their marriages to influential pagan warlords.[52]

In the twelfth century, tales of Christian tribes in central Asia—and of Christian kings in Ethiopia—inspired the enduring European legend of Prester John. John, the immensely powerful Christian priest-king who lived far beyond the boundaries of the known world, was reputedly descended from one of the three Magi. According to a bogus letter that surfaced in Europe in the 1140s, Prester John declared that he was "a zealous Christian and universally protected the Christians of our empire, supporting them by our alms. . . . Seventy-two provinces, of which only a few are Christian, serve us. Each has its own king, but all are tributary to us." It was a dream, but the notion of a Christian kingdom beyond the caliphate was not wholly fanciful.[53]

A European comparison suggests the relative speed, as well as the scale, of Christian growth in the East. In fact, Eastern achievements in such vast areas look all the more impressive when set beside the relatively slow pace of European conversion. Although Christianity reached the European continent in Saint Paul's time, the religion took a long while to move beyond the Mediterranean world. The Franks who conquered Roman Gaul accepted the faith in the early sixth century, the Anglo-Saxons during the seventh, but that still left a great deal of Europe unevangelized. (In each case, of course, the dates for conversion refer to the formal acceptance of Christianity by the political elites, and paganism maintained an underground life for decades afterward.) At the end of the eighth century, Charlemagne was fighting a long war to conquer the pagan Saxons who dominated central Germany, and the conversion of the Slavs and Scandinavians took at least two hundred years more. Only in 987 did the Russian kingdom based in Kiev accept the Orthodox Church, after considering the rival attractions of Islam and Judaism. Poland accepted Christianity in 966, while Norway and Sweden were in the process of conversion only around 1000. The continent's conversion from paganism was only completed when the powerful state of Lithuania accepted the new religion, as late as the 1380s.

The continuing strength of Christianity in Asia is obvious if we look at the distribution of the world's believers around the year 1000, roughly at the halfway point in the story of the faith. Still, at that point, Asia had 17 to 20 million Christians, with a further 5 million in Africa. The European continent as a whole had some 40 million people, including Russia. Of those Europeans, at least a quarter either were still pagan or else lived in countries that had only very recently undergone formal conversion. That overall total would also include the Muslim inhabitants of Spain and Sicily, perhaps 4 or 5 million, in addition to European Jews. By this point, a reasonable estimate would suggest that Europe had some 25 to 30 million Christians, many whose faith was very notional indeed compared with the ancient churches of Asia and Africa.[54] Many Europeans were still in the first or second generation of the faith, a situation comparable to that of modern-day Africa. Most Asian Christians, in contrast, stemmed from Christian traditions dating back twenty-five or thirty generations. If raw numbers favored Europe, Asia could still properly claim the leadership of the Christian world.

3

Another World

In the year 1639 [AD 1328] that is the Dragon Year. This is the grave of Pesoha the renowned exegetist and preacher who enlightened all cloisters through the light—extolled for wisdom, and may our Lord unite his spirit with the saints.

—Syriac grave inscription from
Kyrgyzstan

To say that millions of Christians lived outside the familiar territories of European Christendom might be an interesting observation, but in itself it tells us little about the nature of the religion. In fact, long after the coming of Islam, rich Christian cultures continued to develop and flourish across the Near East and Asia, with their own distinct literature, art, liturgy, devotion, and philosophy, and these cultures often recall the earliest Christian ages.

Heaven and Earth

Some statements apply across the various theological traditions, from the Orthodox to the Nestorians and Jacobites, and the Copts. All these churches were strongly liturgical and hierarchical, with glorious liturgies that presented not just displays of the church's wealth but, literally, foretastes of heaven. Across the creedal spectrum, churches offered their followers experiences designed to appeal to all the senses, from the sounds of bells and music to the visual splendors of icons, images, and illuminated books, and the smell of incense. In one Syriac liturgy, the celebrant prays: "May the sweet aroma which wafted from you, O my Lord, at the time when Mary the sinner poured fragrant oil upon your head, be joined with this incense which we offer to your honor and for the pardon of our debts and sins." Adding to the power of these liturgies was their genuine antiquity, their authentic connection with the earliest Christian ages: the Syriac Anaphora of the Apostles Addai and Mari is the oldest Christian liturgy still in use.[1]

All these churches, moreover, saw monasticism as the highest form of the Christian life. Monasticism probably originated in third-century Egypt, spreading to Mesopotamia through the work of Saint Eugenios, Mar Augin. Some claim, though, that it arose independently in the Syriac-speaking lands, where ancient Christian traditions preached withdrawal from the world and rejection of the flesh. Whatever its origins, monasticism soon became integral to Eastern Christian practice. Throughout the East, Christians were entranced by the vision of saints as ascetic holy men and women, spiritual warriors who were uniquely qualified to confront the demons who threatened humanity at every stage of life. Thomas of Marga told how

> the ascetic fathers went forth into the wilderness and the mountains to preserve the virginity and holiness which had been handed down to them by the apostles, and to battle against principalities and powers and with the evil spirits which are under heaven.[2]

Syrian and Mesopotamian Christians were influenced by Persian dualist ideas that were so commonplace in local culture. This promoted "a religion of intense moral seriousness, of spiritual athleticism, that spoke to a community marked by the eternal conflict of the principles of Light and Darkness and by the realities of death and judgment." Although most monks were affiliated with organized communities, many others pursued lives of individual asceticism. At least through the end of the eighth century, the Syriac churches still had stylites, solitaries dwelling high on pillars. And the old ways continued deep into the high Middle Ages. About 1270, for instance, we hear of Bar Sauma, a Nestorian monk in China who

> set apart a cell for himself and he shut himself up therein seven years; and after that [period] he decided to remove himself from the children of men, and to practice himself in the ascetic life in the mountain, in a place which was wholly isolated, so that he might rest there [undisturbed] in his life as a recluse.[3]

Nothing suggests that this demanding piety was seen as exceptional.

References to the monastic "fathers" obscures the undoubted role of women religious, and from the earliest ages, both Egypt and Mesopotamia had their spiritual mothers, *ammas*, as well as fathers, *abbas*. The Jacobite scholar Gregory Bar-Hebraeus tells us the exemplary story of Mother Sara, who so rejected the world that although she lived in an upper chamber overlooking the river, she never once looked out to enjoy the view of the river that passed by her cell. Another celebrated woman, Shirin, served as spiritual director for both male and female religious. Neither in Egypt nor in Mesopotamia, though, are women religious well recorded, and we depend for their history on such chance references. Another story by Bar-Hebraeus acknowledges this discriminatory treatment. He reports two women lamenting that men had the freedom to visit prostitutes while women's sexuality was strictly controlled: one explains that "the kings, and the judges, and the lawgivers are all men; and they have therefore acted the parts of advocates of their own causes and have oppressed the women." And they have largely omitted women from the historical record.[4]

The Elect and Solitary

Within the monasteries and hermitages, these spiritual athletes pursued intense mystical practices that surprise us because, according to some scholars, they should have ceased centuries before. According to Elaine Pagels, for instance, the growth of the institutional church in the Roman Empire from the fourth century led to a steep decline in the mystical practice that the Gnostics had richly cultivated. In this view, the collapse of such individual mysticism was symbolized by the suppression of the Gospel of Thomas, which had taught "the elect and solitary" to cultivate silence, to seek God within themselves. In contrast, later Catholic piety was church centered and church approved. Again according to Pagels, particularly condemned were any attempts to seek union with God, to erase the boundaries between the human and divine—an idea that at this point seemed heretical and blasphemous.[5]

Laments about the loss of the Gospel of Thomas and the Gnostic worldview read strangely when we look at the near-obsessive nature of the Eastern Christian mystical quest over the following millennium. In fact, the Eastern churches had lost virtually nothing of the ancient mysticism that so attracts many modern readers to the world of the Gnostics. Ideas of solitude, inner contemplation, and even the quest for divinity pervade the stories and teachings of the Egyptian hermits, stories that were passed down over the centuries and are easily available in the work known as the *Philokalia,* collected during the eighteenth century. The widely used hymns of Ephraem the Syrian included one proclaiming, "Glory to the Silence that spake by His [Christ's] voice." The Syriac churches—the most credible claimants to Thomas's heritage—were intimately acquainted with the ancient doctrine of "the elect and solitary." Indeed, such mystical ascetics were quite commonplace throughout the Middle Ages, and had a well-known name: we call them "monks."[6]

Mainstream Eastern churches taught daring ideas about the potential of approaching God so closely as actually to become divine. Athanasius, the great Alexandrian patriarch so often presented as the enforcer of narrow orthodoxy in the age of Constantine, preached that "God became man so that men might become gods." He had many successors, especially in Egypt and Syria, where *theosis,* or deification, became a common goal of the spiritual life. The spiritual masters saw deification not as a distant goal, but as a constant process by which the soul achieved its resurrection even while it was attached to a mortal body.[7] So often in these writings, we find ideas that sound purely Gnostic—the inner resurrection, the emphasis on silence and rest, the return to Eden—though they are attached to an orthodox theology and a total loyalty to the teachings and traditions of the churches. Nor are these themes presented with any disguise or subterfuge. The modern neglect of this potent mysticism provides yet another example of the utter oblivion into which non-European Christianity has fallen, which leads even scholars to believe that the faith had lost most of its diversity and creativity after the fourth century. An equally strong case could be made that this was the era when, far from fading away, Christian spirituality was entering its richest and most daring phase.[8]

The Age of Miracles

Personal sacrifice and asceticism led to sanctity, which was manifested in healings and miracles. Cosmas, a seventh-century bishop of Amida, "performed marvelous miracles like Elijah the Tishbite and the first apostles." All forms of Christianity, East or West, emphasized charismatic and miraculous themes, to a degree that separated them from more rationalistic Muslim contemporaries. In the late ninth century, an elderly Egyptian monk shocked his Muslim listeners when he explicitly denied that Christianity could be supported purely on the grounds of reason, and agreed that ideas like the Trinity and the crucified God flatly contradicted reason. Instead, he said, "I find the proof of the truth of Christianity in its contradictions and inconsistencies which are rejected by intelligence and repelled by the mind because of their difference and contrast. Analysis cannot help it, though the intelligence and perception enquire and search into it." Yet despite all these contradictions and absurdities, many kings and sages accepted the faith: "they do not accept or practice it except for proofs which they have witnessed, signs which they have known, and miracles which they have recognized, which compelled them to submit to it and practice it." Jacobite philosopher Yahya ibn 'Adi agreed that Christianity "is only received and believed in by the signs and miracles which its missionaries showed. . . . The acceptance by those who received it must have been because of the witness of what the missionaries did in the way of signs opposed to human nature."[9]

The best argument for Christianity was that its holy men and women were so close to God that they could defy the laws of nature and demonstrate divine power through acts of miracle and healing. The Kerait king converted when he believed he had been rescued from death by a vision of Saint Sergius.[10] Such ideas clearly carried weight, or the churches would not have made as many converts as they did. Yet, one obvious weakness presented itself: if material success proved the truth of a religion, how would Christians cope when their kings suffered defeat after defeat, when their cities and churches were destroyed and plundered? As we will see, although Christians did their best to explain away these secular disasters, the constant sequence of catastrophes in the later Middle Ages proved devastating to hopes of Christian survival.

Scholarship

For all their challenges to reason and mere human wisdom, the Eastern churches remained passionately committed to learning and scholarship, building chiefly upon local traditions and languages. For centuries after the conversion of the Roman Empire, Christianity was polyglot. In western Europe, Christian culture and thought developed in Latin; in the eastern Mediterranean, the dominant medium was Greek; Syriac dominated in the Asian churches; Egyptians spoke Coptic. The easterners traced their origins to Edessa, which pioneered Christian scholarship and was the birthplace of Syriac Christian writing. Syriac grew in use as Eastern churches became more disaffected with the Orthodox churches and the imperial regime, and Nestorians and Monophysites naturally developed Syriac liturgies.[11]

Syriac scholarship found its primary home in Nisibis, which by the sixth century had developed a school that was the closest the Christian world possessed to a great university, a worthy successor to the academies of ancient Greece. Persia's Sassanian kings favored this school, together with a counterpart at Jundishapur, which became a refuge for dissident Christian scholars uncomfortable with Byzantine rule. The fame of Nisibis spread around the world, supplying a model for the pioneering Latin Christian scholar Cassiodorus in far-off Italy. It was at Nisibis that much of the ancient world's learning was kept alive and translated, making it available for later generations of Muslim scholars, and for Europeans after them. Among other classical works, Nisibis preserved the writings of Aristotle and his commentators. In 1026, Nisibis was the scene of a famous debate between the Nestorian bishop Elijah and a Muslim vizier. Arguing for the superiority of Syriac over Arabic, the bishop made the seemingly incontestable claim that Arabs had learned most of their science from Syriac sources, while the reverse had seldom occurred.[12]

Indicating just what riches were still available when the Arabs arrived is the work of "the holy bishop Severus who is named Seboukt of Nisibis," who headed the Jacobite monastery of Kenneshre (Kennesrin) on the Euphrates. In the mid–seventh century, he wrote extensively on cosmography, on the causes of eclipses, and on geometry and arithmetic: he offers a classic account of the astrolabe. He also wrote commentaries on Aristotle's logic, translating the *Analytics*. Like Bishop Elijah, he was very proud of the Syriac achievement, claiming that the Greeks had taken all they knew from the Chaldeans, whom everyone knew to be really Syrians. However, he was admirably open to crediting the contributions of other cultures. "If those who believe, because they speak Greek, that they have reached the limits of science should know these things, they would be convinced that there are also others who know something." Had not the Indians designed a system of nine wonderful signs that could be used to express all numbers? Although he does not seem to know of the existence of zero, that is the first reference in the West to the revolutionary Indian numbering system, which we know as Arabic numerals. Though the system would not be widely publicized until the ninth century, Syriac Christians had known it long before that.[13]

The Arabs also learned much from Jundishapur. From the eighth century through the eleventh, the Persian family of Ibn Bukhtishu regularly served as physicians to successive caliphs, bringing with them the skills of Jundishapur. Their Christianity was deeply ingrained. The founder's name apparently meant "Jesus has saved," and one of the greatest representatives, Yuhanna (John), became bishop of Mosul. Other denominations also participated in cultivating Arab learning: the Maronite Thawafil (Theophilus) ibn Tuma translated parts of the *Iliad* into Arabic.[14]

For a thousand years, Syriac Christians produced scholars and thinkers who could be set beside the best of their Greek or Latin contemporaries, and who shaped the emerging world of Islamic science and philosophy. Among the greatest scholars produced by the Jacobite church was Jacob of Edessa (640–708), a historian and a superb biblical interpreter who has been compared with Jerome in the West. His colleague and successor was George of Akula, bishop to the Arab nomads in Mesopotamia and commentator on Aristotle's logic. Both were alumni of Kenneshre. Also from the Jacobite tradition was the tenth-century philosopher Yahya ibn 'Adi, who was born in Tikrit and who translated Aristotelian works from Syriac into Arabic. Among the monuments of Nestorian learning was the *Gannat Busamé,* an enormous commentary on the lectionary, which is a gold mine of classical as well as patristic learning. Isho'dad of Merv records an overwhelming mass of stories drawn from classical, Jewish, and early Christian lore, many not recorded outside the Syriac tradition.[15]

A catalog of Syriac writers compiled around 1300 includes over a hundred authors whose works were then available, and some of the lists of works awe by their sheer scope:

> Babai the Great wrote eighty-three books, in one of which he gives an account of the origin of the Feast of Palms, a dissertation on the union of Christ's humanity and divinity, and an exposition of the Book of Hundreds. . . .
>
> Bood Piryadotha wrote poems on the Faith, a treatise against the Manichees, and another against the followers of Marcion. He also wrote a work in Greek, entitled *Alep-Megheen,* and it was he who translated *Kalilah and Dimnah* from the Indian language.[16]

The Syriac clergyman (*periodeutes*) Bodh of Seleucia was the conduit for the Sanskrit animal fables and folktales that would be best known in their Arabic form, and which subsequently spread into many other cultures. Otherwise, though, tragically little of such writing survives today, suggesting the devastation that later overwhelmed Eastern Christian culture.

The Last Flowering

Eastern Christian learning survived well into the high Middle Ages, and some of the finest scholars were working between the eleventh and the thirteenth centuries. In many ways, the situation was more difficult than in Timothy's time, around the year 800. Just in terms of numbers, Muslim advances had reduced the following of the Eastern churches. Christianity had retreated from some areas, particularly in Arabia, while the traditional languages of the churches were falling back before the spread of Arabic. Particularly from the eleventh century, warfare and invasion ruined many traditional centers of Christian learning. Yet for all these setbacks, the Eastern churches after 1100 seemed set for a new glorious age.

Among other triumphs, the so-called Syriac renaissance produced one of the greatest medieval historians, Michael Syrus, Michael the Syrian, Jacobite patriarch of Antioch. Born in Melitene, he spent much of his career at the nearby monastic house of Mar Barsauma, where he died in 1199. Michael wrote a world history—in Syriac, naturally—that takes events up to the end of the twelfth century, and which is a leading source for the era of the Crusades. As he was drawing so extensively on earlier histories that are now lost, he is also a major source for the early medieval era, and modern historians often use his extraordinary detailed records of climate change no less than social history. Historian Peter Brown stresses how Michael's works, and those of his contemporaries, draw on an uninterrupted tradition dating back to the fifth century: "To read them is to catch an unmistakable echo of the world of Late Antiquity in contemporaries of Richard Coeur de Lion, Saint Louis and Marco Polo."[17]

Other scholars of this age were just as impressive. Also from Melitene, Jacob Bar Salibi became the Jacobite metropolitan of Amida, and his extensive biblical commentaries drew copiously on seven centuries of Syriac learning. He wrote homilies, liturgical texts, and polemics against Muslims and heretics. As late as the fourteenth century, Nisibis was still the home of a great Nestorian scholar—namely, the metropolitan 'Abdisho' (Abd Yeshua) bar Berikha. His main surviving work is the *Marganitha* (*Pearl*), a sweeping summary of Christian theology, but he also wrote extensively on canon law, science, and philosophy:

> Abd Yeshua, my vile self, wrote a Commentary on the Bible, the book of the Paradise of Eden, a collection of Synods in Arabic, the book entitled *Marganitha* on the Truth of the Faith, a treatise on the Mysteries of the Grecian Philosophers, and another called *Scholasticus,* against heresy. I also collated a book of Church Laws and Discipline, and another consisting of twelve treatises on knowledge in general, besides Consolations, antiphons, and anthems, for various occasions, an explanation of the Epistle sent by Aristotle to Alexander the Great, also a work solving many difficult questions, and one of arguments, proverbs, and riddles.[18]

Virtually all these works are now lost.

The brightest star of a dazzling era was the Jacobite Gregory Bar-Hebraeus (1226–86), who is sometimes called "the encyclopedia of the thirteenth century." Gregory was the son of a Jewish physician from Melitene who converted to Christianity, and the son became bishop and Maphrianus, resident at Mar Mattai in Mosul. He managed in a single life to be "philosopher, poet, grammarian, physician, Biblical commentator, historian, and theologian," and he can reasonably be mentioned in the same breath as his contemporaries Thomas Aquinas and Roger Bacon. His *Chronicle,* a history of the world, is a major source for his own time, and he published work on logic and theology, a treatise on astronomy, and a commentary on Aristotle. Bar-Hebraeus somehow managed to accomplish all this while the rest of the known world was being torn apart by the Mongol invasions and the ensuing wars. He even wrote a collection of witty sayings and tales, the *Laughable Sayings,* which are striking for the very broad range of settings and cultures on which they draw. Living in the cosmopolitan Mesopotamia of his day, he drew on the wit of Persian, Indian, and Hebrew sages, Greek philosophers, Christian recluses, Muslim kings, and Arab ascetics—not to mention irrational beasts, clowns and simpletons, lunatics and demoniacs.[19]

Amazingly, given the political crises of the era, the Syriac churches were not unique in this late flowering. For the other Eastern Christian cultures, too, the twelfth and thirteenth centuries are remembered as golden ages. Georgians recall the late twelfth century as the age of Queen Tamara, who subdued neighboring Muslim states and presided over the great age of Georgian writing and poetry. Armenians, too, spoke of a renaissance, a Christian cultural resurgence led by clergy like the catholicos Nerses IV and the poet and theologian Vartan the Great. In the early thirteenth century, monk and teacher Mkhitar Gosh earned the title of doctor of the Armenian church, for work that included the codification of Armenian law; he also wrote an influential volume of fables.[20] These medieval glories are commemorated in the building booms at royal centers like Armenian Ani and Georgian Mtskheta (not to mention Ethiopia's Lalibela). Eastern Christian culture did not just steadily decline from late antiquity onward, shrinking ever more timidly before Muslim advances: it continually showed striking powers of renewal.

From the Earliest Ages

While the potent Christian presence in Asia is remarkable enough in its own right, these churches also had a claim to a direct tradition from the apostolic age at least as strong as those boasted by Rome and Constantinople. In the Roman and Byzantine worlds, of course, Christianity adapted to accommodate the dominant cultures, and was increasingly distanced from its Semitic roots. In contrast, the Nestorians, Jacobites, and others stemmed from Syria and Mesopotamia, and their culture was founded in a Semitic tradition that would have been intimately familiar to the apostles. The more we look at the world of these *Nasraye,* the more despairing we should feel, in contrast, about any modern effort to "get back to the world of the New Testament," to restore the values or character of apostolic times.[21]

This Semitic character is obvious from the personal names that emerge in the records, which follow the ancient practice of declaring an individual's relationship to God. Obadiah, for instance, means "Servant of God," while Ezekiel signifies "God Strengthens." Nestorian church leaders bore names like Sabr-isho' (Hope-in-Jesus), 'Ebed-yeshu' or 'Abd-isho' (the-Servant-of-Jesus). Isho'dad probably signifies "Jesus has befriended." Although the Chinese remembered the pioneering missionary in their country as "Olupun," that name may have been a corruption of his title: rabban ("Master").

Further reinforcing a sense of connection with the historic roots of Christianity, the Eastern churches felt that the places in which they lived were exactly the sites in which the prophets and apostles had walked. Residents of Saint Catherine's monastery in Sinai need only look upward to see the great mountain on which, reportedly, God commanded Moses. The thirteenth-century Nestorian writer Solomon of Basra described the fate of the various apostles in strictly local terms:

Simon Zelotes was from Galilee, of the tribe of Ephraim. He preached in Samosata, Perrhê, Zeugma, Aleppo, Mabbug, Kenneshre. He built a church in Cyrrhus, and died and was buried there.

James, the son of Alphaeus, was from the Jordan, of the tribe of Manasseh. He preached in Palmyra, Kirkesion and Callinicos, and came to Batnân of Sarug, where he built a church, and died and was buried there.[22]

Accepting such traditions meant that whoever visited the familiar Syrian churches was literally following in the footsteps of apostles. Syria and Mesopotamia were both richly endowed with ancient tombs and martyrdom sites, and a few were well authenticated. Mosul boasted the tombs of three biblical prophets: Obadiah, Nahum, and Jonah.

Legendary trappings already surrounded other early founders. While the Western church based its authority on the inheritance of Peter and his successors, Asian Christians venerated the apostle Addai, or Thaddeus. According to a widely credited legend, when Abgar, king of Edessa, was suffering from an incurable disease, he wrote seeking the help of "Jesus, the Good Physician Who has appeared in the country of Jerusalem." Jesus replied with his own letter, saying that he could not come personally, but that he would send his apostle Addai. [23]

We need not believe in the literal truth of these traditions, but the Syriac-speaking churches had a surprisingly plausible claim to a direct link with Jesus's first followers, and with the very earliest leadership of the emerging church. We see this in the record that the Nestorian church preserved of the apostolic succession of its patriarchs or catholicoi. According to a list written down around 1500:

- Addai was buried in Edessa.

- Mari (was buried) in the convent of Koni.

- Abris, called in Greek Ambrosius; the place of his grave is unknown; he was of the laying on of hands of Antioch.

- Abraham was of the laying on of hands of Antioch; he was descended from the family of Jacob the son of Joseph; his grave is in Ctesiphon.

- James, of the laying on of hands of Antioch, was also of the family of Joseph the husband of Mary; his grave is in Ctesiphon.

- Aha-d'abuhi was of the laying on of hands of Antioch; his grave is in Ctesiphon.[24]

Later incumbents were "of the laying on of hands of Ctesiphon," and thereafter, the catholicoi were based in that city until they formally moved to Baghdad.

No historian in modern times has taken the tale of Abgar seriously, nor are the later names necessarily reliable; but parts of this tradition might well have a historical foundation.[25] What this account claims is that Christianity reached Edessa very soon after the death of Jesus, and that the earliest missionaries stemmed from Antioch. Given the relationship of the cities and trade routes, that general pattern is overwhelmingly likely. The third and fourth leaders of this church were of the family of Joseph, the husband of Mary, and early historians like Eusebius confirm that kinship with Jesus gave a special warrant for authority in the earliest church. Near the end of the first century, the Roman emperor Domitian sought out the "relatives of the Lord," the *desposynoi,* whom he suspected of sedition. On examination, though, the surviving relatives proved to be hard-working small farmers whom the emperor judged to be unworthy of his attention, and so he let them live.[26] That investigation might well have persuaded any remaining kin to migrate beyond the limits of Roman power, to Parthian Ctesiphon—which is just what the Nestorian record suggests. The story also fits well with what we know about Jews relocating to Babylonia in these same years. The account is plausible, in a way that European legends of early apostles and saints are not: no serious historian thinks that Joseph of Arimathea came to Britain, Mary Magdalene to France, or the apostle James to Spain. But the Nestorian sequence does, in contrast, suggest a trajectory that is perfectly credible for the first and second centuries.

In terms of their impact on later history, it does not matter whether in fact the Syrian churches genuinely could claim such awe-inspiring connections, but the churches that expanded into Mesopotamia,

Persia, and beyond probably did carry an inheritance from the oldest phases of the Jesus movement. In the earliest account of Christianity in India, Eusebius claims that missionaries speaking Aramaic or Hebrew had already reached the country before the second century and had left an original manuscript of the Gospel of Matthew. Though that particular text of Matthew probably never existed, the story suggests once again that from early times, the churches moving east spoke (and wrote) Semitic languages rather than Greek.

Our knowledge of Syriac origins is severely limited by the political disasters that later overcame those bodies and that left so many of the monasteries and their libraries in ruins by the fourteenth and fifteenth centuries. In the nineteenth century, intrepid European and American travelers visited the declining monasteries of the upper Tigris and commented on how often Kurds and other Muslim tribes raided the premises, taking papers and parchments that they might use for loading rifles or starting fires. Nor, by that stage, were the Christian clergy themselves able to read or appreciate most of their older documents. In 1840, one American traveler reported seeing at Mardin fifty dust-covered volumes that had apparently never been opened; ten years later, another Westerner to the same site found only a hundred or so manuscripts.[27] We can only speculate what these collections might have contained at their height, and what was in those fifty lost volumes; but a German traveler to an Egyptian monastery in the same years found there one of the most precious early Bible manuscripts, the Codex Sinaiticus. Elsewhere in Egypt, another traveler discovered the Curetonian Gospels, the most ancient testimony to the Old Syriac Bible text, probably written down in the fifth century. Given their ties to the most ancient churches, the Mesopotamian monasteries probably once contained comparable or even greater treasures, which are now irretrievably lost.

Church and Bible

Throughout the Middle Ages, Syriac Christian scholars continued to use thoroughly Semitic literary styles and approaches to scripture, which often gives their work a startlingly primitive feel. These churches had a boundless veneration for the Bible, which they read in their own Semitic language. In Nestorian epitaphs from China and central Asia, the highest praise is reserved for those who interpreted the scriptures. From the year 1316, "year of the dragon," we find a commemoration of "Shliha the celebrated commentator and teacher, who illuminated all the monasteries with light, son of Peter the august commentator of wisdom. His voice rang as high as the sound of a trumpet."[28]

The "light" that such scholars spread was the Bible in Syriac, an ancient translation that dates back to the time of the proud Assyrian Tatian. Around the year 170, Tatian created a Syriac version of the four canonical Gospels combined into a single harmony, the Diatessaron, the "Through Four." This was the moment at which "Christianity began to spread outside the Greek-speaking cities into the Asian countryside. . . . The first translation of a major section of the New Testament into any language was made in Asia." Later scholars continued the process of translation, which culminated in the *Peshitta* Syriac text of the whole Bible, so called because it was the "simple version." In the Old Testament, this represents a direct translation from ancient Hebrew texts, probably done in Edessa or Arbela. The *Peshitta* remained the standard version for the Eastern churches, just as the Latin Vulgate did for the Western church.[29]

The Syriac Bible was a conservative text, to a degree that demands our attention. In recent years, accounts of the early church claim that scriptures and gospels were very numerous, until the mainstream Christian church suppressed most of them in the fourth century. This alleged purge followed the Christian conversion of the emperor Constantine, at a time when the church supposedly wanted to ally with the empire in the interests of promoting order, orthodoxy, and ecclesiastical authority. According to modern legend, the suppressed works included many heterodox accounts of Jesus, which were suspect because of their mystical or even feminist leanings.[30]

The problem with all this is that the Eastern churches had a long familiarity with the rival scriptures, but rejected them because they knew they were late and tendentious. Even as early as the second century, the Diatessaron assumes four, and only four, authentic Gospels. Throughout the Middle Ages, neither Nestorians nor Jacobites were under any coercion from the Roman/Byzantine Empire or church, and had they wished, they could have included in the canon any alternative Gospels or scriptures they wanted to. But instead of adding to the canon, they chose to prune. The Syriac Bible omits several books that are included in the West (2 Peter, 2 and 3 John, Jude, and the book of Revelation). Scholars like Isho'dad wanted to carry the purge further, and did not feel that any of the Catholic Epistles could seriously claim apostolic authorship. The only extraneous text that a few authorities wished to include was the Diatessaron itself. The deep conservatism of these churches, so far removed from papal or imperial control, makes nonsense of claims that the church bureaucracy allied with empire to suppress unpleasant truths about Christian origins.[31]

Although they did not include them in the canon of scripture, all the Eastern churches knew many ancient Christian texts, including apocryphal Gospels and apocalypses, and many scholars quote from now-lost patristic texts and commentaries.[32] One major influence for Syriac writers was the Diatessaron, which was widely used in Eastern churches before many bishops decided to abandon it on the grounds of Tatian's heretical leanings. Nevertheless, Syriac scholars continued to know and cite the work at least through the thirteenth century, giving them access to what might have been authentically ancient New Testament readings that were lost in later texts. Through the Diatessaron, for instance, scholars like Isho'dad and Bar Salibi knew the ancient story that at the moment of Christ's baptism, "a great light shone" over the Jordan.[33] Even at the end of the thirteenth century, 'Abdisho' bar Berikha not only knows the Diatessaron, but lists it as part of the canonical New Testament.

The Task of Interpretation

The Syriac churches inherited the approach to Bible criticism associated with Antioch, which demanded that texts be put into proper historical and cultural context, rather than (as in Alexandria) being used as the basis for spiritual allegories. Bar-Hebraeus saw little value in reading or hearing the scriptures unless one approached them with a view to true understanding. "As hunger is not satisfied by water, nor thirst by bread, so the Initiate, who wishes to look within the Sinaitic cloud [the Divine], gains small profit by hearing the Scriptures being read." Well into what Europeans call the high Middle Ages, scholars approached the scriptures with what seems to a modern readership like good sense. In the 1220s, Solomon of Basra responded wearily to the painful literalism with which many lesser thinkers read biblical metaphors:

> The things which certain stupid men invent, who indulge their fancy, and give bodily form to the punishment of sinners and the reward of the just and righteous, and say that there is at the resurrection a reckoning and a pair of scales, the Church does not receive; but each one of us carries his light and his fire within him, and his heaviness and his lightness is found in his own nature. Just as stone and iron naturally possess the property of falling to the earth, and as the air naturally ascends upward on account of its rarity and its lightness; so also in the resurrection, he that is heavy and lying in sins, his sins will bring him down; and he that is free from the rust of sin, his purity will make him rise in the scale.[34]

To paraphrase Solomon, the Bible is a complex text that makes rich use of metaphor and other literary devices, so that we hear of the gates of hell, the fires of hell, or of souls being weighed in the balance. But only an idiot understands these images in the sense of real, literal gates, scales, or fires instead of thinking spiritually how sins shaped one's destiny.

In other ways, early and medieval Eastern Christians read the Bible in ways that now seem strange, especially in the thorough integration of the worlds of the Old and New Testaments, so that every aspect of the life of Christ was foreshadowed somewhere in the Law or Prophets. The Bible was a seamless whole in which all prefigures Christ. Thomas of Marga found warrant for monasticism in the Old Testament, in the stories of Moses, Elijah, and others who retired to mountains: "and there, by the glory with which [Moses'] face was clothed, was it indicated that virginity and holiness should spread abroad in later times and be exalted."[35]

Working and thinking in Semitic languages, Syriac Christians always retained an approach to the text that would have much in common with Jewish readers, not least in their fascination with the etymology of words. Syriac scholars like Isho'dad and Bar Salibi operate in a thought world identical to that of the Talmudists, and they are just as likely to produce explanations that are ingenious, if not actually correct. Explaining the origins of Satan's name, the sixth-century author of the *Book of the Cave of Treasures* tells how

the Rebel . . . was swept away out of heaven and fell, and the fall of himself and of all his company from heaven took place on the Sixth Day, at the second hour of the day. And the apparel of their glorious state was stripped off them. And his name was called *Sâtânâ* because he turned aside [from the right way], and *Shêdâ* because he was cast out, and *Daiwâ* because he lost the apparel of his glory.[36]

In this case, the familiarity with Semitic wordplay yields incorrect results—both the Hebrew word *Satan* and the Arabic *Shaitan* really imply "accuser" or "enemy." Yet the wordplay exactly follows the Hebrew and Aramaic tradition that is so obvious throughout the Hebrew Bible and the Talmud. Mary Magdalene's name offered another rich field for possible interpretation. Not content with the simple explanation that she was from an obscure village called Magdala, Syriac commentators assumed that she had some connection with a tower, *migdala;* or that she was famous for the plaiting of hair, making her a hair dresser. Isho'dad speculated on which possible tower could have given rise to her name. Such readings continued through the Middle Ages.[37]

Christian and Asian

But just as the Asian churches never forgot the Semitic roots of their faith, so they adjusted readily to the many new cultures they encountered on their travels, especially across Asia. They were not unique in this. When the lands of western Europe became Christian, churches adapted their forms of doctrine and devotion to the cultures they found there, so that Jesus became a blue-eyed warrior king, and by the eleventh century, theologians tried to understand the Atonement in terms familiar from a feudal society.[38]

But the Eastern churches had to deal with very different cultural traditions, associated with major religious systems and ancient literatures, and they accommodated them just as wholeheartedly: witness the Nestorian tablet at Ch'ang-an. When Nestorians were pressing across central Asia during the sixth and seventh centuries, their paths crossed those of the missionaries and saints of an equally confident and expansionist Mahayana Buddhism. Those ventures left a mighty visual symbol in the great Buddha statues of Bamyan in Afghanistan, which in 2001 were destroyed by the Taliban regime, in a despicable act of cultural vandalism. The statues were built in the sixth century, and stood where they did because they overlooked the Indian branch of the Silk Road. This was a world in which Buddhist and Christian monasteries were likely to stand side by side, as neighbors and even, sometimes, as collaborators. As we have seen, Nestorians helped Indian Buddhists translate their sutras into Chinese. Although this is controversial, some historians believe that Nestorian missionaries influenced the religious practices of the Buddhist religion then developing in Tibet. When seventeenth-century Catholic travelers speculated that the lamas they encountered were distant spiritual descendants of ancient Christian churches, they may have been more right than they knew.

Nestorian interactions with Buddhism have been controversial, as some critics charge that the Eastern Christians watered down their faith in order to appeal to Chinese or Indian societies. Naturally, Christians presented their faith in the form of sutras, on the lines already made familiar by Buddhist missionaries and teachers, and a stunning collection of Jesus Sutras has come to light in modern times in caves at Dunhuang. Some Nestorian texts certainly do draw heavily on Buddhist ideas, and in the early sutras (probably from the seventh century), the Christian phrase "angels and archangels and hosts of heaven" is rendered as "all the Buddhas as well as the Kinnaras and the superintending Devas and Arhans." Even if the missionaries did not fully understand the Buddhist worldview, that sounds like a major concession to other faiths. Generally, though, these early texts do offer a systematic account of the distinctively Christian message, however much they draw on the language available in the dominant culture. One moving visual token of the Nestorians' effort to make their faith intelligible is the combined lotus-cross symbol that appears widely—for instance, in stone crosses from Kerala in southern India, and on tombstones from China's Fujian Province.[39]

These surprising interactions have left many traces, including one of the most popular legends in medieval Europe—that of the hermit Barlaam and the young prince Iosaph. Iosaph's tyrannical father persecuted the church but lived in dread of a prophecy that his own son would become a Christian. Accordingly, he kept Iosaph secluded from the world, until the son was converted under the influence of Barlaam. The tale has an elaborate history in its own right, and one that illustrates the mingling of the great Asian cultures—Buddhist, Muslim, and Christian. In its original form, the prince was Gautama, who became the Buddha. In the Mahayana version, he was remembered as the Awakened Being, the Bodhisattva, the name that was eventually transformed into the Christian Iosaph. Presumably through Nestorian connections, the Buddhist tale spread to Baghdad, and by the eleventh century it was translated by a Georgian Christian monk. It soon reached western Europe, where it became the religious pulp fiction of its day, and both Barlaam and Iosaph were informally canonized.[40]

Bar Sauma's Dream

Around the year 1275, two Nestorian monks from China began a pilgrimage together to the Holy Land. One, Markos, was an Uygur, or perhaps a member of the Onggud Turks, born near Beijing. The other, Bar Sauma, may also have been an Onggud. In different ways, their spectacular careers epitomize the opportunities open to Christians under the Mongol Peace: they also offer a snapshot of a Christian world enjoying its last flowering.[41]

Both men could travel comfortably through the lands that the Nestorians had so thoroughly colonized in the vast expanse between China and Syria. Reaching Mesopotamia, they decided to visit the ancient centers of the faith that had spread across Asia. They were delighted at the abundant evidence of Christian piety they saw all around them, in what they still saw, not implausibly, as the heart of the Christian world:

And they arrived in Baghdad, and thence they went to the great church of Koke [at Ctesiphon] . . . and they went to the monastery of Mar Mari, the apostle, and received a blessing from the sepulchers [or relics?] of that country. And from there they turned back and came to the country of Beth Garmai, and they received blessings from the shrine [or tomb] of Mar Ezekiel . . . which was full of helps and healings. And from there they went to Arbela, and thence to Mosul. And they went to Sinjar and Nisibis, and Mardin; and were blessed by the shrine [containing] the bones of Mar Augin, the Second Christ. And . . . they were blessed by all the shrines and monasteries, and the religious houses, and monks, and the fathers in their dioceses.[42]

When the patriarchate fell vacant in 1281, Markos was elected. He was horrified, and not just as a token of becoming modesty, but from real concerns that his Syriac was scarcely up to the job. But the fathers of the church wisely recognized that "[t]he kings who held the steering poles of the government of the whole world were [Mongols], and there was no man except [him] who was acquainted with their manners and customs."[43] As patriarch from 1281 to 1317, under the name Yaballaha III, he "exercised ecclesiastical sovereignty over more of the earth's surface than even the pontiff in Rome." He established his patriarchal seat at Maragha near Tabriz, the capital of the Mongol Ilkhan dynasty, and from there he ruled thirty provinces and 250 bishoprics. Hoping for further Mongol conversions, he began a large monastery at Maragha itself.[44]

Bar Sauma himself had a diplomatic career. In 1287, the Mongol overlord of the Middle East, the Ilkhan, sent him on a journey to enlist the help of Christian Europe in a potential combined assault on Muslim Egypt. This mission also, it seems, had the support of the allied Mongol regime in Beijing, under Kublai Khan. At the courts of Catholic Europe, Bar Sauma created a sensation. European kings and bishops were amazed to find that this strange creature was a Christian bishop, who seemed perfectly orthodox. Interestingly, in light of the dismissive "Nestorian" name, he stated his creed in terms they found perfectly acceptable, and the king of England himself took Communion from his hands. Yet the good rabban owed his loyalty not to a Roman pope or a Byzantine patriarch, but to a catholicos residing in Mesopotamia. Europeans were further shocked to discover that the Christian world stretched much farther than they had ever dreamed, to the shores of the Pacific, and their visitor seemed confident that his church might be on the point of still greater expansion. Bar Sauma told them how "many of our Fathers have gone into the countries of the Mongols, and Turks, and Chinese and have taught them the Gospel, and at the present time there are many Mongols who are Christians." Christianity, it seemed, was a truly global phenomenon. Suddenly, tales of Prester John seemed not a bit improbable.

Bar Sauma's mission offers a glimpse of an encounter between radically different versions of Christianity, each with its ancient traditions, each with its own linguistic and cultural inheritance, each shaped by very different encounters with rival faiths. The difference between the two worlds, Catholic and Nestorian, is that the Asian churches stood on the verge of annihilation.

4

The Great Tribulation

What a frightful decline! Read all and you shall greatly lament. . . .
Fifty-one metropolitanates, eighteen archbishoprics and 478 bishoprics
are desolate. . . . And not only were those metropolitanates,
archbishoprics, bishoprics, the monasteries and churches desolate; but also
the provinces of the three patriarchs of Alexandria, Antioch and
Jerusalem. Neither will you find a single metropolitan there, nor other
Christian, layman or clergy. But on the thrones of those patriarchates
you will find barely a few priests, monks and laymen. Because the
churches of their provinces have been obliterated completely and Christ's
people, that is the Christians, have been utterly destroyed.
                                   —anonymous Greek churchman, c. 1480

Although Egypt's Christians had often been subject to outbreaks of persecution, the events of 1354 reached an alarming new intensity. Mobs demanded that Christians and Jews recite the Muslim profession of faith upon threat of being burned alive. The government struck at churches and confiscated the estates of monasteries, destroying the financial basis of the Coptic Church. And unlike in previous conflicts, the persecution now reached the whole country, rather than being confined just to Cairo. Under increasingly violent conditions, many Christians accepted Islam, in a massive wave of conversions. Muslim historian Al-Maqrizi reports the unprecedented scale of the change:

> Many reports came from both Upper and Lower Egypt of Copts being converted to Islam, frequenting mosques and memorizing the Quran. . . . In all the provinces of Egypt, both north and south, no church remained that had not been razed; on many of those sites, mosques were constructed. For when the Christians' affliction grew great and their incomes small, they decided to embrace Islam. Thus Islam spread among the Christians of Egypt and in the town of Qalyub alone 450 persons were converted to Islam in a single day. . . . this was a momentous event in Egyptian history.[1]

Not just in Egypt, this was a catastrophic time for the Christians of the Middle East, and it is ironic that such events should have occurred so very soon after Bar Sauma's predictions. So disastrous, in fact, were the cumulative blows against the churches in these years that we can properly see the fourteenth century as marking the decisive collapse of Christianity in the Middle East, across Asia, and in much of Africa.

The story of Christianity's collapse outside Europe runs contrary to many assumptions about the shape of religious history. Though everyone knows that Christianity emerges in the Middle East, and that that area subsequently becomes Muslim, the chronology of that change remains hazy. Popular depictions of that history—for example, in the maps presented by television documentaries—usually show Islam spreading rapidly over the formerly Christian Middle East and North Africa, and the implication is that conversion to Islam was a swift and painless process. Presumably, infidels rapidly came to acknowledge the superior virtues of Islam. Yet the Egyptian persecutions came several centuries afterward, during and after the age of Dante, as western Europe was entering the early Renaissance.

Shaping our views of the religious change are the many recent books that stress the tolerant nature of Islam and its reluctance to impose its beliefs by force. Karen Armstrong regularly contrasts Muslim tolerance with the bigotry so evident in Christian history. Writing of Islamic Spain in the ninth century, for instance, she remarks: "Like the Jews, Christians were allowed full religious liberty within the Islamic empire and most Spaniards were proud to belong to such an advanced culture, light years ahead of the rest of Europe. . . . As was customary in the Muslim world, Jews, Christians and Muslims had coexisted there for centuries in relative harmony."[2] The persecutions would also surprise the many Americans who derive their view of Muslim tolerance from the widely seen PBS documentary *Empires of Faith,* or the film *Kingdom of Heaven,* about the First Crusade. In reality, the story of religious change involves far more active persecution and massacre at the hands of Muslim authorities than would be suggested by modern believers in Islamic tolerance. Even in the most optimistic view, Armstrong's reference to Christians possessing "full religious liberty" in Muslim Spain or elsewhere beggars belief.

To make that point does not necessarily mean shifting to the opposite extreme: if Muslim rulers were not all saints, neither were they the spawn of Satan. We need not subscribe to the account of unrelieved Islamic violence proposed by modern authors for whom every war or conquest involving Muslims automatically becomes a manifestation of religiously motivated jihad. Such accounts err in portraying extreme brutality to noncombatants as a distinctive mark of Islamic fanaticism, when it was in fact the common currency of medieval or early modern warfare, whatever the religious coloring of the participants. Christian Byzantines and Franks committed acts of massacre and ethnic cleansing when they had the opportunity, and were as willing to justify their actions in religious terms.[3]

Nor, by the standards of the time, were Muslims unusual in the discriminatory laws they imposed upon conquered peoples. At the time, it seemed quite natural for the victors to institutionalize their higher status—demanding, for instance, that a higher compensation be paid when one of their own was killed than one of the subject peoples. Germanic tribes in the West set higher man-prices for their own peoples than for Romans or Celts, and Arabs likewise valued their own people at double the rate of Copts or Syrian Christians. As occupiers, early Muslim regimes at least were seldom as oppressive or destructive as many European Christian states: they were much more easygoing than, say, the Normans who conquered England in 1066, the Germans who subjugated Prussia, or the English occupiers of Ireland.

Another problem with focusing on Muslim evils, with the endless accounts of religious warfare and persecution, is that it is impossible to reconcile with the long periods of good interfaith relations that prevailed in many areas. Nor, more important, can it account for the very long survival of Christian communities under Muslim regimes. In contrast, some Christian states did not even permit such minorities to exist on their soil. Legally, Jews were prohibited entry into England from 1290 until the 1650s, and Christian Spain expelled both its Muslims and its Jews.

Oppression and persecution were not integral to Islamic rule; but such conditions could and did develop at particular times, and when they did, they could be devastating. At their worst, we can legitimately compare the conditions of Christians under Islam with that of Jews in contemporary Christian Europe, and the Egyptian campaigns of the fourteenth century look almost identical to contemporary European anti-Semitism. Though Muslim regimes could tolerate other faiths for long periods, that willingness to live and let live did fail at various times, and at some critical points it collapsed utterly. The deeply rooted Christianity of Africa and Asia did not simply fade away through lack of zeal, or theological confusion: it was crushed, in a welter of warfare and persecution.

New Masters

Reading sympathetic accounts of the spread of Islam, we can forget that this was a movement of armed conquest and imperial expansion, which on occasion involved ferocious violence. The battle of Yarmuk in 636, which gave the Muslims control of Syria, was one of the great military massacres of antiquity, costing the lives of perhaps fifty thousand soldiers of the Christian Byzantine Empire. And while cities were generally spared, the invaders showed little mercy to surrounding villages and settlements.[4]

In most cases, however, conquest was not quickly followed by Islamization, or the destruction of church institutions. Partly, this resulted from the speed of the conquest, as Arab forces struck at the two empires, Byzantine and Persian, which had exhausted each other in a century of struggle. A fast conquest meant that cities largely survived intact, and so did their social and ecclesiastical structures.

TABLE 4.1.
CHRONOLOGY OF EARLY ISLAM

610	First revelation to the Prophet Muhammad
622	Hijra: Muhammad migrates from Mecca to Medina
632	Muhammad dies
635	Conquest of Damascus
636	Battle of Yarmuk gives Muslims control over Syria
636	Muslims defeat Persians in battle of Qadisiya
637	Muslims enter Jerusalem
642	Capture of Alexandria
643	Conquest of Azerbaijan
647	First Arab invasion of North Africa
651	Muslims complete conquest of Persia
661	Creation of Umayyad Caliphate, based in Damascus

Table 4.1 *(continued)*

674–77	Unsuccessful Muslim siege of Constantinople
685–705	Abd al-Malik caliph
692	Dome of the Rock in Jerusalem completed
698	Muslims take Carthage
706–15	Caliph Walid builds Great Mosque of Damascus
709	Arabs conquer Ceuta
711	Conquest of Spain
717	Second siege of Constantinople
722	Caliph Yazid II orders destruction of Christian images
732	Charles Martel defeats Muslims at Tours
750	Creation of Abbasid Caliphate
751	Battle of Talas River: Muslims defeat Chinese
762	Foundation of Baghdad

The great exception to this statement was in North Africa, the modern lands of Tunisia and Algeria, a puzzling case to which I shall return later. In short, the North African church based in Carthage had at its height been one of the most powerful and influential in the whole of Christianity, yet very soon after the Muslims took Carthage in 698, that church vanished almost totally. This, however, was an extreme and atypical case, and it is not clear just how Muslim persecution or interference contributed to the Christian collapse here. Probably, most African Christians simply fled, rather than being killed or expelled.[5]

Elsewhere, the Muslims were received surprisingly well. The occupiers distinguished themselves by their contrast to earlier Persian invaders, who had been notorious both for the extensive destruction they caused and for their deep animus against Byzantine clergy and monks. The Persian sack of Jerusalem in 614 had provoked a ferocious Jewish rising against Christians: tens of thousands perished. In comparison, the Arab occupiers of Jerusalem and Alexandria were thoroughly restrained. When the caliphs established themselves at Damascus in 661, they looked like a civilized Byzantine successor state, employing Christian and Jewish civil servants.[6]

Also making the transition easier, it was far from obvious at the time that the Muslim conquest would mark a permanent transformation: countries like Syria and Egypt were well used to passing empires. History suggested that the Roman Empire tended to strike back very successfully against intruders, even though retaliation might take centuries. Of all the barbarian invaders who had seized portions of the Western empire in the fifth century, the Byzantines conquered or expelled some, while the others all accepted Catholic Christianity by the eighth century. After seeing the Persians overrun their whole eastern empire by 616, the Romans had staged a stunning comeback in which they in turn destroyed Persian power. Even when Roman armies were not obviously in the neighborhood, the empire had an impressive ability to project its power through allies and proxy states, using diplomacy and intelligence. The Muslims suffered a traumatic setback in 717–18, when the Byzantines threw them back from the approaches to Constantinople. Adding to the shock, the Romans owed their victory to their secret weapon, which they called "Greek fire"—a kind of napalm that wrought havoc with enemy ships and must have had a daunting effect on Muslims with an apocalyptic mind-set. Hadith (reputed sayings of Muhammad) composed about this time suggest real concerns that a revived Byzantine and Christian power might be able to roll back Islam to Mecca and Medina. As late as the tenth century, these prophecies seemed to be fulfilled when the Byzantines reoccupied most of Syria and northern Mesopotamia, threatening Jerusalem and Baghdad. By the end of the tenth century, the Byzantines had high hopes for ultimate victory in the new millennium.[7]

Nor did the Muslims' religious identity make them unwelcome. As we will see, Muslims were slow to identify themselves as a distinct religion wholly separate from Jews and Christians. Matters were seen rather in ethnic terms, and early chronicles speak not of

Muslims and Christians but of Arabs and Syrians.[8] This lack of religious conflict made Arab rule attractive to those Christians who had previously been subjects of the Persian Empire, and who found more in common with the Muslims than they had with the old regime, dominated as it was by Zoroastrians—dualists whose worship focused on the sacred fire. Both Persian and Roman empires had mixed attitudes toward tolerating religious minorities, and sporadically launched persecutions. In contrast, through most of their conquered territories, the new Muslim rulers had little interest in forcing conversions, and in the early stages did not even encourage them. Non-Muslims after all survived as conquered tributary peoples, paying special taxes, so that it literally paid to keep these people in their infidel state.[9]

Christians were treated rather better than other groups, who did not qualify as approved and tolerated People of the Book. In theory, we might expect the Zoroastrian religion to have been persecuted from the beginning, as the Quran condemned fire worshippers as pagan. In fact, Muslim attitudes were initially more favorable, and only gradually were harsher standards applied. Increasingly, Muslims destroyed the fire temples and built mosques on the sites; churches, in contrast, operated publicly. Ordinary Zoroastrian believers made the best accommodation they could. The few modern followers of the old Persian religion are found among India's Parsis, descendants of those who emigrated in the ninth or tenth century. Muslim regimes were much harsher toward Manichaeans, whom they hunted and killed.[10]

Moreover, many Eastern Christians—Nestorians, Jacobites, and others—were not sorry to witness the fall of the Byzantine authorities who had so persecuted them over the decades, and the followers of the Arab prophet would not necessarily be more heavy-handed as rulers. In the 650s, the Nestorian patriarch Isho'yahb wrote: "The Arabs to whom God has granted at this time the government of the world ... do not persecute the Christian religion; on the contrary they favor it, honor our priests and the saints of the Lord and confer benefits on churches and monasteries." Many similar comments can be found from senior clergy over the following centuries. Later in that century, a Mesopotamian monk praised the caliph Mu'awiya lavishly: "Justice flourished in his time and there was great peace in the regions under his control. He allowed everyone to live as they wanted." One ninth-century Nestorian chronicle was lyrical: "The hearts of Christians rejoiced at the ascendancy of the Arabs. May God affirm and make it triumphant!" Whatever the faults of the Arabs, at least they were not Christian Byzantines.[11]

Beyond simple relief at the withdrawal of Byzantine power—however temporary it might be—many Christians saw the Arab victory as a sign of divine judgment. A later Coptic history offers this interpretation: "And the Lord abandoned the army of the Romans before him, as a punishment for their corrupt faith, and because of the anathemas uttered against them, on account of the council of Chalcedon, by the ancient Fathers." As late as the twelfth century, after long experience of Muslim rule, Michael the Syrian (a Jacobite) had a simple explanation for the Muslim triumph:

> The God of vengeance ... seeing the wickedness of the Romans who, wherever they ruled, cruelly robbed our churches and monasteries and condemned us without pity, raised from the region of the south the children of Ishmael to deliver us by them from the hands of the Romans ... it was no light advantage for us to be delivered from the cruelty of the Romans.

(In fairness, it should be said that the Monophysites had certainly persecuted the Orthodox when they had the opportunity.) Despite all their defeats at Muslim hands, the Byzantines rarely attempted to see all Christians as allies in a common religious struggle. In the eleventh century, a Byzantine Empire desperate to keep out invading Turks often showed contempt for its Monophysite Armenian allies, although these were militarily crucial. On the other side, once the Turks captured Jerusalem, they actually "employed for the administration of the country a Christian man, a Jacobite, a lover of Christ, known as Mansur al-Balbayi . . . and he was of assistance to every one who arrived in Jerusalem from among the Christians of Egypt and of the countries besides it."[12]

Even Orthodox clergy had mixed feelings about the rise of Muslim power. Church Father Saint John Damascene could write freely against the theological errors of the Byzantine emperors because he was safely ensconced at the court of the caliph, who did not interfere in such intra-Christian bickering. The Byzantines called him *Sarakenophron,* "Saracen-minded." In 869, the Melkite (Orthodox) patriarch of Jerusalem wrote of the Muslims, "They are just, and do us no wrong or violence of any kind."[13]

Dhimmis

Matters would change over time, as Muslim self-identity grew and tolerant attitudes weakened. In the 690s, the regime imposed the poll tax on Syria's non-Muslims, "and all the calamities began to emerge against the Christian people." Rivalry between the two faiths intensified after the failed Muslim assault on Constantinople in 717–18, and in 722 the caliph Yazid II prohibited the display of religious images, destroying the public displays in many churches. A rigorous fanatic, Yazid ordered the extermination of unclean animals across his realm.[14]

In Egypt especially, this crisis provoked a real persecution of Christian monks and clergy, who were targeted because of their overwhelming prestige within Egyptian society. At least for the first two centuries after the conquest, Egypt was still effectively a Christian society under a Muslim military elite. Laws reduced the number of churches while introducing a ferocious regime for monks. In 718, Muslim authorities

commanded the monks not to make monks of those who came to them. Then [the governor] mutilated the monks, and branded each one of them on his left hand, with a branding iron in the form of a ring, that he might be known; adding the name of his church and his monastery, without a cross, and with the date according to the era of Islam. . . . If they discovered a fugitive or one that had not been marked, they brought him to the Amir, who ordered that one of his limbs should be cut off, so that he was lame for life.

However, this extraordinary situation soon passed, and the official history of the Coptic patriarchs records the relief that later caliphs granted to Christians. One, Hisham, was praised as "a God-fearing man, according to the method of Islam . . . the deliverer of the orthodox."[15] Thereafter, the history carries on to record monastic life proceeding much as it had ever done, with the customary range of apparitions and healings. The ban on images proved equally short-lived. For much of the eighth century, Christian icons and paintings were much safer under Arab rule than they were in Byzantine territory, then dominated by the Iconoclastic movement.

Before the eleventh century, incidents of persecution were local and sporadic, and usually ran counter to official wishes. Some, however, were traumatic. One of the worst disasters suffered by the Egyptian church was the sacking of the beloved monasteries of Wadi el-Natrun. Over the centuries, nomads occasionally attacked these houses, and matters grew worse after the Arab conquest, when raiders saw monasteries and churches as easy targets for plunder. The "holy desert" was devastated around 818, when the Alexandrian patriarch Mark was appalled to see

what they suffered at the hands of the miscreant Arabs, through their having taken possession of them and driven out our holy fathers who dwelt there, and killed many, and burnt the churches and the . . . cells, with fire. In consequence of this slaughter, the monks were dispersed among the cities and villages and monasteries, in the various provinces of Egypt and the two Thebaids.

Most of these houses never recovered. Although a disaster for the Egyptian church, the incident reflected the lower standards of law and order now prevailing in the countryside, rather than persecution specifically targeted against Christians. Nor could monasteries now count on the aura of sanctity that might have deterred earlier free-booters, who notionally held Christian loyalties.[16]

Nor can we see explicit systematic persecution in other instances of violence around this time. Riots destroyed churches in tenth-century Palestine and Syria, though in most cases Muslim rulers helped rebuild the destroyed structures. Describing these incidents, Christian accounts were as likely to denounce Jews as Muslims: according to these reports, Jews led and joined in these persecutions, urging Muslim rulers to suppress icons and other visual depictions of the holy. Christian complaints about tyranny and extortionate taxation often prove to be describing injustices imposed on all religions alike, as part of the standard procedure of early medieval governments. After cataloging the horrors of Abbasid taxation, an eighth-century Christian chronicler says that if Christians alone were affected, he would have been quick to write of martyrdom. In the event, the disasters affected "Arabs and Syrians . . . poor and wealthy, all mixed together." At such moments, oppression knew neither creed nor color. Significantly, the first few centuries of Muslim rule did not produce any substantial number of martyrs commemorated by the churches, although Christians at the time were profoundly sensitive to issues of sacrifice and sanctity, and would have been on the lookout for new spiritual heroes and role models. Most of the known martyrs were isolated individuals who had converted to Islam and then tried to reconvert to Christianity. The chief lapse into public violence came in the mid–ninth century, when an aggressive Christian campaign within Muslim Spain led to a number of martyrdoms in Córdoba, but again, these incidents stand out because they were so atypical. Christians had to go out of their way to provoke martyrdom, usually by aggressive public denunciations of Islam.[17]

The glaring exception to official toleration came at the end of the tenth century, when the Egyptian-based caliph Hakim launched an unprecedented systematic persecution of Christians and Jews, and three thousand churches were destroyed or converted into mosques— an important move in a country where village churches were still at least as common as Muslim sites. Sensationally, in 1009 he destroyed Jerusalem's Church of the Holy Sepulcher, and Christians were forbidden to visit the site for forty years. He demanded that all non-Muslims constantly wear a mark of their religions, a large wooden cross for Christians or a symbolic golden calf for Jews. Only at the end of his rule did he relent, restoring the churches and allowing those who had been forcibly converted to return to their original faiths. Yet however burdensome Hakim's rule was, his decisions can be traced to the extreme mental instability of a man who eventually proclaimed his own divinity, speaking of himself as Allah: he was duly assassinated. His policies grew from insanity, not Islam.

Other forms of discrimination were more enduring. Accounts of early Muslim history record the establishment of the *dhimma,* the pact of security, which governed the status of non-Muslims within Islamic society, and over time these regulations became more specific, and harsher. By the ninth century, governments were ordering Jews and Christians to wear distinctive badges or clothing, and it was probably around this time that scholars retroactively invented the terms of subjection supposedly imposed on Christians during the initial conquests, the codes associated with the caliph Umar. Often, these laws were adapted from late Roman regulations imposed on Jews, who were required to avoid any ostentatious acts that could offend Christians. In practice, though, this dhimmi legislation—including the dress code—was not enforced consistently. New churches continued to be built throughout the first centuries of Muslim rule, although dhimmis were specifically forbidden to undertake such new construction.[18]

Moreover, the "protected" status of subject peoples meant something very different from the kind of protection offered by modern-day crime syndicates. Although offering nothing like equality, the arrangement had a firm contractual basis that gave people real, enforceable rights: it really was a pact, not just a euphemism. In the late twelfth century, the great king Saladin proclaimed relatively tight restraints on unbelievers. However, he added a stern proviso:

> When we ordered the dhimmis to wear the distinctive clothing which distinguishes them from Muslims ... we heard that gangs of thugs inflamed by hatred attacked the dhimmis with words and detestable actions in contravention of their rights under the dhimmi pact. We strongly disapprove of this and we forbid either fomenting or executing such things.[19]

As all sane people knew, Saladin's orders were not lightly ignored.

Survival

At least before the twelfth century, the Eastern churches found little difficulty in maintaining their organizations, in operating their churches and monasteries, or in launching new mission ventures beyond the borders of Muslim political authority. Ancient empires had regularly granted minority communities a large degree of self-government, extending to issues of personal law, and even their own courts, and this had usually been the situation of Christians within the Persian Empire. The Muslims took over this situation quite seamlessly. In fact, Christian legal autonomy might actually have increased under Muslim rule, as Christians formally codified their civil laws to match the Quranic law of the occupiers. As Peter Brown remarks, in the early Muslim centuries, "Islam rested as lightly as a mist along the contours of what had remained a largely Christian landscape." In remoter areas like Upper Egypt and northern Iraq, "local Christian elites remained firmly in control for centuries. They administered the taxes and proudly maintained the churches and great monasteries of the region." Bishops continued to rule their flocks, with extensive civil powers over religious matters, broadly defined: when Mesopotamians followed a man who claimed to be Christ returned, his bishop simply threw him into prison, without appeal. Why would any Muslim ruler trouble himself with such a purely internal matter?[20]

Not only did church hierarchies remain in place, but new bishoprics and metropolitans were created, even in Arabia itself. Church leaders became important figures at the different Muslim courts, so that Christian primates "were often used as ambassadors, consulted for political advice, or even solicited for prayer." From the eighth century, the patriarchs usually lived at the new Muslim capital of Fustat, and about 1080 they formally moved their seat to the rising center of Cairo. Church-state connections remained startlingly favorable. One thirteenth-century Coptic patriarch prayed, "May God—praised be He—make victorious their sultan, and he is our sultan, and their imam, and he is our shepherd."[21]

The Nestorian catholicos was just as much a fixture at the court of Baghdad, where some incumbents of the office became favorites of the caliphs of the day. In a characteristic document from 1138, a caliph recognized a new catholicos, giving him authority over the various Christian sects: "thou art empowered to act as their head, and the head also of those Greeks, Jacobites and Melkites, whether represented here or not, who might oppose them in any country." Senior clergy also became adept at the art of bribing Muslim officials, but such gift giving was a standard political practice.[22]

The caliphs were surrounded by Christian or crypto-Christian courtiers, including many doctors, scribes, and scholars. The scribes are an interesting group, as both in Egypt and the East these were members of a hereditary profession: these medieval Christian scribes may well have been distant descendants of the ancient servants of pharaohs and Babylonian kings. Christians represented sizable minorities in such great Muslim cities as Baghdad, Damascus, and Cairo. In Baghdad, they were so numerous that their demands for fish during fasting season had an inordinate impact on the price. Strictly orthodox Muslims complained about the conspicuous wealth and power of Christians. When Muslim activist al-Jahiz denounced Christians in the ninth century, his main complaint was that they were too rich and that the people respected them too much for their business dealings. Furthermore, his complaints about aggressive Christian rhetoric suggest a real openness in religious debate that is difficult to reconcile with images of grinding Muslim oppression. Christians, he complained,

> hunt down what is contradictory in our traditions, our reports with a suspect line of transmission and the ambiguous verses of our scripture. Then they single out the weak-minded among us and question our common people concerning these things . . . and they will often address themselves to the learned and powerful among us, causing dissension among the mighty and confusing the weak.[23]

Below the level of the leadership, it is not easy to assess the continuing appeal of the churches, and historians of Islam differ widely in their estimates of how rapidly the populations of Muslim-ruled countries converted to the new dominant faith. Undoubtedly, Islam attracted followers in what had been Christian lands. In the first century or so, conversion was difficult, and new Muslims had to be fitted into the Arab tribal system through a kind of fictitious adoption. Matters changed when the Abbasid Caliphate took power in 750. Around 775, a monkish chronicler from Tur Abdin commented sadly on the fickleness of his Christian neighbors, even in Edessa the Blessed:

> Without blows or tortures, people slipped towards apostasy with great eagerness, in groups of twenty, thirty, one hundred, two hundred or three hundred without any compulsion. . . . They used to come down to Harran, to governors, and aposta-

size to Islam. They would boast and look down on us saying to us "You are godless and you are holding, as it were, onto a spider's web". . . . [Satan formed] a great crowd from the regions of Edessa, Harran, Resaina. . . . Dara, Nisibis, Sinjar and Callinicum.

They "turned to paganism [i.e., Islam] faster than sheep rushing to water." In the ninth century, one of the most active Muslim controversialists against rival faiths was the Persian Ibn Rabban, whose name indicates that he was the son of a Nestorian clergyman.[24]

But how rapidly did the churches decline? The most systematic calculation is that of historian Richard Bulliet, who used a large biographical sample to track the rate of conversion through Islamic history, and based on this, he proposed a "conversion curve." According to this view, Islam made little impact on populations outside Arabia before the mid–eighth century, but then grew steadily. Within the regions ruled by Islamic governments, Muslims reached 40 percent of the population by about 850, and close to 100 percent by 1100. In Egypt, Syria, and Iraq, "the primary conversion process was essentially complete by 1010." Bulliet's daring attempt was based on the best available evidence, but the use of biographies is dubious because of the many biases that would have led early compilers to underplay non-Muslims and social outsiders. The evidence is also patchy for territories removed from official gaze, where minorities tended to hang on. His sources thus tell us too much about the behavior of Muslim elites, and his theory works best for Persia, where Zoroastrians were at a real disadvantage in the new order. Nor can we rely too heavily on naming practices, as non-Muslims certainly did adopt Muslim-sounding names.[25]

The "conversion curve" ignores the substantial minorities who clearly survived into the twelfth and thirteenth centuries. If only from the later accounts of their destruction, we know that thousands of churches were still operating in Egypt in the eleventh century, many more in Mesopotamia and Syria, and all these lands still possessed their diocesan networks as well as many functioning monasteries. If Egypt and Iraq in 1300 had large Muslim mobs to riot against Christians, there were still plenty of Christians to be rioted against. When we read about sheep rushing to water, we should also realize that in the early years, it was far from obvious that conversion to Islam—or any other faith—need be a one-way process, a commitment for the span of one's whole life, let alone one's whole family. We hear of people converting to Islam to secure a particular legal benefit, and then returning to their customary faith. A few years after the "sheep" reference, the caliph al-Mahdi commanded that apostates and turncoats from Islam be subjected to the death penalty, suggesting a need to prevent convenience conversions.

Putting the evidence together, a neat conversion curve seems unlikely, and the evidence is better suited to what evolutionary theorists call *punctuated equilibrium*. Instead of moving at a steady gradual pace, conversions to Islam would have moved in surges that coincided especially with social upheavals, such as revolutions and changes of dynasty: one boom occurred in the late eighth century, another in the early eleventh. Once Muslim numbers reached a new plateau, religious loyalties would remain fairly steady for decades or even centuries before another sudden upward movement. The process of conversion would also be rather later than sometimes argued, and we should probably date the rise of a solid Muslim majority in Egypt to the late ninth or tenth century, and a hundred years later in Syria and Mesopotamia. Even so, large minorities persisted into the thirteenth century, when we see a decisive movement toward absolute Muslim hegemony.

The Collapse Begins

Apart from its continuing strength in the Muslim-ruled realms, Christianity still flourished as the dominant religion in those regions still under the control of the Byzantine Empire. Within the empire and beyond, Asian and African Christianity were still powerful forces in 1200, yet within at most two centuries that presence had crumbled. In this brief time, some of the most ancient Christian communities were all but annihilated.

Different factors explain the collapse of the churches in different regions, and initially at least we see little evidence of religiously motivated persecution. This was true even in Asia Minor, which between the eleventh century and the fifteenth suffered a radical and near-total destruction of church institutions, and the massive destruction of Christian populations. As the perpetrators were Muslims, from the central Asian people of the Seljuk Turks, it would be tempting, but misleading, to see this as a clear manifestation of Muslim holy warfare, of an exterminationist jihad. Rather, the Seljuks followed the same pattern of aggressive expansion followed by many Eurasian tribes before and since, and their main military activities were directed against the Byzantine Empire, which happened to be Christian. In contrast to the earlier Arab invasions, however, the Seljuk conquests were a very long, drawn-out process, lasting for centuries rather than a few years, and the ensuing wars devastated Christian society.[26]

Asia Minor remained thoroughly Christian through the Byzantine era, but matters changed rapidly after 1050. The Seljuks subjugated the Armenian kingdom in 1064, forcing survivors to create a new Armenian state in Cilicia. And in 1071, the Turks won an epochal victory over the Byzantines at the Battle of Manzikert. Throughout the twelfth and thirteenth centuries, war raged across Asia Minor and the Levant, largely due to the pressure of incoming Turkish forces on the Byzantine Empire, and only incidentally because of Western crusader attempts to reverse their victories. The collapse of Byzantine power in the thirteenth century left a power vacuum filled by warring Muslim states, and the Mongols added a new and vastly destructive element to the mixture.[27]

Though the Western sack of Jerusalem in 1099 is rightly notorious—forty thousand people may have perished—such massacres were far from rare, and Turks were at least as guilty as crusaders. Michael the Syrian recorded the destruction of his hometown, the Christian bastion of Melitene, in 1057. The Turks "began to massacre without pity" and "to torture the men that they might show them hidden things; and many died in torment. . . . The Turks stayed at Melitene for ten days, devastating, and pillaging. Then they burnt the wretched city, devastating the surrounding area . . . and burning the whole country." Cities were raided and sacked, often repeatedly, and society came close to collapse. By 1080, we hear that

> [e]verywhere the Christians had been delivered to the sword or into bondage interrupting thus the cultivation of the fields so that bread was lacking. The farmers and workers had been massacred or led off into slavery and famine extended its rigors to all places. Many provinces were depopulated.

The border regions between warring sides became "deserts." Populations fell steeply, and any families who could flee to safer parts of the world did so. Asia Minor, which probably had 12 million people in the early Byzantine period, had barely half that by the thirteenth century.[28]

These changes naturally had religious consequences, as ancient Christian centers were devastated. In the 1140s, the Turks took Edessa the Blessed, killing or enslaving virtually its entire population, then estimated at forty-seven thousand. Even some decades later, Michael the Syrian lamented that

> Edessa remained a desert: a moving sight covered with a black garment, drunk with blood, infested by the very corpses of its sons and daughters! Vampires and other savage beasts ran and entered the city at night to feast on the flesh of the massacred, and it became the abode of jackals; for none entered there except those who dug to discover treasures.

Decades later, most of the city remained in ruins, including some seventeen unrestored churches, and travelers noted that the city had been without a priest for years. Reading such accounts, we can only speculate about the books and manuscripts that must have been lost in the catastrophe that overwhelmed cities like Edessa and Ephesus, which must once have contained treasure troves of records of the earliest Christian communities.[29]

Such destruction—and Edessa represents only an extreme example of what occurred to most cities in the region at some point in this era—meant the crippling or elimination of the structure of dioceses, each of which had been based in a city and had controlled rural life through a network of subordinate parishes. In 1283, Bar-Hebraeus mocked the charge that he might have ambitions to be Jacobite patriarch. Why would anyone want such a thing, he asked, when "the dioceses of the West are laid waste"? Antioch was "in a state of lamentation and tears." Was he supposed to covet Aleppo, Edessa, or Harran, "all of which are laid waste"? Or "the seven dioceses which are round about Melitene, in none of which doth a single house remain"? Or other once-flourishing towns that now had not even a wall to piss against?[30] Meanwhile, the spiritual life of the Eastern churches had depended on the once-thriving network of monasteries, which provided wonderfully lucrative targets for Turkish raiders.

No less profitable for raiders were pilgrimage centers, where grateful visitors had often donated precious gifts. From the eleventh century onward, the Christian landscape of Asia Minor was destroyed piecemeal: gone was the church of Saint Basil of Caesarea, the shrine of Saint Nicholas of Myra (the legendary original Santa Claus), while the Turks desecrated the churches of Antioch when they captured the city in 1085. The church of Saint John at Ephesus survived as long as it did only because it was fortified and walled.[31] The situation recalls the Viking raids on the churches and monasteries of western Europe, where the raiders chose targets for economic motives rather than out of any specific malice against Christianity as a religion.

At least before the later thirteenth century, Turkish forces did not target Christian churches or sects consistently or systematically, and they treated different bodies selectively. The Syrian and Armenian churches were more likely to be left alone, while the Greeks suffered as representatives of the Byzantine Empire, a hostile power. Worst treated of all were the Latin Catholic clergy, who were seen as interlopers and who were massacred wholesale when opportunity arose. But although we cannot talk of direct persecution, the effects of war were cataclysmic enough. Whatever their intentions, the Turks shredded Christian ecclesiastical institutions beyond repair. And an impoverished church could not offer poor Christians the kind of material aid they had been accustomed to receiving during times of famine and crisis. This dereliction of duty disappointed believers while opening the way to Muslim organizations that could offer such charity. Muslim rulers speeded the process of assimilation by favoring dervishes from Sufi orders, who began aggressive evangelization of the remaining unbelievers in the countryside.[32]

Meanwhile, at least some of the conquerors did directly force Christians to accept Islam. This kind of compulsion was not uniquely Muslim, as the successful Byzantine emperors of the ninth and tenth centuries had succeeded in bringing Muslim cities and leaders over to Christianity. For later generations, though, most of the spiritual traffic lay in the other direction. One later source reports that when the city of Comana was taken, its people were forced to accept Islam, and the new governor acted forcefully to ensure that the conversions were not merely feigned: "He compelled the inhabitants to perform the five daily prayers and all those who refused to go to the mosque were brought there by threat of physical violence. Those who continued to drink wine were flogged, and other violations of Islamic law similarly treated." When Christian forces approached, the inhabitants revolted against their occupiers, and replaced the mosques with monasteries. Other evidence of forced conversion is strictly contemporary. A twelfth-century canonist reports how "many others who were forcibly circumcised by the Hagarenes [Muslims] and done other things or suffered impieties were received by the church after sincere confession and suitable penance."[33]

False Dawn

As time went by, religious hostility became acute, so that Muslims increasingly targeted Christian sites and populations as a matter of systematic policy: persecution and massacre became an issue of faith. One recurring factor driving persecution was warfare, and the sense that Muslim nations faced a genuine threat to their existence from unbelievers. Several such dangers appeared from the eleventh century onward. In response, Muslim states penalized or expelled Christians as potential subversives.

The best-known of these new assaults on Islam grew from the crusading movement, originally launched by the pope in 1095 with the goal of recapturing the Holy Land from the Turks. Over the next two centuries, a series of ventures mobilized many thousands of European Christians to military adventures in the Levant, and at their height, crusader statelets occupied much of Palestine, Lebanon, and Syria. Western hopes in the region ended only with the Muslim capture of the city of Antioch in 1268, and of Acre in 1291. What made the crusading movement particularly painful for Middle Eastern Christians was the constant pressure it involved, and the repeated provocations to Muslim authorities. Instead of one main incursion, which might have been forgotten in time, new surges followed every few decades: in the 1090s, the 1140s, the 1190s, and so on. The effects were obvious in the domestic politics of Egypt and other states, which tightened and strictly enforced the old dhimmi laws, closed churches, and sometimes forced conversions. Repeatedly, only state intervention held off mobs trying to close churches or persecute Christians. The already strong pressure to convert intensified.[34]

In Spain, too, crusading Christian powers made steady gains in reconquering the peninsula, building on their capture in 1085 of Toledo, the old Visigothic capital. As warfare escalated, both sides were strengthened by an influx of harder-line believers from neighboring countries, motivated by new waves of religious zeal. In the Muslim case, these militantly pious outsiders were the Almoravids of the late eleventh century, and the Almohads of the mid-twelfth. Both showed much less tolerance for non-Muslim subjects, but their attitudes were not altogether new in Moorish Spain, however much we may romanticize that society as a haven of interfaith tolerance. In 1066, an anti-Jewish pogrom in Granada reportedly killed five thousand, a massacre on a scale equal to anything in the Christian lands, and Córdoba's Jews suffered a notorious massacre in 1148. Once the *Reconquista* began in earnest, authorities began mass deportations of Christians and Jews. The worst instance came in 1126, when a threatened invasion from Christian Aragon provoked reprisals against the native Christians of Andalusia. Ten thousand of these Mozarabs fled to the Christian north, while thousands more were deported to Morocco, where they remained for decades. A second wave of deportations followed in 1137, reportedly leaving very few Mozarabs in Andalusia. Although later Christian Spain became notorious for its expulsion of religious minorities, that regime was doing nothing different from what its Moorish predecessors had done in earlier centuries.[35]

The story of the Crusades is well known, but less celebrated is the much more acute challenge to Muslim power caused by Christian attempts to create an Eastern Front against Islam. During the thirteenth century, the Muslim states suddenly found themselves under attack from a lethal enemy whose activities made the Western Crusades look like fleabites. The Mongol assault on the Islamic world began in 1219 when the forces of Genghis Khan attacked the Khwarezmid Empire of central Asia, taking such great cities as Bukhara and Samarkand. Over the next forty years, Mongol power extended over most of western Asia, through a series of campaigns in which they devastated ancient cities. When Merv fell in 1221, the Mongols slaughtered virtually every man, woman, and child in the city, not to mention many thousands of refugees from surrounding areas. Contemporary accounts claim that the dead ran into the hundreds of thousands, or even millions. Ani in Armenia never recovered from the sack of 1236, while Mongol devastation ended the golden age of the Christian kingdom of Georgia. In 1258, the Mongols under Hulegu, Genghis's grandson, perpetrated a historic massacre in Baghdad itself, ending the caliphate and conceivably killing eight hundred thousand residents. Over the next century, Hulegu's successors ruled the Ilkhanate, one of the Mongol successor states, a vast empire stretching from the boundaries of India to western Anatolia. When modern-day Iraqis denounce American occupiers as the New Mongols, they are invoking memories of the direst moment of their history. The Mongol threat remained acute until 1303, when Egyptian forces decisively defeated them in Syria.[36]

The Mongol Faith

The Mongol invasions posed what was unquestionably the greatest threat ever to the existence of Islam. The Mongols were not Christianized, but they knew both Christianity and Buddhism as mainstream central Asian faiths, and their coalition included such Christianized peoples as the Keraits, Ongguds, and Uygurs. In his youth, Genghis Khan was under the patronage and protection of the Kerait chieftain Toghrul. After Genghis overthrew Toghrul, he used the Christian nieces of his defeated enemy as marriage partners for his own family. He married one sister himself, and gave the others to his own sons. The most important of the Kerait sisters was Sorghaghtani-beki, whose son Hulegu may have identified himself as a Christian. Sorghaghtani's other children included the Chinese ruler Kublai Khan, whom Bar-Hebraeus lauded as "the just and wise king, and lover [or friend] of the Christians." Hulegu's Christian wife ensured that the invaders single out Baghdad's mosques for destruction, while churches were protected. Reportedly, she wanted "to put the Saracens into such slavery that they dared not show themselves any more." The Mongols actually turned one of the caliph's old palaces into an official residence for the catholicos, and it became the site of a new church. In this ambience at court, it is not surprising that some Mongol leaders converted, while others had Christians in their immediate family, which meant that they usually had priests or monks in attendance.[37]

Noting this religious context, Asian Christians hoped for a glorious future. In the 1220s, at the height of Genghis's conquests, Solomon of Basra wrote an apocalyptic tract prophesying the fall of Islam. He imagines "Ishmaelite" (Muslim) tyranny growing ever worse, until they proclaim, arrogantly, that

> "[t]he Christians have neither a God nor a deliverer"; then all
> of a sudden there shall be raised up against them pains like
> those of a woman in childbirth; and the king of the Greeks
> shall go forth against them in great wrath, and he shall rouse
> himself like a man who has shaken off his wine. He shall go
> forth against them from the sea of the Cushites, and shall cast
> the sword and destruction into the wilderness of Yathrib
> [Medina] and into the dwelling-place of their fathers. . . . All
> the wrath and anger of the king of the Greeks shall have full
> course upon those who have denied Christ.

Bar-Hebraeus later eulogized the genocidal Hulegu and his wife as "great luminaries and zealous combatants of the Christian religion." Beleaguered Western crusaders were delighted to hear of such potential allies approaching from the East, and some tried to ally with the Mongols. Though the popes forbade a formal pact, the surviving crusader states were sympathetic to Mongol schemes to conquer Mamluk Egypt in 1260, and they agreed neither to hinder the invasion nor to warn the Egyptians. The Mongol general Kitbuqa was himself a Kerait Christian. The decisive Egyptian victory at Ain Jalut was a devastating reversal of Christian hopes.[38]

Still, Mongol rulers continued to cultivated Christian ties. Hulegu's own son married a Byzantine princess, and he favored Christianity and Buddhism over Islam. Over the following decades, while the Mongols did not actually persecute Muslims, they did impose upon them what was seen as a grievously oppressive burden—namely, that they would no longer be able to treat Christians as subject peoples. Partly, this policy reflected Mongol favor to the Christians, but it was also a straightforward political decision: as long as subject peoples paid their taxes, their religious attitudes were irrelevant. Christians across the Middle East took advantage of the newfound liberty and the prospect that the situation would survive indefinitely under sympathetic Mongol rule. With Hulegu and his heirs in power, Christians publicly did the things that had been forbidden under Islam, including carrying the cross in public processions, drinking wine, and erecting churches in towns where none had been permitted. In 1268, in Baghdad itself, the catholicos ordered a man publicly drowned for converting from Christianity to Islam. Scandalized Muslims responded with mob attacks where possible, but the Mongol regime strictly limited such outbreaks. This was the political environment at the time of Bar Sauma's visit to the West, and the reason for his optimism.[39]

Continued toleration depended entirely on the attitudes of the Mongol rulers, whose religious attitudes drifted increasingly toward favoring Islam. Although there was no one moment when the ruling family converted to Islam—some rulers were solidly Muslim, others not—the overall trend was clear. In 1295 the new khan, Mahmud Ghazan, persecuted Christianity and Buddhism, and his successors followed his policies. Particularly severe was Ghazan's brother and heir, Oljeitu (1304–16); originally baptized a Christian under the name Nicholas, he now became a fervent Muslim, taking the name Muhammad. After an interlude of a few decades, the Christians found themselves under the control of a Muslim superstate, but with their position radically changed. In contrast to the generally easygoing policies of the Arab caliphate, Christians were now subjected to intense persecution.

Worse, Christians could no longer hope to counter their loss of influence in the Middle East by missionary expansion into central Asia, as the Mongol invasions had so devastated the traditional urban centers. Moreover, all the Mongol successor states soon fell under heavy Muslim influence. By the mid–fourteenth century, Islamized Mongol princes ruled not just the Ilkhanate but also most of the other states. These included the Chaghadai Khanate that dominated the lands between Persia and China, and the Golden Horde of the steppes. Even after accepting Islam, the Chaghadai rulers continued to tolerate a Christian presence at their capital of Almaliq until 1338, when all Christians in the city were killed. Traces of Christianity among the Keraits and Uygurs did not last long into the fifteenth century.[40]

After half a millennium in which any of three great religions could reasonably hope to win the religious loyalties of the central Asian peoples, that contest was now firmly resolved in the cause of Islam. Arguably, that victory was even more critical for the long-term relationship between Islam and Christianity than the original Arab conquests of the seventh century. And the historic Christian association with the central Asian peoples now came back to haunt them.

The Great Persecutions

Egyptian Christians initially bore the brunt of the new intolerance. From the start of the thirteenth century, Egypt had been the primary target of Western Crusades, and governments occasionally retaliated against the Copts. By 1250, Egypt was ruled by the Mamluk dynasty, which from its earliest history was in armed conflict with Christians and their allies. The first sultan came to power through a war with French crusading invaders, and the greatest Mamluk leader was the general Baybars, the scourge of both crusaders and Mongols. Baybars hated Christians generally, but his loathing knew no bounds where Latin Europeans were concerned. When he captured Antioch in 1268, he wrote to the city's crusader ruler that, had he not escaped,

> [y]ou would have seen the crosses in your churches smashed, the pages of false Testaments scattered, the patriarchs' tombs overturned. You would have seen your Muslim enemy trampling over the place where you celebrate Mass, cutting the throats of monks, priests and deacons upon the altars, bringing sudden death to the patriarchs and slavery to the royal princes.[41]

This brutal attitude—so radically different from the tone of earlier Muslim-Christian wars—partly reflected his fury at the Christian alliance with the Mongols. After the sack of Baghdad, it was not far-fetched to imagine a world in which Egypt would stand alone as the last remaining Muslim great power, in a Middle East dominated by Christian Mongols. And the more explicitly Islamic the Mamluk campaigns became, the more tempting it was for local Christians to act as a fifth column for Mongol forces, which in turn called forth worse displays of Muslim revenge.

This intolerance was increasingly evident in Egyptian policies toward their still substantial Christian minority. Persecution was not new in Egypt, but matters deteriorated sharply after the Mamluk-Mongol wars. Between 1293 and 1354, the government launched four separate campaigns intended to enforce the submission of Christians and Jews, and to drive them to accept Islam. Each wave of violence became more intense and better organized. In 1293, an initial persecution fizzled when the sultan's officials realized that the Christians they were on the point of executing largely ran and controlled the country's finances, not to mention being the most competent scribes; but later movements were more success-ful. In 1301, a vizier arriving from Morocco was appalled at the ob-vious wealth and status of the Egyptian dhimmis, both Christians and Jews. Unlike in his own country, where the dhimmis were firmly repressed, in Egypt they held high public offices, they wore sumptu-ous clothes, and they rode the most elegant mules and mares. The vizier's views impressed local officials, who came to believe that putting the subject peoples in their place would advance the cause of Islam.[42]

A wave of repressive laws followed, and one ordinance in 1301 tried to close all the churches and synagogues outside Cairo. Though this was not permanently enforced, some ancient churches were demolished and the relics of their saints publicly burned. Dhimmis were dismissed from public employment and were forced to wear distinctive clothing—blue turbans for Christians, yellow for Jews. In a powerful statement of their symbolic inferiority, dhimmis were forced to ride donkeys rather than mares or mules, and even then they had to dismount when a Muslim approached. Travelers still commented on the enforcement of these rules into the nineteenth century.

The effects of this crisis linger to the present day, as the rigorous Muslim legalism that emerged in just these years has largely shaped modern fundamentalist movements. From the 1290s, Muslim jurists produced ever-harsher interpretations of the laws governing mi-norities, particularly through the work of militant and puritanical scholars like Ibn Taymiyyah. Ibn Taymiyyah's life was shaped by the disasters of the Mongol wars, which forced him into exile in Egypt, and he saw his goal as the militant restoration of Islam in the face of its enemies at home and abroad. His work has had a long afterlife. Ibn Taymiyyah is regarded as the spiritual godfather of the Wahhabi movement, and of most modern extremist and jihadi groups. Among many others, Osama bin Laden cites him as a special hero.

The new Muslim hostility was reflected in outbreaks of extreme anti-Christian violence. In 1321, Muslim mobs began looting and destroying Cairo's Coptic churches. Commonly, a holy man would give the signal for the attacks by mobilizing crowds in the mosques under the cry "Down with the churches." Muslim historian Al-Maqrizi recorded:

> Then they destroyed the Church of St. Mennas in the Hamra, which had from ancient times been much revered by the Christians . . . the people climbed the walls, opened the gates and took money, vessels and wine jars out of the church; it was a terrible occurrence. Thereupon they went from the church in the Hamra after they had destroyed it to the two churches near the Seven Wells, one of which was called the Church of the Maidens, and was inhabited by a number of Christian girls, and by monks.

Though the sultan initially tried to keep order, killing many rioters, the general hatred of Christians was too powerful to contain. Shortly afterward, Christians were blamed for setting fires across Cairo, allegedly aided by Byzantine monks armed with ingenious incendiary bombs. When some of the accused confessed under torture, the authorities were forced to support the popular movement. At one point, the sultan faced a mob some twenty thousand strong, all calling for the suppression of Christians. In order to safeguard his rule, the sultan permitted a purge. Al-Maqrizi went on to catalog the churches wrecked in the ensuing violence: "six churches in the province of Al-Bahnasa; at Suyut, Manfalut and Munyat Ibn al-Khasib eight churches; at Kus and Aswan eleven churches. . . . A great number of monasteries were also destroyed." The government further proclaimed that anyone who found a Christian was permitted to beat him and take his goods.[43]

By midcentury, Muslim writers had access to a whole catalog of anti-Christian charges that bear close resemblance to scabrous anti-Jewish tracts like the later *Protocols of the Elders of Zion*. According to writers like al-Asnawi, Christians were spies ever on the lookout for opportunities to betray the Muslim cause; and cases in both Egypt and Syria proved they were serial arsonists: "They display great cunning in their schemes to burn down mosques, many of which have been destroyed in this way, and many men, women and children burnt to death." Some Christians were even reported to have planned to bomb the great mosque of Medina. Given modern-day stereotypes of Islam in the West, it is ironic that Christian minorities were then so feared because they were allegedly plotting terror bombings against prestigious symbols of Muslim power. On a lesser scale, it was said, Christian agents in government systematically tried to plunder Muslim property, to ruin mosques, and to transfer property to churches. Such stories reinforced demands for tight restrictions upon dhimmis.[44]

In a society so founded upon honor and family pride, the cumulative humiliations of the new policy were too much to bear for the many wealthy urban Christians who now converted to Islam. Other, poorer Christians proved firmer, particularly if they were located in rural areas where government policies were slower to penetrate, but subsequent waves of intimidation wore down this resistance. The violence of the 1320s reduced Christian numbers and prepared the way for the disasters of 1354. From the end of the fourteenth century, Egypt's Coptic Christians were reduced to the minority status that they would retain until the present century, constituting perhaps 10 percent of the Egyptian people. The Coptic Church entered a period of "hibernation" that lasted until the mid-nineteenth century.[45]

When Al-Maqrizi surveyed Egypt's monasteries in the early fifteenth century, he was recording a blasted landscape, particularly on the Nile's eastern bank. The entries become monotonous: "now deserted"; "fallen into decay"; "no one lives there"; "now likewise destroyed." "In the district of Al-Bahnasa there were many monasteries now destroyed." These elegiac sketches offer a bitter taste of what had once been. Near Suyut, "on both the dams there are said to have been 360 monasteries and the traveler went from Al-Badraishin to Asfun, continually in the shade of the gardens. Now this part is laid waste, and deserted by the inhabitants." The houses near Asfun "are all destroyed and forgotten, though in former times they were so populous and their monks so numerous, their estates so large, and the offerings made to them so valuable." What were once the thousand monks of Bu Fana were now reduced to two.[46]

Once their Mongol rulers converted to Islam, conditions became equally difficult for the Christians of Mesopotamia and Syria. Between 1290 and 1330, the story of Christianity in these parts, like that in Egypt, becomes a litany of disasters and ever-more draconian penal laws. One edict commanded that

> the churches shall be uprooted and the altars overturned and the celebrations of the Eucharist shall cease and the hymns of praise and the sounds of calls to prayer shall be abolished; and the chiefs of the Christians and the heads of the synagogues of the Jews and the great men among them shall be killed.

Churches suffered mass closure or destruction, even at such ancient centers as Tabriz and Arbela, Mosul and Baghdad. Bishops and clergy were tortured and imprisoned. Mobs attacked and tortured the patriarch Yaballaha III.[47]

Some laws struck directly at ordinary believers, rather than just the institutions or the hierarchy. Some of these edicts came from the khans themselves, while others came from the initiative of local governors, but the effects were just as damaging. Even when the khans tried to limit persecution, they could hardly stem the zeal of local officers. In some cities, local laws ordered forcible conversion to Islam and prohibited the exercise of Christianity, upon pain of death. One Muslim ruler in Armenia began by inflicting ruinous taxes, and finally ordered that any man who refused to convert to Islam should suffer branding, blinding in one eye, and castration.[48]

Yet even the more limited sanctions were severe enough, especially when they were reinforced by mob action. Christians, like Jews,
were to be instantly recognizable. As one new law commanded, "No
Christian henceforth should go out without a waist-belt and . . . all
Jews should wear a conspicuous mark on their heads." In this atmosphere, "a Christian man [in Baghdad] dared not appear in the
market but the women went forth in public and bought and sold
since they could not be distinguished from Saracen women; and if
they were recognized they were burdened at once with trials and
contumely and even received blows and beating." In the words of
one contemporary, "The persecutions and disgrace and mockings
and ignominy which the Christians suffered at this time, especially
in Baghdad, words cannot describe." The persecution reached its
height with wholesale massacres, at Arbela in 1310 and at Amida in
1317. At Amida, where twelve thousand were carried into slavery,
the destruction of churches and monasteries was so thorough that
the fires reputedly burned for a month.[49]

These persecutions had a greater effect on the churches of the
Middle East than any other event since the conversion of the
Roman Empire. The succession to the ancient hierarchies fell into
disarray, interrupting sequences that had remained unbroken since
the time of the apostles. The office of Nestorian catholicos remained vacant from 1369 to 1378, and possibly longer, and the
Jacobites remained without a head from 1379 to 1404. Whole Christian communities were annihilated across central Asia, and surviving communities shrank to tiny fractions of their former size. As
late as 1340, Merv was still the setting for a Christian training
school for Tatars, but by this stage the city was finding it difficult
to maintain even the shreds of its former glories. Christianity now
disappears in Persia, and across southern and central Iraq. The
patriarchs "of Babylon" now literally headed for the hills, taking
up their residence on the safer soil of northern Mesopotamia. In
later centuries, patriarchs made their home at the Rabban Hormizd
monastery in the mountains near Mosul.[50]

Becoming Turkey

In Asia Minor, meanwhile, the growing centrality of religious moti-
vations made the endemic cycle of violence still more bitter, as
Turkish forces became even harsher to Christian enemies of all
sects and denominations. In 1304, Turkish forces obliterated the
city of Ephesus, where Paul once confronted a mob chanting the
glories of Artemis: all Christians were either killed or deported.
When a metropolitan arrived in 1340—the first to enter the city in
thirty-five years—he operated not from the historic cathedral but
from cheap lodgings in the house of an old Turkish woman. Most
of his flock consisted of thousands of Christian prisoners and
slaves, among whom were many priests and monks. By 1387, the
few remaining believers were too poor to maintain a priest. When
Ibn Battuta visited Ephesus about 1330, his travel diary recorded
that "[t]he cathedral mosque, which was formerly a church greatly
venerated by the Greeks, is one of the most beautiful in the world. I
bought a Greek slave girl here for forty dinars."[51]

Large areas of Asia Minor were now effectively dechristianized.
As we have seen, this area was once under a well-organized hierarchy of metropolitans and bishops, but by the twelfth century, many
bishops appointed to serve sees in the Anatolian war zone found it
all but impossible to leave Constantinople to visit their dioceses.
Local church administration and supervision lapsed. Many cities remained without bishops, while some bishops served areas that were
cities only in name, glorified villages. In many sees, sequences of
bishops and metropolitans that began in Roman times dried up suddenly in the fourteenth century. Over the decades, metropolitan
after metropolitan, diocese after diocese, vanishes from the Notitia,
the roster of church leaders. By the late fifteenth century, the
number of bishoprics in Anatolia contracted from three hundred
seventy-three to just *three,* compared with one hundred fifteen in the
empire's European provinces. Though metropolitans were still
listed, many of these names were honorary titles, preserved only

because nobody in the church of Constantinople could bring himself to record that a center as prestigious as Ephesus had actually ceased to exist as a Christian community.[52]

By the fifteenth century, then, when the Ottoman Turks completed the conquest, Christians were already a small minority outside Constantinople and perhaps a couple of other major cities, and the rural areas were ripe for Islamization. By the early sixteenth century, tax records suggest, Christians made up just 8 percent of the population of Anatolia, although that figure is an underestimate, as it does not include slaves, and many of those were certainly Christian. Two-thirds of the recorded Christians lived in just one of the five Anatolian provinces.[53]

Spreading Ruin

The new Muslim militancy had dreadful consequences for the network of smaller Christian states that had existed on the fringes of the Muslim world—Armenia and Georgia, Ethiopia and Nubia. After 1250, the Mamluks pursued their jihad not only against European crusaders, but against neighboring Christian regimes. After 1260, the Mamluks expanded into Syria and began pressing on the Armenian state. In 1293, the Mamluks again raided Armenia, destroying the seat of the Armenian catholicos. Like other Christians, the Armenians still found the Mongols preferable to their old Muslim enemies, and Armenian forces joined the Mongols in their great invasion of Syria in 1303. The Mamluks, however, decisively defeated both. In 1375, the Mamluk conquest of Cilicia ended the last independent Armenian kingdom and demolished the beloved ecclesiastical capital of Sis. As one historian writes, "After 1375, Armenia as an autonomous political entity ceased. . . . The Armenian church, deprived of its traditional upper-class support, and divided by dissension, accommodated itself to Islamic tutelage in order to endure intact beyond this destructive era." Armenians recall the following two hundred years as a dark age for their nation, the beginning of their great diaspora. Very little Armenian historical writing survives from the years between 1450 and 1650.[54]

The newly Muslim regime of the Ilkhanate became just as intolerant of Christian neighbors. In 1307, the khan Oljeitu ordered the Georgians to give up Christianity upon pain of destruction, and a savage war ensued.[55] The campaigns of Timur after 1380 destroyed much of Georgia, especially the churches and monasteries, and one king allegedly accepted Islam. What had once been a great regional kingdom fell apart in the fifteenth century, succumbing to Turkmen and Persian raids. By the sixteenth century, both Georgia and Armenia were partitioned between the Ottoman and Persian empires. Otherwise, only two Christian states remained in Asia. One was the Byzantine Empire itself, although by 1400 this magnificent label applied only to a tiny region around Constantinople proper, together with some small fragments of Greece. The Black Sea kingdom of Trebizond, "the last Greek empire," limped on until 1461.

African Christianity also suffered. In 1275, Baybars conquered Nubia, capturing the capital, Dongola. His forces sacked churches and forced the king, David, into exile. Repeated attacks weakened the state, while the growing crisis of the Egyptian church prevented Coptic authorities from supplying the bishops and priests essential to maintaining church life. By 1350, the royal church in Dongola had become a mosque, and around 1372, we hear of the ordination of the last Christian bishop. Within a few decades, Nubia was both dechristianized and Arabized in language and culture, although a tiny Christian statelet lingered on until the late fifteenth century. Sixteenth-century travelers were told that Nubia's Christians "had received everything from Rome [i.e., Constantinople] and that it is a very long time since a bishop died whom they had received from Rome. Because of the wars of the Moors, they could not get another one, and they lost all their clergy and their Christianity and thus the Christian faith was forgotten."[56]

Only Ethiopia remained as a bastion of African Christianity, and that came under increasing military pressure. Christian kings generally expanded the hold of the religion during the fourteenth century, but calamity was to follow. A long series of defeats and disasters culminated in the early sixteenth century, when the mighty jihad of Ahmed Gran threatened to annihilate the nation. The Muslim invaders proclaimed a sultanate of Habasha (Abyssinia), and many Christians defected to Islam. The nation's monasteries were sacked, its art and manuscripts destroyed or plundered, so that much of our knowledge of earlier Christian Ethiopia perished forever. One modern historian of African Christianity has aptly termed this "a systematic campaign of cultural and national genocide." Ethiopia barely survived the crisis, scraping through with Portuguese assistance. Although Christianity survived, it did so in vastly impoverished form.[57]

The destruction of Christian states like Nubia and Armenia meant that surviving minorities living under Muslim rule no longer had even the faint hope that outside forces might someday come to their aid. During the persecutions of the early fourteenth century, the only external power that the Egyptian government seriously needed to conciliate was the Spanish kingdom of Aragon, which meant that churches near the coast were less likely to be suppressed. For the first time, Middle Eastern Christians looked to European powers for protection, a linkage that would often prove treacherous.[58]

Farther afield, too, the contraction of Mongol power withdrew the friendly tolerance to which Christians had become accustomed. In 1368, the nationalist Ming dynasty overthrew the Mongol regime. The new authorities cracked down on foreign religious bodies, especially those associated with the defeated Mongols. As had occurred in the ninth century, the Nestorian mission was largely destroyed, and the much thinner Catholic missions disappeared: most of the Catholic clergy present at the time simply vanished without a trace. For almost two centuries, China lacked an obvious Christian presence.

A Colder World

We can identify specific political reasons for the new harshness to Christians. A reaction against Western crusading zeal played some role, but that is not of itself an adequate explanation. Looking at other parts of the world suggests that intolerance was becoming a marked feature of widely separated cultures around the world and not just in Asia. The chronology of Christian sufferings under Islam closely mirrors that of Jews in Christian states. It was in 1290 that England expelled all its Jews, followed by France in 1306, and pogroms reached appalling heights across western Europe during the 1330s and 1340s. Other groups likewise suffered from growing paranoia, and this was the era in which the great European witch persecutions began. The papacy formally listed witchcraft as a heresy—that is, as an evil alternative religion—in 1320, and women were soon being accused of the familiar package of crimes, including devil worship, poisoning, and black magic. In 1307, the French king arrested the members of the Knights Templar on trumped-up charges of devil worship, heresy, and conspiracy, destroying what had been the greatest crusading order. In 1320–21, southern France and Aragon suffered two outbreaks of hysterical violence, the Shepherds' Crusade and the Lepers' Plot. Around 1300, the world was changing, and definitely for the worse.[59]

If we seek a common factor that might explain this simultaneous scapegoating of vulnerable minorities, by far the best candidate is climate change, which was responsible for many economic changes in these years, and which increased poverty and desperation across the globe. Populations had swelled during the warming period between the eleventh and thirteenth centuries. Europe's population more than doubled during these prosperous times, forcing settlers to swarm onto marginal lands. In the late thirteenth century, however, Europe and the Middle East entered what has been described as the Little Ice Age, as pack ice grew in the oceans, and trade routes became more difficult both by land and by sea. Summers became cooler and wetter, and as harvests deteriorated, people starved. The world could no longer sustain the population it had gained during the boom years. Europe suffered its horrific Great Famine between 1315 and 1317, with reports of widespread cannibalism in 1318–20. Populations contracted sharply across Eurasia, and grossly weakened societies lingered on to face the horrors of the Black Death in the 1340s.

Aggravating matters was the environmental collapse in large sections of the Middle East. From Carthage to Persia, societies had waged a constant battle between "the desert and the sown," with irrigation as the critical weapon. Incessant wars and massacres, social and governmental breakdown all took their toll, making it impossible to maintain irrigation, and thus to defend the arable lands won a thousand years earlier. Some argue that the Mongols deliberately destroyed irrigation works as a kind of environmental warfare, leading to the spread of desert conditions. The main victims of the transformation were settled farmers and city dwellers, while nomads inherited much of the region: Bedouin cultures spread over what had been fertile lowlands. When Ibn Battuta traveled across the Middle East in the 1320s, he listed all the once-great cities now characterized as only "a total ruin" or "totally uninhabited." Seeing a fine mosque at Basra, he is told that

> Basra was in former times a city so vast that this mosque stood in the centre of the town, whereas now it is two miles outside it. Two miles beyond it again is the old wall that encircled the town, so that it stands midway between the old wall and the present city.[60]

Against this social background, states foundered, kings were murdered, and popular revolts and uprisings became commonplace. (This age of crisis is the backdrop to the Scottish national revolution portrayed in the film *Braveheart*.) Whatever the religious coloring of particular societies, this was a world that directly attributed changes in weather or harvest to the divine will, and it seemed natural to blame catastrophes on the misdeeds of deviant minorities who angered God. Bitter experience taught governments of all faiths not to try to stem the rage of mobs against hated minority groups. The anti-Christian persecutions in Egypt in 1354 followed shortly after the visitation of the Black Death, which killed a third of the residents of Cairo.[61]

As persecutions grew, it became ever more difficult for religious minorities to survive. In some cases, minorities were thoroughly uprooted. We think of the Jews of England, or the survivors of the western European pogroms of the 1340s. After the Black Death, many Jews migrated to the less-developed, eastern regions of the continent. By the end of the fourteenth century, Europe's Jewish population was largely concentrated in the united kingdom of Poland and Lithuania, which included much of what later ages would know as Belorussia and the Ukraine. In Muslim societies, too, Christian areas chiefly maintained themselves in remote or marginal communities where they could escape the attention of the suspicious majority. Both Christian and Jewish minorities were forced to exercise evergreater discretion in their daily lives, seeking to avoid any possible acts of provocation, and living in constant fear of violence. In such a world, religions could hope to flourish only in the context of a state that identified fully with that faith, and supported its cause. Except possibly in India, after 1300 it became difficult to practice Christianity outside the protections of a Christian state.

It was a Muslim ruler who administered the coup de grâce to the Christian Middle East. In the 1360s, the warlord Timur began a career that would make him khan over most of Asia, and his homicidal policies toward captured cities followed closely those of his Mongol predecessors. His distinctive custom, his trademark, was to exterminate the population of any city that resisted him, and to erect a giant pyramid built from the skulls of his victims—men, women, and children. Considering the much smaller population of the world at that time, Timur's depredations probably inflicted greater slaughter, in relative terms, than would either Hitler or Stalin in their day.

His career marks the end of the urban Middle Eastern society that had flourished since Hellenistic times. Only in Timur's time, for instance, did the ancient Silk Road finally cease to function.[62]

The once-Christian lands of Asia fared no better. About 1400, Timur's forces massacred the city dwellers of Syria and Mesopotamia. Disaster overcame such venerable Christian areas as Damascus, Amida, Ani, Tikrit, Arbela, Mosul, and Tur Abdin. In 1402, Smyrna's population was transformed into yet another pyramid of skulls. Even in remote areas like northern Mesopotamia, Timur's forces sought out refugees who hid in caves, setting fires and thus killing them by asphyxiation. Although by this point the Christian element of the population must have been quite small, Timur did consciously target non-Muslims, boasting of "washing the sword of Islam in the blood of the infidels." Any Christian remnants in Samarkand and central Asia were finally destroyed by Timur's grandson, Ulugh Beg. The Asian churches—Nestorian, Jacobite, and others—barely survived even in name.[63]

On May 29, 1453, Ottoman Turkish forces stormed and captured the city of Constantinople, destroying the last remnants of the Roman Empire. Hagia Sophia, the Church of the Holy Wisdom, lost its status as the world's largest church, becoming instead a mosque. The traumatic religious implications can be suggested if we imagine a world in which Christians or Jews annexed and converted the cities of Mecca and Medina, demolishing the Ka'ba and turning the Great Mosque into a splendid cathedral or synagogue. The very thought would be blasphemy for pious Muslims; and for Christians throughout eastern Europe and the Middle East, likewise, the fall of Constantinople was "the day the world ended." Yet for all its symbolic weight, this event was of little practical importance in a world in which the Ottomans had already absorbed virtually all the old Byzantine lands. And at least as a majority faith, Christianity had long since lost its importance. From the fourteenth century, Islam had gained a decisive role as the dominant faith in the Middle East, and the only remaining question was how long Christians could retain any presence whatever.

5

The Last Christians

The bloodstained annals of the East contain no record of massacres more unprovoked, more widespread or more terrible than those perpetrated by the Turkish Government upon the Christians of Anatolia and Armenia in 1915.

—James Bryce, the 1st Viscount Bryce

In 1933, Muslim forces in the new nation of Iraq launched a deadly assault on the few surviving communities of the Nestorian or Assyrian peoples, in what had once been the Christian heartland of northern Mesopotamia. Government-sponsored militias cleansed much of the far north of Iraq of its Assyrian population, killing thousands, and eliminating dozens of villages. As the catholicos protested:

Men, women and children were massacred wholesale most barbarously by rifle, revolver and machine gun fire. . . . Priests were killed and their bodies mutilated. Assyrian women were violated and killed. Priests and Assyrian young men were killed instantly after refusing forced conversion to Muhammadanism. . . . Pregnant women had their wombs cut and their babies destroyed.[1]

Although the crimes were anything but new in their nature, the coming of modern media meant that, unlike on previous occasions, the events now reached the attention of a wider world, raising demands for Western intervention.[2]

So shocking were the anti-Christian purges that they demanded a new legal vocabulary. Some months afterward, Polish Jewish lawyer Raphael Lemkin used the cases of the Assyrians, and the Christian Armenians before them, to argue for a new legal category to be called *crimes of barbarity,* primarily "acts of extermination directed against the ethnic, religious or social collectivities whatever the motive (political, religious, etc.)." Lemkin developed this theme over the following years, and in 1943 he coined a new word for this atrocious behavior—namely, *genocide.* The modern concept of genocide as a uniquely horrible act demanding international sanctions has its roots in the thoroughly successful movements to eradicate Middle Eastern Christians. Lemkin recognized acutely that such acts might provide an awful precedent for later regimes: as Hitler asked in 1939, "Who, after all, speaks to-day of the annihilation of the Armenians?"[3]

The very recent character of these events, of this genocide, must be stressed. We tend to assume that the world we grow up with has always been in existence, so that it can be difficult to realize just how remarkable present-day conditions might look to someone from the past. This is especially true of the region we call the Middle East, which many Westerners see as an overwhelmingly Muslim land that is sharply demarcated from the historically Christian West by the Bosporus. The city of Istanbul thus stands at the far western limits of the Islamic world. Within that world, which stretches east as far as India, no rival religions of any significance are believed to exist, with the obvious exception of the Jewish state of Israel.

Such a vision would have puzzled an observer just a century ago, for whom the Middle East was characterized by bewildering religious diversity—an area in which Christians remained a familiar part of the social and cultural landscape. And that picture had remained true in essentials for half a millennium. Particularly startling for our time traveler from 1900 would have been the almost inconceivable vision of modern-day Turkey as an almost wholly Muslim land. A hypothetical time traveler from just a century ago would be just as amazed that Greek no longer served as a convenient lingua franca around much of the Mediterranean. Only very recently, in historical terms, Christians were quite as familiar a part of the Middle Eastern scene as Jews are in the modern United States, or indeed Muslims in contemporary western Europe. Middle Eastern Christians in 1900 actually represented a much larger part of the overall population (some 11 percent) than do American Jews today (2 percent) or European Muslims (4.5 percent). The removal or destruction of that community represented a historic transformation for the region, no less than for the Christian world.

The decline of Christianity in the Near East occurred in two distinct phases, two distinct "falls." In the first, in what Europeans call the Middle Ages, Christians lost their majority status within what became Muslim-majority nations. Different groups suffered to varying degrees—the Syriac sects worst of all, the Copts least. But once reduced to minorities, these groups proved very durable, with no obvious reasons why they should not last indefinitely: witness the Coptic experience in Egypt. In the second phase, however, which is barely a century old, Christians have ceased to exist altogether—*are* ceasing to exist—as organized communities. We can argue about the causes of that change, whether they can legitimately be described as religious rather than political, but the result was to create a Muslim world that was just as Christian-free as large sections of Europe would be Jew-free after the Second World War. And in both instances, the major mechanism of change was the same. For all the reasons we can suggest for long-term decline, for all the temptations to assimilate, the largest single factor for Christian decline was organized violence, whether in the form of massacre, expulsion, or forced migration.

Conquered Christians

When we look at the Christian communities surviving in the Middle East so many centuries after the Muslim conquest, we might be tempted to see this as evidence of Muslim willingness to tolerate other religions, and in some cases, that interpretation would be fair. Yet we also need to remember that the millennium-long saga of Muslim conquest was constantly bringing in new infusions of Christian subjects, which compensated for older Christian communities that had ceased to exist.

The most important force in that story of conquest was the Ottoman Empire, which began as a small power in Asia Minor. After the Mongol invasions destroyed the great Seljuk state, the Ottoman Turks used the ensuing wars to create a power base in Asia Minor, and they gradually spread over what had been the Byzantine Christian world. Already by the time they took Constantinople, the Ottoman Empire included most of the Balkans, and by 1500 they controlled the whole Black Sea region. By 1520 they ruled most of the Muslim world west of Persia, as far as Algiers, and thus became the main antagonist for Christians, in Europe or beyond. Their European conquests advanced rapidly through the sixteenth century, under such aggressive leaders as Selim I (1512–20) and Suleiman the Magnificent (1520–66). In 1526, the Turks conquered Hungary, destroying what was then one of the major European powers. Turkish advances were not reversed until the Christian victory at Vienna in 1683.[4]

Although some rulers were more explicitly motivated by religion than others, the Ottomans were often more aggressively anti-Christian than were the original Arab conquerors of the Middle East. Selim I in particular took the title of caliph, and took his role as head of Islam very seriously. He ordered the confiscation of all churches, many of which were razed, and Ottoman authorities forced many thousands to accept Islam. A century later, the sultan Ibrahim contemplated the extermination of Christians. From the fifteenth century onward, the pressure to convert to Islam was substantial, especially when the regime made such massive use of converts throughout its administrative and military system: Europeans termed this an "empire of renegades." Throughout the Christian territories, too, the Turks levied the "tribute of children" (*devshirmeh*), by which Christian families were required to give a proportionate number of their sons to be raised by the state as slaves, but also as elite soldiers, and this system continued through the mid–seventeenth century. Usually, these janissaries ("new warriors") would convert to Islam. Although the system provided a kind of social advancement for subject peoples, it clearly represented a high degree of religious compulsion, and Bulgarians recall the system as the Blood Tax.[5]

Reinforcing such demands, Ottoman warfare was extremely destructive, not because it was "Islamic," but because it drew so heavily on methods that stemmed from the Turkish heritage in central Asia. Ottoman forces carried out notorious massacres against Christian populations, and particularly targeted Christian clergy and leaders. In 1480, the Turks destroyed the Italian city of Otranto, killing twelve thousand and executing leading clergymen by sawing them. The destruction of Nicosia in Cyprus in 1570 may have inflicted still more casualties. Accounts of Ottoman warfare and punishment include such gruesome techniques as impaling, crucifixion, and flaying. The Christian leader who most effectively deployed such tactics against the Turks themselves was Vlad of Wallachia, "the Impaler," who is remembered in Western folklore through tales of Dracula.[6]

From the fifteenth century through the nineteenth, the Turks ruled over a substantial Christian population on European soil, and enforced the kinds of forms of religious discrimination that had been commonplace throughout the Middle East. Turks termed Balkan Christians *rayah*, "the herd," as animals to be sheared and exploited as necessary. As a Bosnian Muslim song declared:

The *rayah* is like the grass
Mow it as much as you will till it springs up anew.

Of course, Christianity survived, partly because the rapid Muslim conquest of the Balkans largely left Christian communities in place and did not destroy ecclesiastical structures: the Orthodox churches would recover, in Greece, Bulgaria, and elsewhere. But we should note just how successful the Ottomans were in establishing Islam in the Balkans, by weakening Christianity and encouraging apostasy; by encouraging conversions to Islam, and by importing immigrant Muslim populations.[7] Even today, after many thousands of Muslims have been removed from southeastern Europe in various population transfers, Islam still commands the loyalty of perhaps a quarter of the region's people.

TABLE 5.1.
MUSLIMS IN CONTEMPORARY
SOUTHEASTERN EUROPE

Country	Total Population (millions)	Muslims (millions)	Percentage
Albania	3.6	2.5	70
Serbia and Montenegro	10.8	2.2	19
Bosnia and Herzegovina	4.1	1.6	40
Bulgaria	7.5	0.9	12.2
Macedonia	2.1	0.6	17
Croatia	4.5	0.2	4.4
Cyprus	0.9	0.16	18
TOTALS	33.5	8.16	24.4

Source: Adapted from Philip Jenkins, *God's Continent* (New York: Oxford University Press, 2007).

Although the Ottomans did not destroy Balkan Christianity, they achieved inroads into Christian loyalty at least as deep as those obtained by the earlier Arab regimes in a comparable time span. If Christianity did not die in this region, it was only because Turkish power did not last quite long enough.[8]

European Expansion

Most of the Orthodox churches now followed their old Nestorian and Jacobite rivals in passing under Muslim rule. But Muslims were not the only threat to their survival. In addition to the constant pressures from expanding Islam, all the surviving Eastern churches also faced real dangers from a newly assertive Western Christianity, which tried to bring these struggling bodies under its own power. The result was an ever-spreading pattern of schisms and internal controversies, which further paralyzed already weakened communities.

As the Near East fell into the control of militant Islamic states, so western European nations had an ever-greater incentive to find alternative trade routes, commonly by exploiting the oceans. Well into the fifteenth century, some explorers still dreamed of linking up with Prester John, and renewing the alliance against Islam. In the mid–fifteenth century, the Portuguese were exploring the Atlantic and the shores of Africa, and by the seventeenth century, the European powers were well on their way to global domination. Rising economic power led to urbanization, and the share of the world's population living in Europe and in white European overseas possessions grew dramatically. Demographic expansion vastly increased the relative power of European Christianity, much as African forms of Christianity are growing in relative importance in the modern world.

Expanding commercial horizons also brought Europe's churches into direct contact with what were by now the tattered shreds of the ancient Eastern Christian groups. Tensions between European and non-European churches were of ancient origin. As early as 1300, Catholic missions in China had met sharp opposition from

Nestorians, who naturally saw the newcomers making inroads on their ancient territories. Now, however, the Latin powers were far stronger than before, and better able to enforce their will. During the great period of Spanish and Portuguese empire building in the century after 1550, the leading edge of Christian expansion was the Roman Catholic Church, now fortified by the militancy of the Counter-Reformation. As Catholic clergy and missionaries roamed the world, they found the remnants of many ancient churches, which they determined to bring under papal and Roman authority.[9]

So long-standing was the separation of Western and Eastern churches that the two sides never stood much chance of a friendly alliance. As Christianity had fallen into such dire straits outside Europe, Europeans and particularly Catholics tended to dismiss foreign traditions as marginal or even unchristian. After the fall of Constantinople, Pope Pius II wrote to the victorious sultan, effectively denying that the non-Catholic churches were Christian in any worthwhile sense: they were "all tainted with error, despite their worship of Christ."[10] He more or less explicitly asserted the identity of Christianity with the Catholic tradition and, even more radically, with Europe itself.

As Western Christians traveled the world, many demonstrated a like skepticism about the Christian credentials of the other churches they encountered. In 1723, a French Jesuit reported "that the Copts in Egypt are a strange people far removed from the kingdom of God . . . although they say they are Christians they are such only in name and appearance. Indeed many of them are so odd that outside of their physical form scarcely anything human can be detected in them." Although Christ had ordained that salvation must be extended to all, Copts seemed a particularly hard case: "in any event we should not omit to teach the ignorant Copts in the faith as incapable as they always are of learning its mysteries without incontestable effort."[11] A Jesuit observer was appalled at the arrogance of the long-isolated Ethiopian church, although his criticisms could equally well be applied to some of his exclusive-minded colleagues:

They are possessed with a strange notion that they are the only true Christians in the world; as for us, they shunned us as heretics, and were under the greatest surprise at hearing us mention the Virgin Mary with the respect which is due to her, and told us that we could not be entirely barbarians since we were acquainted with the mother of God.

So bizarre were the customs of these Easterners, so puritanical, that Ethiopians even looked askance at the Portuguese habit of spitting during church services.[12]

Latins were troubled by the pretensions of these threadbare Christians, who nevertheless claimed such grand titles. In 1550, a Portuguese traveler reported that the forty thousand Christians of the Indian coast owed their allegiance to a head in "Babylon," the catholicos. Bafflingly, they had not so much as heard of a pope at Rome. Some years later, envoys dispatched by the Vatican were appalled to discover that India's Nestorians called "the Patriarch of Babylon the universal pastor and head of the Catholic Church," a title that in their view belonged exclusively to the Roman pontiff. How dare a non-European church make such extravagant claims?[13]

For the first time, many Asian and African churches now found themselves under a European-based regime, and were forced to readjust their patterns of organization and worship accordingly. Distinctively local African and Asian forms now found themselves under heavy pressure. Catholicization incited sharp controversies within the churches, driving schisms and defections, and reducing any chance of local revival.

Around the world, we see similar attempts at harmonization. From the 1550s, factions in the Nestorian church sought Roman support, and much of the church accepted Roman rule under a new patriarch of the Chaldeans. Like other Eastern churches, the Catholic Chaldeans retained many of their customs and their own liturgy, but this compromise was not enough to draw in other Nestorians who maintained their existence as a separate church. The Jacobites split on similar lines, with an independent church remaining aloof from the Catholic "Syrians." Other mergers and acquisitions followed. In 1596, the Union of Brest-Litovsk brought many European Orthodox believers into communion with Rome, but following their own rite and customs, and many Near Eastern Orthodox followed shortly afterward. They thus became members of the so-called Uniate churches. In 1624, Roman missionaries even brought Ethiopia into the papal fold, though the union lasted only for a few years before national traditions reasserted themselves. Thereafter, any Catholic clergy found in Ethiopia stood an excellent chance of being martyred, albeit by fellow Christians.[14]

The most controversial moment in this process occurred in 1599, when Catholic authorities in southern India sought to absorb the ancient Syriac-founded churches of the region, the Thomas Christians. The main activist was Aleixo de Menezes, archbishop of the Portuguese colony of Goa, who maneuvered the Indian church into a union with Rome at the synod of Diamper. In Indian Christian memory, de Menezes remains a villainous symbol of European imperialism, who began the speedy Romanization of the church, enforced by Goa's notoriously active inquisition. The synod ordered the burning of books teaching Nestorian errors or "false legends," as well as texts teaching practices that the Europeans deemed superstitious or magical. A substantial body of Syriac and Nestorian tradition now perished. Many local Christians reacted against the new policy by forming separate churches, and in later years the Thomas Christians would be deeply fragmented.[15]

Under New Masters

Yet despite all these disasters, this double pressure from Muslims and Catholics, Eastern Christian communities survived. At its height, the Ottoman Empire encompassed the Middle East, the Balkans, and North Africa, and especially in Europe included millions of subject Christians. Even in 1900, Muslims made up just half the empire's overall population: Christians comprised 46 percent; Jews, 3 percent. Christian numbers were obviously smaller in the Asian territories, the lands east of Constantinople, but they were still thriving.[16]

This survival may seem amazing when we think of the accumulated military catastrophes and defeats between 1300 and 1600, and the tyranny of sultans like Selim I. Yet for all these horrors, the Ottomans also found it in their interest to maintain a stable imperial order, and a semblance of legality. After Sultan Mehmet II took Constantinople, he formally invested the new patriarch with his cross and staff, just as the Christian emperors had done previously: Mehmet was, after all, both sultan and Caesar. Christian numbers now stabilized as the Ottomans granted them the status of millet communities, under a system dating back to the ancient Persians. As a millet, a nation, each denomination or theological tradition was recognized as a community under its own laws and courts, and governed by its own particular clerical structures. Orthodox Christians became the Rum Millet—the Roman nation—under a patriarch who was both religious and civil head, the ethnarch, and this system endured into the 1920s.[17]

Christians enjoyed nothing like what modern Americans construe as religious liberty, and there were stringent limits on any kind of Christian expansion, yet at least this legal position granted them some degree of protection and stability. The patriarchate became a fixture of the Ottoman system of government, so that sultans resisted efforts by more rigid Islamic forces to revoke minority rights. The empire proved flexible about enforcing restrictions. Notionally, for instance, Christians were not allowed to build or rebuild churches, but permission was granted as a special reward for loyalty, or to encourage settlement in new areas. Around 1620, one Armenian traveler claimed that at least in western Asia Minor the Turks discriminated against no one, Christian or Jew, though matters were more perilous farther east, and away from the coasts. The fact that the sultan was also the caliph, head of Islam, placed such flexibility beyond criticism.[18]

Within limits, then, Christians often flourished, to the puzzlement of western Europeans, who could not understand the distinctive Ottoman mix of tolerance and persecution. Particularly baffling was the extensive use that the empire made of non-Muslims, who were in so many other ways denied the most basic rights. Sultans regularly used Christians and former Christians as administrators, partly because such outsiders would be wholly dependent on the ruler's pleasure: eight of the nine grand viziers of Suleiman the Magnificent were of Christian origin. Greek political influence in the imperial administration reached its apex during the eighteenth century, the era of the Phanariotes, the residents of Phanar, the Greek quarter of Constantinople. At lower levels, too, certain communities dominated their niches in the Ottoman world: Greeks were the sailors; Armenians, the merchants and traders.[19] Although the Orthodox church cherishes its list of neo-martyrs from this period, most cases involved exceptional violations of Ottoman law. Most commonly, these were either Muslims who attempted to convert to Christianity, or converts to Islam who changed their minds and tried to revert to their old faith.[20]

Making their life under the new order more acceptable, Christians actively proved their loyalty. Above all, Orthodox believers were not likely to work with foreign Catholic powers to subvert Turkish rule. The Orthodox found the Muslims no more obnoxious than the Catholic nations, whose activities in recent centuries had left horrendous memories. Apart from the Latin sack of Constantinople in 1204, later Catholic invaders like the Venetians had been almost as tyrannical to their Orthodox subjects as were the Turks. Even in the last days of the empire, a Byzantine official famously declared, "Better the Sultan's turban than the [Catholic] Cardinal's hat!" Matters deteriorated further when the Orthodox saw how Catholics treated members of their church and Uniate believers, in eastern

Europe and elsewhere. When a Syrian cleric visited the Ukraine in the seventeenth century, he was appalled, writing, "God perpetuate the empire of the Turks! For they take their impost [tax] and enter into no account of religion, be their subjects Christians or Nazarenes, Jews or Samaritans." The oppressive Poles, in contrast, were "more vile and wicked than even the worshippers of idols, by their cruelty to Christians."[21] Few Orthodox Christians had any dreams of being liberated by these hated Catholic foreigners. The sultans encouraged these divisions by favoring those Orthodox leaders most opposed to Catholic influences.

Within this delicate system, some churches coped better than others. The largest Christian group in Asia was the Orthodox, who had of course been the dominant religious and cultural force under the Byzantine Empire, but who found themselves reduced to a minority under Ottoman rule. This was also the status of the Copts in Egypt, and of several churches in Syria (a term that for several centuries included what we would today call Lebanon and Israel). In the 1670s, an English diplomat saw in the sturdy faith of these oppressed churches powerful evidence in favor of Christian belief:

> The stable perseverance in these our days of the Greek church ... notwithstanding the oppression and contempt poured upon it by the Turk, and the allurements and pleasures of this world, is a confirmation no less convincing than the miracles and power which attended its first beginnings. For indeed, it is admirable to see and consider with what constancy, resolution and simplicity ignorant and poor men keep their faith.[22]

By far the worst sufferers from the carnage of the fourteenth century were the old Eastern Syriac churches, precisely because they had once been so powerful and had posed a real danger to Muslim supremacy. Neither Jacobites nor Nestorians ever recovered from the time of Timur. If we combine all the different branches of these churches, we find barely half a million faithful in all by the early twentieth century, scattered from Cyprus and Syria to Persia. (India had a further six hundred thousand "Syrians.") The implosion in numbers led to a steep decline in morale and ambition. Instead of trying to convert the whole of Asia, the Syrian churches survived as inward-looking quasi-tribal bodies within the Near East. Succession to the Nestorian patriarchate became hereditary, passing from uncle to nephew. Intellectual activity declined to nothing, at least in comparison with the glorious past. Many clergy were illiterate, and the church texts that do survive are often deeply imbued with superstition and folk magic. In the early twentieth century, the *Catholic Encyclopedia* pronounced, harshly, "From the fourteenth century, Syriac literature produced no works of value." Suggesting just how isolated and exotic the Nestorians seemed, nineteenth-century Anglo-American travel accounts bracketed the church's followers with the Yezidi "Devil-Worshipers" who lived nearby.[23]

Within the Ottoman realm, we have good estimates for Christian numbers around 1900. As by this stage they would have been under such intense pressure for several centuries, it is reasonable to assume that the figures would have been much higher in earlier years. (As recently as the mid-1890s, Christians had suffered widespread massacres.) Even so, by 1900, Christians still constituted 15 or 20 percent of the population of Asia Minor. In Constantinople itself, Christians in 1911 made up half the population—at least four hundred thousand strong—compared with 44 percent Muslim and 5 percent Jews. The city's population was 17 percent Greek Christian, 17 percent Armenian. As for other places in Asia Minor, a 1911 encyclopedia commented simply, "Modern Smyrna is in all but government a predominantly Christian town," which was known to the Turks as the city of the *giaour*, the infidels. About the same time, Trebizond "has 50,000 inhabitants, among whom are 12,000 Greeks, 10,000 Armenians, some Jews, and a few hundred Catholics." Christians made up 31 percent of the people of greater Syria.[24]

In 1907, the *Catholic Encyclopedia* reported in loving denominational detail on the enormous diversity that still prevailed in much of the Middle East. The city of Amida, modern Diyarbakir, was still 40 percent Christian, with a polyglot gaggle of bishops and higher clergy:

> It has about 35,000 inhabitants, of whom 20,000 are Mussulmans (Arabians, Turks, Kurds, etc.), 2,300 Catholics (Chaldeans, Armenians, Syrians, Melchites, Latins), 8,500 Gregorian Armenians, 900 Protestant Armenians, 950 Jacobite Syrians, 900 Orthodox Greeks, and 300 Jews. Diyarbakir possesses an Armenian Catholic bishop, a Syrian Catholic bishop, a Syrian Jacobite bishop, a Chaldean Catholic archbishop, and a Greek Orthodox metropolitan under the jurisdiction of the Patriarch of Antioch.[25]

Shrinking Numbers

If we take the Middle East to include all the land from Egypt to Iran, and including Anatolia and the Arabian Peninsula, Christians represented 11 percent of the total population. That degree of survival is impressive, but the absolute numbers of these communities were still quite small. Even including the Copts, the Armenians, and the Greeks living in Asia Minor, we are thinking only of some 5 million believers. (See table 5.2; this table understates the number of Armenians, which was probably closer to 2 million.)

TABLE 5.2.
CHRISTIANS IN THE MIDDLE EAST AROUND 1910
(including Egypt and Persia but excluding Ethiopia)

Denomination	Numbers
	(in thousands)
Greek Orthodox	1,662
Armenian Orthodox	1,073

Table 5.2 *(continued)*

Denomination	Numbers (in thousands)
Copts	600
Maronites	309
Nestorian	143
Melchites	142
Protestant	100
Armenian Catholic	94
Jacobite	78
Chaldean	67
Syrian	40
Latin	47
TOTAL	4,355

Source: Catholic Encyclopedia, s.v. "Asia," http://www.newadvent.org/cathen/01777b.htm.

This small scale reflected the political and economic decline of this once-crucial ancient region, which sank into near insignificance compared with the newly ascendant worlds of Europe and North America. In 1800, the population of the whole Middle East region was perhaps 33 million, a number that had grown only to 44 million by 1900. That 1900 figure was about the same as the national population of France, and considerably below the population of Germany. Ironically, this historic center of urbanization had utterly failed to compete with the growth of cities in the West. Still in 1900, only Constantinople could compete with the booming cities of Europe, while cities like Damascus, Alexandria, and Baghdad had a mere two or three hundred thousand residents apiece.

Christians in the Middle and Near East found themselves ever more marginalized, not only in their home societies, but in the Christian world at large, as the proportion of the world living in Christian or Christian-ruled states grew vastly. The combined populations of Europe (including Russia) and North America represented 22 percent of world population in 1800, and 32 percent by 1900.

TABLE 5.3.
THE CHRISTIAN WORLD AROUND 1900

Continent	Number of Christians (in millions)	Percent of overall total
Africa	10	2
Asia	22	4
Europe	381	68
Latin America	62	11
Northern America	79	14
Oceania	5	1
TOTAL	559	100

Source: David B. Barrett, George T. Kurian, and Todd M. Johnson, *World Christian Encyclopedia,* 2nd ed. (New York: Oxford Univ. Press, 2001).

By 1900, 68 percent of the world's Christians lived in Europe alone, besides a further 25 percent in the Americas. Although Christians made up a respectable share of the Middle Eastern population, their overall numbers were tiny compared with the churches of England or France, to say nothing of emerging nations like the United States and Canada. By this stage, the whole Middle East accounted for just 0.9 percent of the world's Christians.[26]

The tiny size of the population would itself be a crucial factor in the area's religious development, as such small groups could so easily be identified, and then expelled or killed. And that represents much of the story of the Middle East's Christians over the past century, as this small population would soon lose even this marginal presence. Reading an account of the Christian Middle East in the early twentieth century—of Smyrna or Trebizond or Diyarbakir—is to excavate a lost world. From the First World War onward, Christian communities were systematically eliminated across the Muslim world, and the Armenian horrors of 1915 are only the most glaring of a series of such atrocities that reached their peak between 1915 and 1925. Although these instances of massacre and persecution have no historical resonance for most Westerners today, they count among the worst examples of their kind.

The Ottoman Crisis

Mass violence was by no means a new factor in Muslim-Christian relations, but matters deteriorated from the early nineteenth century, as Muslim societies felt themselves under increasing threat from the Christian West. As so often in history, the persecutors saw their actions as fundamentally defensive in nature, and the sense that a majority community was facing grave threats to its very existence drove them to acts of persecution and intolerance against convenient minorities. And although this certainly does not excuse the later violence, Turkish fears of predatory Christian rivals were by no means an illusion.

From the mid–eighteenth century, the vast Ottoman Empire began to crumble at the edges. From the 1760s, the Russians pushed into the Crimea and the Caucasus, establishing a strong foothold on the Black Sea. The ease with which Napoleon's armies routed Muslim forces in Egypt in 1798 suggested the West's immense technological and military superiority, and through the nineteenth century, Britain and other colonial powers progressively grabbed more and more outlying corners of the Ottoman world. By midcentury, only the rivalry from British and French interests prevented the Russians from taking over the heart of that empire and establishing themselves in Constantinople. The Russian czars presented themselves as the protectors of the Orthodox Christians within the Ottoman Empire. In 1850, an experienced British traveler was just reflecting the common wisdom when he predicted the imminent Russian takeover of the Middle East:

> From Mount Ararat to Baghdad, the different sects of Christians still retain the faith of the Redeemer whom they have worshipped according to their various forms, some of them for more than fifteen hundred years; the plague, the famine and the sword have passed over them and left them still unscathed, and there is little doubt but that they will maintain the position which they have held till the now not far distant period arrives when the conquered empire of the Greeks will again be brought under the dominion of a Christian emperor.[27]

Partly in response to such hopes, Christian minorities became ever more assertive, and the more Christian subjects struggled against the Ottoman Empire, the more brutally their aspirations were suppressed. The savagery of Muslim regimes must be understood as a manifestation of the shock and outrage they felt at the resistance of peoples they had come to view as natural inferiors. Moreover, the Turks associated the menace from domestic dissidents with the external danger from rival empires, so that Christian rebels were portrayed as agents of foreign aggression. Anti-Christian policies began a vicious circle. The more brutally the Turks treated their minorities, the greater the Western clamor for intervention to protect the victims. The closer the harmony of interests between domestic and foreign enemies, the greater the Turkish hostility to Christian minorities.

Violence escalated during the Greek revolt that began in 1821, when mass killings claimed the lives of tens of thousands of Muslims on Greek soil. These acts left a lasting memory, suggesting the likely fate of Turkish minorities should Ottoman rule ever weaken. Across the Greek-speaking world, the Ottomans responded by a series of massacres, and many clergy died in the ensuing repression.

The patriarch of Constantinople was hanged outside his cathedral—on Easter morning!—and other archbishops and patriarchs were hanged or beheaded, at Adrianople and Thessaloniki, and across Cyprus. Turkish massacres culminated in the slaughter on the island of Chios, where perhaps twenty thousand Christians were killed. Unlike the earlier atrocities, which had occurred far from the Western gaze, this incident generated horror across Christian Europe, and Lord Byron and Victor Hugo both helped mobilize public anger. Eugène Delacroix painted a famous work with the emotive title *Scenes from the Massacres at Chios: Greek Families Awaiting Death or Slavery*. Anti-Turkish feeling provoked armed intervention by Britain, France, and Russia, who combined to crush the Turkish navy in 1827.

As the rulers of an ever-weaker Ottoman Empire realized how desperate their situation was, they tried to modernize and often to grant more rights to minorities. Most dramatically, in 1856 the empire was just emerging from a war in which Britain and France had fended off yet another Russian advance. Partly in response to Western demands, the sultan issued a historic law granting religious liberty, including the right to change religions. The thought that anyone would want to leave Islam for Christianity had not really registered with the Ottoman rulers. Christian missionaries now became active in the Ottoman realm, and the converts they made sometimes invoked the support of the Christian powers.[28]

These concessions infuriated conservatives, who blamed precisely those minorities for the plight of Muslims within the empire and beyond. The more reforms threatened to undermine the privileged positions of Muslims, the angrier those old elites became. Also angered were secular-minded modernizers, who had hoped for a strong new nation but who now saw a future of collective humiliation and subjection. Looking at the unintended consequences of these liberalizing pressures, modern observers might draw analogies with Western states forcing Middle Eastern nations to grant democracy and freedom of speech, only to find that the greatest beneficiaries of this openness are radically anti-Western Islamist parties.

Purging the Christians

Looking at acts of pogrom and massacre, it is not easy to identify specifically religious motives, to tell which acts of violence were targeted against Christians as Christians rather than as rebels against the regime. Whatever the initial reasons, Turkish forces and mercenaries commonly did choose Christian leaders and properties for special attention during Balkan counterinsurgency campaigns, burning churches and killing clergy. Religious themes became still more explicit in the Middle East proper as Christian communities increasingly fell prey to sectarian attacks by Muslims, violence that made Christian survival ever more difficult. In 1860, Druze and Muslim forces massacred ten thousand Maronite Christians in the land that would later become Lebanon, raising fears of the wholesale extermination of one of the largest surviving Christian groups in the region. A pogrom in Damascus killed thousands more, besides those driven from their homes or starved. The "Massacres of '60" (*Madhabih al-Sittin*) still live in the Maronite consciousness.[29] Other sects suffered comparably. Muslim forces attacked Assyrian and Nestorian Christians between 1843 and 1847 and again in the 1890s, killing and enslaving thousands. Many more Christians perished during the Bulgarian wars of the 1870s.

The Bulgarian situation provoked an international crisis that decisively shifted the religious balance in the Ottoman world. In 1877–78, the Russians won an overwhelming victory over the Turks, who were saved from total destruction only by British intervention. The outcome placed an expansionist Russia perilously close to the Turkish heartland; and immediately over their border, the Russians could look to sympathetic Christian populations, especially the numerous and influential Armenians. For the Ottomans, the prospects for the near future looked dire. If the Russians could create an independent Bulgaria within their sphere of influence, why should an independent Armenia not be next, followed by a Christian Assyria? However loyal most Armenians remained within the empire, radical nationalists made no secret of their hopes for Russian aid. Making matters worse, the Russo-Turkish war was followed by a widespread ethnic cleansing of Muslims in Bulgaria. And the French were already carving out a Christian protectorate around Mount Lebanon. Christian communities within the Turkish Empire looked like a clear and present danger to the survival of Ottoman and Muslim power.[30]

Unrest among the Armenians led to an official clampdown, which led to the so-called Hamidian massacres of 1894–96. Reportedly, the sultan's regime directly inspired extremism, as envoys gathered Muslims together in local mosques, telling them that Armenians were preparing to rise against Islam. The main killings were then undertaken by the Turkish military, supported by Kurdish irregular forces. Probably a hundred thousand Christians perished. Armenians were the primary targets, as "the murderous winter of 1895 saw the decimation of much of the Armenian population and the devastation of their property in some twenty districts of eastern Turkey." A killing spree occurred in Urfa—ancient Edessa—where Armenians made up a third of the population. Eight thousand were killed, including three thousand who were burned alive in the cathedral where they had sought sanctuary. A thousand more were killed in Melitene. The Syriac Christians of northern Mesopotamia also suffered during the red year of 1895, especially in the ancient sanctuaries in and around Amida and Tur Abdin. The French ambassador reported at this time that "Asia Minor is literally in flames. . . . They are massacring all the Christians without distinction."[31]

As in the Middle Ages, Christians and Jews both suffered from the new wave of harsher and more paranoid popular attitudes. In Damascus in 1840, the anti-Jewish blood libel surfaced in the Muslim world, with allegations that Jews kidnapped and murdered Gentiles in order to use their blood for ritual purposes. In this instance, the scandal arose with the disappearance of a Christian cleric, a Capuchin friar, and other Christians took the lead in denouncing the Jews. Soon, however, the charge entered Muslim thought and inspired Ottoman authorities to launch copycat persecutions in many other regions; and the story still circulates in the Arab world today. Many Jews died in the Damascus rioting in 1860.[32]

The Year of the Sword

Such conflicts provide the essential prehistory for the Armenian genocide of the First World War years, which represented an escalation in intensity, rather than a departure from previous tolerance. Although the regime in power at the time of the actual massacres was the nationalist Young Turks, the actual violence had many resemblances to the Hamidian killings of twenty years earlier. As before, Turkish forces attacked a community believed to be sympathetic to external enemies, at a time when European powers were threatening not just the defeat of the Turkish state, but its partition among rival imperial powers. After a century of combining to restrain Russian advances, in 1914 the British and French were actually allied with the czar, making it virtually certain that a peace settlement would see the Russian empire expand toward Constantinople. Britain and France also had their own designs on Ottoman territories, and they used the promise of lands in Asia Minor as a means of rewarding their Italian and Greek allies. For the Turks, losing the war would potentially cost them everything, including any shade of national independence.[33]

The violence that began in 1915 killed perhaps half the Armenian Christians in the region. Although the accumulated stories of massacre numb after a while, some of the atrocities cry out particularly. One of the worst storm centers was the *wilayet,* or province, of Diyarbakir, under its brutal governor, Reşid Bey. Here, "men had horse shoes nailed to their feet; women were gang-raped." One source placed the number of murdered Christians in this province alone at 570,000. In the summer of 1915, the *New York Times* reported that "the roads and the Euphrates are strewn with corpses of exiles, and those who survive are doomed to certain death. It is a plan to exterminate the whole Armenian people." During the 1915–16 era, at least

1 million Armenians were displaced, and plausible estimates for those actually killed range from eight hundred thousand to 1 million. If the word *genocide* has any meaning whatever, it certainly applies to these events.[34]

Other Christian communities reported horrendous losses from similar events. Lord Bryce alleged that the Turkish government was pursuing a "plan for exterminating Christianity, root and branch," which equally targeted "the minor communities, such as the Nestorian and Assyro-Chaldean churches." Claiming to have lost two-thirds of their own people during their own wartime genocide, the Assyrians recall 1915 as *sayfo,* "the Year of the Sword." In the Christian-majority region of Lebanon, the Turkish military deliberately induced a famine that left a weakened population unable to withstand the ensuing epidemics: a hundred thousand Maronite Christians died. All told, including Armenians, Maronites, and Assyrians, perhaps 1.5 million Christians perished in the region.[35]

Far from anti-Christian purges ceasing with the official end of war in 1918, they actually intensified during the ensuing war between Greece and Turkey. In its origins, this war stemmed from aggressive Greek claims to territory in Asia Minor, which at their most extreme amounted to a return to something like the Byzantine Empire. As matters turned out, the Turks turned the conflict into their own war of independence, in which they evicted foreign invaders. In the process, the Turks purged the Greek Christians of Asia Minor, as ethnic cleansing continued through the early 1920s. The campaign reached its horrifying peak in the destruction of Smyrna in 1922, allegedly causing the deaths of a hundred thousand Greek and Armenian Christians in what had been the City of the *Giaour.* The area around Trebizond was the setting for what Greeks and Armenians today recall as the Pontic Genocide of Christians.[36]

As with most other incidents described here, historians differ widely in how they interpret these events, and we can attribute most of the deaths in Smyrna to the results of war and social breakdown rather than deliberate anti-Christian persecution. Elsewhere, religious motivation was more explicit: in Iraq by 1933, it was "the universal belief of the Arabs that the war was between the Crescent and the Cross. . . . Hundreds of thousands of Arabs volunteered to fight a handful of unbelievers and infidels."[37] Whatever the reasons, the long-term effects would be the same: across the Middle East, Christian communities vanished one after the other, like lights being switched off. Before 1914, Christian pockets were numerous and widespread, while by 1930, most had vanished or were in the process of disappearing.

Asia Minor now became, definitively, Turkey—a Muslim land, freed of virtually all Greeks and Armenians. Constantinople, which had over four hundred thousand Christians in 1920, today has perhaps four thousand. The city's final Greek remnants largely vanished during a sweeping race riot in 1955. Multiethnic Smyrna became Muslim Izmir; Trebizond is now Trabzon; Melitene is Malatya. A recent writer comments, "On the eve of their forced mass exodus in 1924, the Syriac Orthodox population of Edessa was approximately 2,500. Today no Christian soul exists in Edessa." Edessa is today Urfa, and is famous as a center of Islamic piety, one of the two main power bases of the nation's ruling Islamist party. Although religious activism here is conservative and traditionalist rather than extremist, Urfa is definitely a capital of the Quran Belt, which resents modernization and Western influence. So is Mardin, deep in the outer provinces of rural Islamic Turkey: in recent years the area has been best known as the rural backdrop for a popular television soap opera depicting life in a Muslim backwater. Recently, the formerly Christian cities have witnessed violent outbreaks that are now exceptional in modern Turkey. In 2006, a young Islamist murdered a Catholic priest praying in a church in Trabzon, and the following year, assassins butchered three Protestants in Malatya.Generally, such attacks target foreign Christians, as very few local believers remain.[38]

Along with the Christians, there also vanished what had once been their abundant heritage of buildings, of art and architecture.

In 1914, the Armenian Patriarchate of Constantinople recorded a total of 2,549 ecclesiastical buildings, including 210 monasteries. By 1974, the locations of only 913 were still known. Four hundred sixty-four had completely disappeared, 252 were in ruins, and 197 were in fairly sound condition. Even this dreadful situation had already deteriorated further by the 1990s. Although theoretically committed to archaeological and historic preservation, Turkish authorities systematically discriminate against preserving Christian remains.[39]

Visiting Diyarbakir in 1997, William Dalrymple reported finding literally the city's last Armenian Christian, "a very old lady called Lucine," who had not spoken since her husband was killed. In the words of one of the Kurdish Muslim brothers who cared for her, "Her mind is dead." Asked about other Armenians, he continued, "There are none. There used to be thousands of them. . . . I remember them streaming out of here every Sunday, led by their priest. But not now. She is the last." Elsewhere, too, we find individuals who are the last of their kind. Mesopotamia's two hundred thousand Syriac Christians, the *Suriani,* had contracted by 1920 to seventy thousand, and to barely four thousand by 1990. A solitary priest was the only Christian inhabitant of one village that was once endowed with seventeen churches. The monasteries of Tur Abdin were home to just two brothers.[40]

The Last Stand

Since the 1920s, the much-reduced Christian populations have tried various strategies to maintain their existence, but none shows great hopes of success.[41] One tactic was the creation of a protected Christian reservation, a state that would be able to defend Christian interests. This separatist goal explains the creation of the nation of Lebanon. After the First World War, with the horrible experience of the Armenians fresh in their minds, the French arbitrarily detached the most Christian sections of Syria as a separate enclave, which achieved independence in 1943 as the state of Lebanon. Though Maronites and other Christian sects initially formed a solid majority, the territory also included substantial Muslim minorities, which grew significantly over time in consequence of their higher birthrates. The lack of representation for poorer groups fostered disaffection and contributed to the bloody civil war of 1975–90. Violence and repression naturally encouraged Lebanese to flee to safer lands, and the fact that better-off Christians were more able to leave contributed still further to the shrinking of the Christian population. Christians today represent at most 40 percent of the nation's people.

Another difficulty with the reservation scheme was that it reinforced the popular association of Christianity with foreign imperialism, and thus with enmity to the nationalism that was rising in the early twentieth century. This problem became evident with the Assyrians, who had sympathized with the Western Allies against the Turks during the war, and who were exiled in large numbers. Most fled to northern Mesopotamia, where they supported the British mandate regime. The British cast the Assyrians as a warrior race, the supposed descendants of the ancient peoples they knew from the Old Testament; and they relied on their loyal (and Christian) Assyrian Levies to suppress Arab and Kurdish insurgencies. By 1932, the British were anxious to withdraw from the lands they had pulled together to form the new kingdom of Iraq. Fearing revenge from their Muslim neighbors, the Assyrians hoped for some form of autonomy, ideally a small nation-state, headed by their patriarch. The Levies would provide the core of a national army. It was this threat of separatism, of disloyalty to the Iraqi national cause, that provoked the massacres of 1933, and that incident ended Assyrian hopes within Iraq.[42]

Seeing little hope in separatism, many Christians took a different course, seeking not to remove themselves from mainstream political life but rather to lead it. They worked to create a progressive and nonsectarian Middle East in which Christians and other minorities would be able to survive in any nation, free of the dangers of Muslim hegemony. In the process, Christians would free themselves of the taint of being potential agents of outside forces, of the enemies of Islam. Far from being traitors to the Arab world, they would prove themselves as Arab superpatriots, and in so doing, they contributed mightily to progressive and radical politics in the region.

Across the political spectrum, Christians became the leaders and thinkers of movements that would move the region's politics in secular directions. We regularly find such leaders bearing such typically Christian names as Michael, Anthony, and George. Some Christians were influential in Communist parties, while others founded influential Pan-Arab movements. A founding text of modern Arab nationalism was *The Arab Consciousness,* published in 1939 by Syrian Christian Constantin Zureiq, who created the idea of the "Arab mission." In 1947, Michel Aflaq, of a Greek Orthodox family, cofounded the Baathist Party, which long ruled Iraq, and which still holds power in Syria. Syria, indeed, represents a real success story for Christian activism, since Christians still enjoy great power under the Baathist regime, and constitute 15 percent of the nation's population, if we count thinly disguised crypto-Christians: Aleppo might be a quarter Christian. Egypt's Copts worked closely with Muslims in the Wafd Party, which from the 1920s strove to eject British imperialism: patriotic banners bore the combined symbols of the cross and the crescent. Christian nationalist thinkers made every effort to accommodate the Muslim sentiments of the Arab majority, agreeing that the Islamic tradition was essential to understanding Arab history, and lauding Muhammad and the Quranic inheritance. Michel Aflaq urged Christians to understand that Islam was inseparable from Arabism.[43]

Christians were prominent in Palestinian nationalist causes— inevitably, since they represented much of the educated professional elite that stood to lose most from the growth of Zionist settlement. At least as much as for Muslims, the creation of the state of Israel was for Christians the *Nakba,* the catastrophe: the war of 1948 caused the exodus of 650,000 Muslim Palestinians, and a further 55,000 Christians. The plight of Palestinian Christians accounts for the long reluctance of the Vatican to establish diplomatic ties with Israel, a step not formally taken until 1993. Otherwise, Arab Christians complain that their existence has been largely forgotten in the West, especially by those evangelicals who pledge uncritical support for "Christian Zionism."[44]

Christians enjoyed a wholly disproportionate role in the leadership of the Palestinian guerrilla movements through the 1980s. Much of the sensational Palestinian terrorism across the globe in the 1970s was planned and orchestrated by Christian commanders like George Habash, Wadih Haddad, and Nayef Hawatmeh, who often operated in alliance with the Baathist regimes. Although he did not invent the tactic, Wadih Haddad was the first Arab guerrilla leader to use airliner hijacking on a major scale. Some notorious Palestinian attacks were aimed at freeing Hilarion Capucci, a Melkite archbishop who was jailed by Israel for running guns and explosives to the Palestinian guerrillas. After his release, the archbishop became a personal envoy for Yasser Arafat, and a member of the Palestine National Council. Another prominent Palestinian nationalist of Christian faith is Hanan Ashrawi, a leader of al-Fatah. Elsewhere, Lebanese Christian novelist Elias Khoury has provided perhaps the greatest literary commemoration of the Palestinian experience.[45]

The Western response to these nationalist movements produced some powerful ironies. From the 1950s through the 1980s, the United States and its European allies viewed the world primarily through the lens of the Cold War confrontation with the Soviet Union, and possible Soviet advances against Middle Eastern oil supplies. Accordingly, the West was alarmed at the progress of secular leftist movements across the Arab world, of Marxist, Baathist, and nationalist currents, many of which featured Christians so prominently in their leadership. Americans in particular found it easy to choose between leftist pro-Palestinian Christians and anti-Communist Muslims. Western governments and intelligence agencies cooperated with the Saudis and other

conservative regimes to promote traditionalist Muslim religious organizations. The result was the spread of Wahhabi- and Muslim Brotherhood–oriented networks, in Europe and elsewhere.[46]

Middle Eastern Christians, in short, tried every possible tactic to
survive and flourish, and their efforts have largely failed. Partly, this
is a matter of sheer numbers. Christian populations, shattered by
the events of 1915–25, have never recovered, and some communities have been eliminated. The survivors face the problem that
wealthier and better-educated communities usually have low birthrates, particularly as they are more likely to follow the lead of secularized Europe. At the same time, the overwhelmingly Muslim
majority population of the region has boomed. The 44 million
people who populated the Middle East in 1900 grew to over 300
million by the end of the century, and the figure will probably rise
to 450 million by 2025. The Christians who constituted 10 percent
of the region's population in 1900 made up at most 3 percent by the
end of the century. Just to take one example, the Turkish city of
Diyarbakir has over the last century grown from thirty-five thousand residents to at least 1.5 million; in the same period, its Christian population has fallen from fourteen thousand to a few hundred.
Baghdad's population grew during the century from one hundred
forty-five thousand to 6 million.

Christians live alongside a Muslim supermajority that has become
more intensely and devoutly Muslim. Radical and fundamentalist
Muslim movements have grown across the region, financed by the
vast oil wealth of the conservative states of the Arabian Peninsula
and the Gulf. Even societies that once aspired to be secular and so-
cialist adopted Islamic values with varying degrees of enthusiasm.
In the last days of Saddam Hussein's regime, even Baathist Iraq declared its support for Muslim values, while a moderate Islamist party
has made advances in secular Turkey. More perilously, the rise of
popular Muslim movements has made life all but impossible for
surviving Christian communities. Since the late 1980s, with the rise

of Hamas, the leading forces in the Palestinian cause have all been Islamist rather than Christian.

Growing religious tension, economic hardship, and the threat of violence have all conspired to drive Christians into exile, chiefly to the United States and Australia. While Arab Christians emerged as celebrated cultural figures, they often achieved these successes overseas: Khalil Gibran, author of *The Prophet,* was a Lebanese American, while prominent intellectual Edward Said was based in the United States. Removing so many exiles left societies in which barely enough Christians existed to act as a visible minority. In 1915, the Arabs of Palestine represented a 15 percent Christian minority, though that figure is now below 1 percent. Even Egypt's Copts, who have withstood so many pressures over the years, are being weakened by emigration. The fact that Egypt's Muslim Brotherhood makes conciliatory remarks about Christians may simply mean that the Copts are no longer considered potential rivals or a cause for concern.[47]

Iraq's Martyrs

The most dramatic catastrophe in recent years has been that of Iraq's Christians, who represented 5 or 6 percent of the population in 1970. That number is now around 1 percent, and it is shrinking fast. As in Syria, Christians did well under the militantly nonreligious Baathist regime, and produced some well-known faces. Saddam's foreign minister and deputy, Tariq Aziz, was by origin a Chaldean-rite Catholic who bore the pure Christian name of Mikhail Yuhanna, "Michael John." He adopted his Muslim-sounding name to avoid offending more rigid Arab counterparts. Christians in the 1980s reportedly made up 20 percent of Iraq's teachers and many of its doctors and engineers.[48]

The nation's economy was, however, devastated by two wars, against Iran in the 1980s and the U.S.-led coalition in 1990–91, followed by painful international sanctions. These events provoked the exodus of everyone who could leave easily, which usually meant those professional groups among whom Christians were well represented. The second invasion, that of 2003, proved the final straw in unleashing Muslim militancy, both Sunni and Shiite, while removing any central policing authority. In the ensuing anarchy, Christians became primary targets of mobs and militias. Christians were regularly kidnapped, and militias demanded protection money, under the euphemism of exacting the *jizya*, the poll tax on unbelievers. When Pope Benedict gave his controversial address in Regensburg in 2006, the "Lions of Islam" retaliated by beheading a Mosul priest, Paulos Iskander. Father Paulos belonged to the Syrian Orthodox church, the denomination anciently known as the Jacobites.

As so much of the story of Middle Eastern Christianity has its origins in northern Mesopotamia, it is appropriate that it should end there. One of the most active priests in Mosul was Father Ragheed Ganni, a Chaldean Catholic of the church that traced its origins to the Nestorians and, before them, to "those of the laying on of hands at Antioch." By 2007, as the situation was becoming desperate, he tried to preserve a note of optimism:

> The young people organized surveillance after the recent attacks against the parish, the kidnappings, the threats to religious; priests celebrate mass amidst the bombed out ruins; mothers worry as they see their children face danger to attend catechism with enthusiasm; the elderly come to entrust their fleeing families to God's protection, they alone remain in their country where they have their roots and built their homes, refusing to flee. Exile for them is unimaginable.

But matters did not improve: soon he was writing, "Each day we wait for the decisive attack, but we will not stop celebrating mass; we will do it underground, where we are safer." As it became increasingly difficult to celebrate services, he admitted, "We are on the verge of collapse." On Trinity Sunday, 2007, Father Ragheed and three subdeacons were kidnapped and killed, their bodies mined with explosives to make their recovery more difficult.[49]

Shortly afterwards, Pope Benedict showed his concern for Middle Eastern Christians by granting cardinal's rank to the Chaldean patriarch of Baghdad. Yet many believe that the church in Iraq is now entering its final martyrdom. In 2008, Islamists murdered Archbishop Paulos Faraj Rahho, head of the Chaldean church in northern Iraq. Just between 2003 and 2007, two-thirds of Iraq's remaining Christians left the country, and the population will certainly sink further in coming years. A traveler in the near future might well encounter someone like "a very old lady called Lucine," who would be the last incarnation of Mesopotamian Christianity.

Christians thus survive in the Middle East, but their collapse in numbers and influence over the past century has been astonishing, and only a wild optimist would predict that the process of decline had finished. The most vulnerable groups are those in Syria, which has since the disasters in Iraq become yet again the refuge for thousands of exiled Christians. Yet any change of regime could easily produce a radical Islamization such as occurred in Iraq, with similarly dreadful effects on minorities. Cynical observers hope for democracy and majority rule to come to Syria, but preferably not in their lifetimes. Perhaps within a decade or two, Egypt itself might find itself under an Islamist regime, driving the remaining Copts to choose between mass migration and conversion.

The remaining 10 million Christians in the Middle East could easily be reduced to a handful, while the story of their churches would continue only outside the region—in Detroit and Los Angeles, in Sydney and Paris. Already, the Syrian Orthodox have created new European monasteries in the familiar tradition: the Netherlands has a Mor Ephrem, while a new Mor Augin rises in Switzerland. In the West, members of these ancient communities are annoyed to be asked just when they converted to Christianity. And they explain, patiently, that their Christian heritage goes back a good deal further than that of their new host countries.

Middle Eastern Christianity will not become extinct in the same way that animal or plant species vanish, with no representatives left to carry on the line and no hope of revival. Even in the worst-case scenario, a few families, a few old believers, will linger on for decades to come. Millions of people from the region will also continue the tradition elsewhere. For practical purposes, however, Middle Eastern Christianity has, within living memory, all but disappeared as a living force.

6

Ghosts of a Faith

Can a religion be said to die because it is given a new name?
—A. Eustace Haydon

Not even in the direst circumstances, however, do religions vanish without trace. When religions fade and die, they leave behind them remnants that are incorporated into the newly dominant culture, and that is especially true when faiths decline gradually over a period of generations or centuries. No less than the natural landscape, human cultures are strewn with the vestiges and fossils of older worlds.

A Christian with any awareness of history knows that many of the greatest monuments of that faith are built on the remains of older religions. Most of the great cathedrals and holy places of Europe stand on the sites of pagan shrines and temples, part of a deliberate attempt to win over the loyalty of a newly Christianized population. We find similar patterns in the New World. The cathedral in Mexico City is one of many Christian centers built on the ruins of an older holy place—in this instance, an Aztec temple. These physical transitions neatly symbolize the appropriation of older rituals and practices, which reshape the victorious religion. Religions that endure build upon the ruins of their predecessors.

However much liberal modern observers might regret such a negative attitude to pagan or primal religions, the religious transformation seems like a part of natural evolution. As older primal religions die, so (in this view) they are replaced by the great world faiths, with their more exalted spiritual and ethical traditions, and their deeper intellectual roots. The old religions devolve into folklore; their gods become demons or fairies. And even if taking over the shrines or rituals was morally wrong or offensive, no representative of those faiths exists to whom one can or should apologize. Driving a religion to extinction means never having to say you're sorry.

Viewed globally, though, the institutions of world religions like Christianity and Islam seem just as vulnerable to supersession as were the ancient primal religions. When Christianity dies in a particular nation or community, it seldom vanishes without a trace, and its buildings often continue as more than merely archaeological remains. We commonly find mosques built on the remains of churches, or vice versa. But religions possess an afterlife that goes beyond bricks and mortar, or cut stone. Just as Christian practice bears within it the imprint of older devotion, so vestiges of Christianity survive within successor faiths.

Even where Christianity has seemingly been eradicated, we find many traces of it on the cultural and religious landscape. A traveler in today's Middle East sees societies that are overwhelmingly Muslim, and in some instances exclusively so. In many cases, though, those Muslims are the lineal descendants of communities that were once Christian, and that often maintained their Christian loyalties for a millennium or more. Even if the connection is not by blood, many other Muslims live in nations in which Christian influence was once predominant and shaped everyday life.

So strong, indeed, are the evidences of continuity from Christianity in Islam and other faiths that we might ask in what sense the old religion actually died at all. If, after a religious revolution, people are following practices very similar to what they had done for centuries beforehand, are we really seeing anything more than a change of label? Assuming for the sake of argument that all religions are equally true, or equally untrue, does the new label make any difference? In fact, solely from a secular perspective, we can find differences of real significance. Two faiths might be similar at an early stage of development, but will grow apart as they mature and develop over time, so that the fact of living in a society that is (for instance) Muslim rather than Christian can in the long term have a vast impact on such basic matters as attitudes to family, gender, property, law, and political arrangements. Yet we should be careful not to apply these distinctions retroactively. No matter how powerful our awareness of these later differences, these various clashes between civilizations, we can still find earlier eras when Christian and Muslim communities—to take the most obvious example—freely interchanged beliefs and symbols. Modern Christians or Muslims can scarcely denounce the practices of the other religion without in the process rejecting a substantial part of their own heritage.

After Christianity

When Christian communities are destroyed, they rarely vanish entirely or immediately, and survivors often maintain a clandestine existence for many years afterward. One spectacular example of such crypto-Christianity occurs in Japan, where seventeenth-century governments extirpated a thriving European Catholic mission that at its height had three hundred thousand followers. The last priests were killed or expelled about 1650, and tens of thousands of laypeople also perished: suspicion of Christian loyalty could lead to the death penalty. Japan remained a closed society until 1853, when a U.S. warship forced the nation to open its borders to external trade and contact. Christian missionaries were among the other Europeans who arrived over the following years, and in 1865, a Catholic priest received some surprising visitors. Nervously, in constant fear of detection, fifteen elderly Japanese peasants wanted to ask him what he knew about the faith they had maintained secretly for so long. They asked particularly about

> *O Deusu Sama, O Yasu Sama,* and *Santa Maria Sama,* by which names they designated God, Jesus Christ and the Blessed Virgin. The view of the statue of the Madonna and Child recalled Christmas to them ... they asked me if we were not in the seventeenth day of the Time of Sadness (Lent); nor was St. Joseph unknown to them.[1]

As we have seen, the remnants of the Japanese churches still survive as hidden Christians, *kakure kirishitan,* having outlasted four centuries of persecution and discrimination.

The Japanese experience finds many echoes worldwide among crypto-believers who ostensibly follow the dominant faith while stubbornly maintaining older practices. Much of the work of the Spanish Inquisition consisted of uncovering and condemning the Jewish or Muslim rituals and practices that people kept alive even after their formal adherence to Christianity. Some preferred or avoided certain foods; they differed from the Christian mainstream in the days of the week or the seasons of the year they kept holy; they favored different styles of dress and hygiene. As so many of these markers involved domestic issues like clothing and food, feasts and fasts, women were a critical factor in preserving underground faith. Under constant intrusive enforcement, most such practices were eventually suppressed, in many cases by expelling the converted families that tried to keep alive the old ways.[2]

Such subterranean religious practice can last for centuries. In China, most sources confidently assert that Christianity was wholly rooted out on at least two occasions, once in the tenth century and again in the fourteenth, before being replanted. Yet despite this, some communities kept the faith alive through long years of persecution. About 1300, Marco Polo reported Christians who had maintained continuity of practice over seven centuries—that is, from the time of the first Nestorian missions. In 1605, Catholic missionary Matteo Ricci told how "[i]n the central region of China there lived for five hundred years a considerable number of Christians and . . . there have remained important traces of them in many places."[3]

Crypto-Christians survived under Muslim rule. After the great conversions of the fourteenth century, mainstream Egyptian Muslims never knew quite what to make of the new Coptic converts, whom they called not Muslims but *masalima*—"pseudo-Muslims" or even "Muslim-ish"—and they treated them with suspicion. As a cynical preacher complained:

> Now look at those who embraced Islam, inquire.
> Do you find them—any one of them—in any mosque?
> If they say they became Muslims—where is the fruit of their
> Islam?

They were never seen to pray, never fasted or went on pilgrimage:

> Or else—you say—they are not Muslims. Then why is poll tax
> not exacted from them, humiliation not imposed upon them?

Across the Middle East, crypto-Christian families and communities were regularly rediscovered in Turkey and elsewhere, long after their supposed acceptance of Islam. The best-recorded examples are found in the Balkans—in Bulgaria, Serbia, and Albania—and hidden Christians maintained links through activity in seemingly Muslim religious activities, especially through certain Sufi orders. Observers commented on the practice of double faith (South Slavic *dvoverstvo,* Greek *dipistia*). One Macedonian congregation, complete with its bishop, formally accepted Islam while pursuing the Christian faith secretly, worshipping by night. After the Turks conquered Cyprus in 1571, official policies created a substantial Muslim population on the island, but perhaps a third of the converts were

Linovamvakoi. They were like a cloth on which cotton (*vamvaki*) was covered by linen (*lino*), so that they showed only one side at a time. Often, such multiple loyalty made good practical sense for communities that remembered just how often borders changed and territories changed hands. In the case of the Balkans, these hopes would be justified in the long term, although the time span would be several centuries. Cyprus's *Linovamvakoi* had to maintain their disguise from the 1570s to the 1870s.[4]

The churches responded ambiguously to such clandestine practice, and some authorities pointed to the stern New Testament passages demanding the open proclamation of faith, at whatever cost. As Jesus warned, anyone who failed to acknowledge him in this world could expect no recognition on the Day of Judgment. Yet as ever more Christians fell under Muslim authority, the desperate situation demanded accommodation. As early as the 1330s, the patriarch of Constantinople unofficially sanctioned "double faith," promising that the church would work for the salvation of Anatolian believers who dared not assert their faith openly for fear of punishment, provided that they tried to observe Christian laws. After the fall of Crete in the seventeenth century, the patriarch of Jerusalem similarly permitted surface conversion to Islam on grounds of "inescapable need."[5] Generally, Catholic authorities adopted a much harder line than the Orthodox, presumably because their hierarchy did not live under Muslim rule, while most of their Orthodox counterparts did. Nevertheless, throughout Ottoman times, Catholic clergy ministered to secret Christian communities in the Balkans.

Christian communities in dissolution also maintain an afterlife through the experience of exiles. As with other diasporas, these refugees play an important pollinating role, spreading ideas and institutions that would otherwise have remained confined to one region. In the early Middle Ages, the clergy of the African churches scattered widely before the growth of Islam, carrying with them long traditions of learning and the distinctive customs and liturgy of the African church. Within decades, we see their influence in Spain, and afterward in Ireland, with its historic oceanic connections to Spain and southern Gaul. A Spanish-Irish cultural axis was well in place by the seventh century, and was reinforced by refugees fleeing the Muslim conquest.[6] Exiles spread Spanish traditions in learning and liturgy across Europe. When Charlemagne initiated his "renaissance," his main aides included Spanish Visigoths, who restructured Western liturgy and church organization according to the models they knew.

Other influential diaspora movements included the Syrians in the eighth century, and the Greeks from Asia Minor from the twelfth century onward. By the time Constantinople itself fell in 1453, Greek scholars had few enough resources to bear with them to help promote learning and culture in the West, but they did at least carry their language. From the late fifteenth century, Greek language and scholarship became an integral part of Renaissance humanism. Arguably the most distinctive European painter of the following century was Doménikos Theotokópoulos, known in Spain as El Greco, "the Greek." Though his native Crete was still in Christian hands during his lifetime, it remained a border territory perilously close to the Ottoman Empire, which actually seized the island some years after his death.[7]

From Churches to Mosques

But even when Christianity dies by any accepted standard—when people no longer form Christian communities, attend religious worship, or acknowledge Christian doctrines—the religion leaves remnants, sometimes material, sometimes not. To take a Japanese example, a beloved center of the Shinto religion is the Suwa shrine in Nagasaki, an ancient holy place thoroughly reconstructed during the seventeenth century. The shrine has at its heart a holy of holies, a place accessible only to priests during certain special times, and here can be found the sacred images or *kami,* which the divine spirits possess during rituals. These *kami* take different forms, but one of the three holy images at Suwa is unique. It is a figure or statue, which was almost certainly inherited from a destroyed Catholic church that once stood nearby. During the great persecutions, Japanese authorities placed this figure in the restored Suwa temple in order to attract the loyalty of those who might have been drawn to the now proscribed religion of the *kirishitan*. The great image at the Suwa shrine, which attracts tens of thousands of faithful Shinto devotees each year, is almost certainly a Spanish or Portuguese statue of the Madonna and child.[8]

The most obvious remains of older Christianity come in the form of churches and other religious structures wholly appropriated to a new faith, and from the nature of the contact between the religions, Islam has usually been the beneficiary. In this practice, Muslims were following long precedent. Through most of history, conquering a territory with a different religion meant that the victors unapologetically took over the places of worship of the losers, or at least the most prominent and significant buildings, and converted them to their own faith. Roman emperors happily confiscated the buildings of Christian sects condemned as heretical, or of pagans, and successor states shared these attitudes. When the pagan kingdoms of Anglo-Saxon England accepted Christianity, Pope Gregory ordered

> that the temples of the idols in that nation ought not to be destroyed, but let the idols that are in them be destroyed . . . let altars be erected, and relics placed [so] that the nation, seeing that their temples are not destroyed, may the more familiarly resort to the places to which they have been accustomed.[9]

Though Gregory was prepared to go far in accommodating former pagans, the thought of allowing temples to operate unmolested was never an option.

Later Christians repeatedly seized and converted mosques—for instance, in Palestine and Syria during the Crusades. The Dome of the Rock became a Christian church, while the Knights Templar established their headquarters in part of the al-Aqsa Mosque. When the Christian Normans took over Muslim Sicily, there was never any doubt that the celebrated Palermo mosque would become a cathedral. Nor would their Spanish counterparts allow mosques to continue operating after they conquered Muslim regions. When Christian England expelled its Jews, old synagogues were reputedly reused as churches.[10]

When they were able, not surprisingly, Muslims performed exactly the same kind of appropriations, and in their early conquests, their demands were moderate. Generally, on taking a city, they demanded that half the churches be transferred to them for conversion to mosques. One of the great Christian shrines of the Near East was the church of John the Baptist in Damascus, which an eighth-century caliph confiscated in order to convert it to a mosque. By this point, Damascus Christians had access to only fourteen of the forty-two churches they once had at their disposal. These Muslim acts of seizure should be stressed in light of claims by modern-day writers anxious to present Muslims as infallibly tolerant of the religious practices of their subjects. And similar appropriations occurred across the region: in the Syrian city of Epiphaneia (modern Hama), the basilica became the central prayer hall of the new great mosque. When Pope John Paul II visited the Great Mosque of Damascus in 2001, he was certainly aware that he was visiting the site of the older church of Saint John, and thus the lost roots of Eastern Christianity.[11]

The best-known case of Muslims annexing a great church involved Constantinople's Hagia Sophia, which subsequently became the principal mosque of the Ottoman Empire. Elsewhere in the Middle East, many of the other great mosques do not stand on Christian foundations, because they were erected in cities that became major urban centers only after the rise of Islam, Baghdad and Cairo being prime examples. Even in Cairo, though, the columns of an older Christian building can be seen in the structure of the ninth-century Ibn Tulun Mosque, one of the world's largest. In older centers, we find hundreds of examples of venerable churches transformed into mosques. The Armenian cathedral of Ani was a mosque for some decades before it was retaken in 1124. In Alexandria, the fourth-century church of Saint Athanasius became a mosque after the Arab conquest, and this fairly small building later evolved into the great Attarine Mosque of a Thousand Columns. Across Asia Minor, most churches—many dating back to early Christian times—became Muslim places of worship. The nave of the church of old Amida became the courtyard of the Great Mosque of Diyarbakir. Many Mesopotamian mosques rise on the sites of older Nestorian or Jacobite holy places: the mosque of Jonah, *Nabi Yunis,* at Nineveh, is probably built over the tomb of a Jacobite patriarch.[12]

Such appropriations of churches are all the more numerous when we take account of areas conquered later by Islam and subsequently retaken by Christian powers, so that they enjoyed only temporary Islamic status. In Córdoba, the eighth-century Muslim conquerors demolished the cathedral of Saint Vincent before erecting on the site the famous Mezquita, which in its day was the second-largest mosque in the world. In the thirteenth century, it was transformed once more into a Christian cathedral.

The process of seizing and reseizing continued as long as Muslim conquests continued, which in some areas meant into the late seventeenth century. When the Ottomans occupied Budapest in the sixteenth and seventeenth centuries, all the churches but one became mosques. In Cyprus, the Gothic cathedral of Famagusta became the Turkish mosque of Lala Mustafa Pasha, named for the leader of the Ottoman conquest of the island in 1570. As late as the 1990s, the Balkan wars witnessed a number of Orthodox churches transformed into mosques. In 1997, William Dalrymple reported visiting what had been the Armenian cathedral of Edessa, which lost its worshippers during the slaughter of 1915. It then remained a fire station until the 1990s, when it became a mosque, with a mihrab punched into the south wall to indicate the direction of Mecca.[13]

Christians who converted to Islam must have had mixed feelings about worshipping in such reconditioned buildings. While lamenting the loss of the symbols that characterized the church, the fact of praying in a familiar structure provided some kind of comfort in continuity. Some evidence from folklore illuminates converts' ambiguous attitudes toward their former faith. In Turkey, stories circulated about church buildings stubbornly resisting conversion, sometimes by having their crosses reappear after being removed. In one case, proximity to a converted church reportedly caused a neighboring minaret to collapse.[14] Church buildings may or may not have been faithfully Christian, but the people who once worshipped in them believed they were, and perhaps felt guilty that they had not been as loyal as their buildings.

As conquerors of both faiths normally had the sense to reuse well-built structures rather than to destroy them, converted buildings often retain physical reminders of their earlier status, including paintings and mosaics in converted churches. Sometimes, indeed, these works of art survive only because the buildings lost their function as churches, as later generations would probably have felt the need to renovate or remove such ancient and outmoded pieces. But the consequence is that some mosques preserve rich galleries of venerable Christian art. At Damascus itself, an impressive shrine in the Great Mosque contains the relic that is the supposed head of John the Baptist, as well as the more authentic tomb of Saladin. In Hagia Sophia, some glorious mosaics were covered with whitewash for centuries, and, when revealed in the nineteenth century, they proved to be some of the great works of Byzantine art. Other treasures, including the giant figure of an all-ruling Christ Pantokrator, probably exist under later Islamic artworks, which would have to be destroyed in order to reveal the original mosaics.

So extensive are the conflicting claims of ownership to sacred structures that any suggestion of restitution is extremely sensitive. As Muslim immigration into Europe has grown in recent years, the issue has resurfaced in the case of great cathedrals—Toledo, Seville, Córdoba, Palermo—that stand on the sites of ancient mosques. Even moderate Muslim groups in Spain and Italy have expressed an interest in reclaiming such properties, or at least gaining the right for prayer space, but the Catholic response has been chilly. Responding to such requests, the president of the Pontifical Commission for Inter-religious Dialogue noted tactfully that "the Vatican has always been very careful not to ask for similar rights with regard to mosques which once were churches." No Christian realistically expects that great mosques in Damascus or Constantinople will ever revert to churches, at least not this side of the Day of Judgment.[15]

Making Islam

Islam retained much more from Christianity—especially in its Eastern forms—than just the buildings, to a remarkable degree for anyone who knows the religions only in their modern forms. Today, an observant Christian who chooses to convert to Islam would face countless cultural issues, and the religious change would affect every aspect of belief and practice, not to mention daily life. That contrast was far less marked in the early centuries of Islam, which took many years to define itself as a separate religion, and which includes in its deepest strata many traces of older Christian (and Jewish) influences. We see this in the oldest texts of the religion, as well as in many of the practices that today seem so unfamiliar and "Oriental."

Early Christian observers had mixed views of Islam, but some at least found much in common with their own faith—admittedly, at a time when forthright criticism would be dangerous. As we have seen, when the patriarch Timothy debated religion with the caliph, he lauded Muhammad as one who "separated his people from idolatry and polytheism, and attached them to the cult and the knowledge of one God." Others suggested a much closer Christian connection. Earlier in the eighth century, indeed, Saint John Damascene saw Islam not as a new religion but as a Christian heresy, the sect of the Ishmaelites or Hagarenes. "From that time to the present," he wrote, "a false prophet named Mohammed has appeared in their midst. This man, after having chanced upon the Old and New Testaments and likewise, it seems, having conversed with an Arian monk, devised his own heresy."[16]

This story of the monk would often resurface in various forms, and has Muslim parallels. Muhammad's early biographer Ibn Ishaq tells how the prophet, as a child, was visiting Bostra, in Syria, where the Christian monk Bahira recognized the child's genius and tried to protect him. Allegedly, Bahira was able to confirm Muhammad's prophetic role from the copies that he possessed of the authentic Christian Gospels, the ones unpolluted by the church. In his story of the Arian monk, John may be turning this preexisting Muslim tradition round into an anti-Muslim legend. In the ninth century, the mysterious monk would be renamed Sergius; and the figure of Sergius often resurfaced in Christian polemic, which presents Muhammad as a plagiarist, one who distorted an old religion rather than founding a new one. Throughout the Middle Ages, Christians saw Muhammad as a schismatic rather than the leader of an alien faith. It is his role as "*seminator di scandalo e di scisma*," sower of scandal and schism, that earns him his place in Dante's hell.[17]

As it stands, the story of monkish borrowing is pure legend, and ignores the complexity of the Quran: it would be absurd to treat Islam as merely a bastardized offshoot of Christianity or Judaism. But just as certainly, Islam arose in dialogue with those other faiths. Speaking about external elements in the Quran itself is deeply controversial, because Muslims take the Quran to be the directly inspired word of God, transcribed (emphatically, *not* composed) by the Prophet Muhammad from about the year 610 onward. But for scholars who do not accept that interpretation, and who try to trace the origins of that text, the Quran seems to grow out of Christian and Jewish sources, and it is often difficult to separate the two influences. Even what appear to be strongly Semitic currents might have flowed from the Syriac-speaking churches.

The Quran tells many familiar biblical stories, featuring Abraham, Moses, and other key figures of the Old Testament, in addition to lengthy passages concerning Jesus and Mary, and of course the Quranic focus on the Last Judgment strongly recalls biblical texts. But generally, the most potent outside influences seem to have come from Eastern forms of Christianity. Most of the Quranic stories about Mary and Jesus find their parallels not in the canonical four Gospels but in apocryphal texts that circulated widely in the East, such as the Protevangelium of James and the Arabic Infancy Gospel. The Quran cites the miracle in which the infant Jesus shaped a bird out of clay and then breathed life into it, a tale also found in the Infancy Gospel of Thomas. The Quran also presents the death of Jesus in exactly the language of those heretical Eastern Christians known as the Docetists, who saw the event as an illusion rather than a concrete reality: "They did not kill him and they did not crucify him, but it was made to seem so to them." One sura includes the common Christian legend of the Seven Sleepers of Ephesus, the saintly young men who escaped a persecution by sleeping many years in a cave.[18]

So strong are these connections that over the past half century scholars have questioned whether the Quran could even have originated in Arabia, or whether it was collected or constructed somewhere else with a prominent Christian and Jewish population, perhaps in Syria or Mesopotamia. In a controversial work, German scholar Christoph Luxenberg suggests that the Quran is a confused translation from earlier Syriac Christian texts, at a time when Syriac was the lingua franca of the Middle East. Significantly, given the radical implications of the work and the possibility of an angry Muslim reaction, the name "Luxenberg" is a pseudonym, and his real identity remains secret. When the Quran was constructed, he notes, the only Arabic schools were in southern Mesopotamia, at al-Anbar and al-Hirah, where "the Arabs of that region had been Christianized and instructed by Syrian Christians." Often, obscure Quranic phrases make sense when understood in the Syriac context, and can be elucidated from the well-known works of Syriac writers like Ephraem the Syrian.[19]

"In its origin," claims Luxenberg, "the Quran is a Syro-Aramaic liturgical book, with hymns and extracts from Scriptures which might have been used in sacred Christian services." The very name Quran, he thinks, derives from the root *qr'*, "to read," and it is equivalent to the Syriac *qeryana*, the church lectionary used to proclaim the gospel in public readings. In his view, "the Quran intended itself first of all to be understood as nothing more than a liturgical book with selected texts from the Scriptures (the Old and New Testament) and not at all as a substitute." Some of Luxenberg's detailed readings produce jaw-dropping results. In the conventional translation, Sura 96—commonly thought to be the oldest part of the Quran—ends with the verse "Nay! obey him not, and make obeisance and draw nigh [to Allah]." Luxenberg's retranslation reads: "You ought not to heed him at all, perform instead your divine service, and take part in the liturgy of Eucharist." Or again, Syriac Christian visions of paradise promised the believers exotic fruits such as white raisins, or *hur*. For Luxenberg, when Syriac texts were absorbed into the Quran, translators made many errors, and believers were now promised not raisins but *houris,* virgins. Hence the seventy-two virgins that martyrs will reputedly receive on entry into paradise.[20]

Luxenberg's work has been much criticized, and not just by defenders of strict Islamic orthodoxy. Some critics think he underplays the influence of Jewish texts, particularly the Targums, while overplaying Christian elements. Others attack his linguistic knowledge. But whatever the scholarly verdict on Luxenberg's theory, there is no doubt that Eastern Christians were a well-known presence in the Arabian world, and influenced the early development of Islam.

Arabs and Christians

Muhammad's world in western Arabia was surrounded by potent Christian forces to north, south, east, and west. Two leading Arab kingdoms were Christian: the Lakhmid state based in al-Hirah, in Mesopotamia; and the Syrian Ghassanids. Al-Hirah had its Nestorian bishopric and its famous network of monasteries. Bostra, the reported setting for Muhammad's encounter with the monk, was an ancient Christian metropolitan see in what is now southern Syria, and long a base for the evangelization of Arabs. Some twenty sees were subordinate to Bostra. The greatest of all Arab shrines was Resafa in Syria, which was also known as Sergiopolis, the shrine city of the third-century Christian martyr Sergius. Perhaps this name contributed to the Christian story of the renegade monk who influenced the prophet.[21]

Other Christians were scattered across the trading communities of the Arab Gulf, along the sea routes that connected Mesopotamia to India. Christianity had deep roots in Bahrain by the fourth century, and this became a Nestorian center, with two bishoprics. The church had other sees in Oman and Yemen. Cosmas Indicopleustes reported that the island of Socotra off the coast of Yemen had "clergy who receive their ordination in Persia, and are sent on to the island, and there is also a multitude of Christians." The Christian presence across Arabia survived at least into the tenth century.[22]

Apart from Byzantine Syria, by far the most powerful Christian presence looming over the Arab world was Ethiopia, and when the first Muslims faced pagan persecution, Aksum was the natural place for them to take refuge. Recording one of the prophet's early acquaintances, the early biographer Ibn Ishaq recorded the saying "The one who teaches Muhammad most of what he brings is Jabr the Christian"—who may have been Ethiopian. This Ethiopian presence was so important because it might explain many of the Jewish-seeming customs found in early Islam. Undoubtedly, Jews were a force in the world of Muhammad, and close Jewish parallels in early Islam indicate direct influences. At the same time, though, when Muslims encountered Ethiopian Christianity, as they must have done, they found a form of Christianity that included many Judaic customs, including circumcision and strict food regulations, which would become standard within Islam.[23]

The Yemen in southern Arabia also had strong Christian communities, and client states here operated under Ethiopian protection. Najran in Yemen became the scene of a mass martyrdom in 523 when a Jewish king slaughtered thousands of Christian believers, a massacre stopped only by Ethiopian intervention. The Ethiopian commander Abraha established himself as an independent king, creating at San'a a fine Christian cathedral, and a pilgrim shrine that rivaled Mecca itself. His career also defined Arab and Muslim historical memory. In 570, Abraha marched on Mecca with an army that included an unforgettably stubborn war elephant, and historians can date the birth of Muhammad because it fell in precisely this celebrated Year of the Elephant.[24]

Against this background, we might return to Saint John Damascene's account of Islamic origins, with the role of the Arian monk. Arian monks were not common in the region at the time, but both Nestorians and Jacobites were. The Quran refers to Christians as *al-Nasrani*, using the archaic term commonly used by East Syrian churches themselves. Muhammad himself favored these Nazarenes, and was appalled when the Persians captured Jerusalem in 614: in his view, pagans had defeated the worshippers (however misguided) of the true God. An early story reports that when he captured the sanctuary of Mecca, Muhammad ordered the destruction of all the idols in the temple, except for a figure of the Virgin and child. Even if the story is not literally true, it is startling that an early Muslim commentator would be comfortable inventing it.[25]

One Quranic passage points to linkages with the Syriac churches and their clergy. In a verse often cited to prove Muslim goodwill toward Christianity, the faithful are told:

Strongest among men in enmity to the believers wilt thou find the Jews and pagans; and nearest among them in love to the believers wilt thou find those who say, "We are Christians": because amongst these are men devoted to learning and men who have renounced the world (*ruhban*), and they are not arrogant.

But the next verse makes it clear that the Quran is not so much lauding Christian monks and hermits, but praising those formerly Christian clergy who have accepted Islam:

And when they listen to the revelation received by the Messenger, thou wilt see their eyes overflowing with tears, for they recognize the truth: they pray, "Our Lord! we believe; write us down among the witnesses."

Surely these "men devoted to learning" did not enter the new faith empty-handed, nor did other monks and scholars who accepted Islam over the following centuries. One Egyptian document from around the year 710 shows how former Christians applied their old categories to the new religion. It contains an early Greek form of the Muslim declaration of faith, with an interesting theological twist: "There is no god except the single God; Muhammad is God's *apostle* [*Maamet apostolos theou;* my emphasis]."[26]

Some of those early converts might well have been from traditions even further removed from Orthodox Christianity than were the Nestorians or Jacobites. Across the Near East, we find a number of Muslim sects that are quite secretive about their doctrines, which on closer examination seem closely related to Christian or Gnostic movements. In the Shiite tradition, for instance, the Alawites make up just 11 percent of the population of Syria, but they hold disproportionate political power under the Asad family and the Baathist Party, which has been in office since 1970. They not only venerate the prophet Ali, but see him as an incarnation of God—an idea that appalls orthodox Muslims. They have a special devotion for Jesus, they celebrate some Christian holidays, and Christian elements survive in their liturgy. They also retain ideas that sound Gnostic, viewing the true believer as one of the people of light, seeking salvation in a world of darkness. In older sources, they are usually called Nusayris, a term that was meant to be demeaning but which may actually be descriptive: it means "little Christians." Other Gnostic-tinged groups on the fringes of Islam include the Druze, who teach reincarnation.[27]

If in fact Islam was a Christian heresy, orthodox believers could learn from it and even try to adopt its more rigorous practices into their own lives. A surprising example of continuing dialogue occurred in the 720s, when the Muslim caliphs proclaimed a strict prohibition of religious images in churches. One might expect Christian powers to have reacted by asserting the importance of images and icons, as a means of distinguishing themselves from Islam, but in fact they took the opposite course. Conceding nothing to Islam in the degree of official piety, the Byzantine emperors themselves forbade the making or veneration of images. Government forces destroyed or desecrated icons and figures at least as thoroughly as Muslims were doing in their own territories, and continued to do so long after Muslim fervor had relaxed. These policies of image breaking (iconoclasm) dominated imperial policy for fifty years. In 754, a council condemned

> every likeness which is made out of any material and color whatever by the evil art of painters. . . . If anyone shall endeavor to represent the forms of the saints in lifeless pictures with material colors which are of no value (for this notion is vain and introduced by the Devil), and does not rather represent their virtues as living images in himself, let him be anathema!

What could Muslims themselves add to such powerful words? Not until 787 were the iconoclasts defeated and condemned in their turn, so that the veneration of images definitively came to mark a cultural boundary between Christianity and Islam. Spanish Christians, meanwhile, were so anxious to refute Muslim charges of tritheism—of worshipping three gods—that they underplayed the unity of God and Christ, creating the so-called adoptionist heresy.[28]

Building Mosques

Muslims drew explicitly from Christians in constructing their new religious buildings, and not just because they had appropriated old churches for their own uses. A modern Westerner might draw an easy and obvious contrast between a medieval Christian church, imagined as a French or German Gothic building, and a Muslim mosque. Even a poorly informed observer can readily identify the features of "Muslim architecture." Originally, though, mosques appeared as they did precisely because they were imitating Byzantine Christian churches of the sixth and seventh centuries. Particularly influential were the *martyria*: churches intended for the display of sacred relics, buildings marked by characteristic domes and colonnades. Constantinople's Hagia Sophia looks exactly like what the West expects a mosque to be, but of course its basic structure—complete with great dome—was completed in the sixth century, when it was meant to be a definitive statement of Christian architecture. Other influences came into play in the design of mosques, especially from Persia, but the major sources were Christian.

As the Arab conquerors had scant experience in monumental architecture, they naturally turned to the available experts to build their mosques, and that normally meant Christian designers and craftsmen. They built what seemed appropriate for them, and those patterns subsequently spread across the emerging Muslim world. In 685, Caliph Abd-al Malik built the Dome of the Rock—designed as a martyrium in the most fashionable Byzantine style—explicitly to compete with the Christian structures that still dominated city skylines across the Middle East:

> For he beheld Syria to be a country that had long been occupied by the Christians, and he noted there are beautiful churches still belonging to them, so enchantingly fair, and so renowned for their splendor, as are the Church of the Holy Sepulcher, and the churches of Lydda and Edessa. So he sought to build for the Muslims a mosque that should be unique and a wonder to the world.

All the more tellingly in this post-Christian setting, the Dome of the Rock includes a series of inscriptions repeatedly denying that Jesus was the son of God, but ending, "In the name of Allah, pray for your prophet and servant, Jesus son of Mary."[29]

If you take a Middle Byzantine martyrium, and take out the icons and images—which is roughly what the iconoclasts did during the eighth century—what you are left with looks uncannily like a mosque. As William Dalrymple notes, "[T]he architecture of the earliest minarets unmistakably derives from the square late antique Syrian church towers." Late-seventh-century Christian travelers to Syria had no difficulty in identifying the structures the "unbelieving Saracens" were building for prayer: they were "churches." Coptic, Syrian, and Byzantine craftsmen worked on the Great Mosque of Damascus, while the tenth-century builders of Córdoba's mosque borrowed skilled Byzantine artisans. Christian continuities also appear in interior details of the early mosques, themes that survive today. From Ethiopian churches, Muslims learned to construct the pulpit, the *minbar*—a raised platform in the mosque from which preachers still deliver Friday sermons.[30]

Christian influences on mosque design continued long after the rise of Turkish power. Even under the Ottomans, converted Greek masons and artisans built some of the stellar productions of that era, like the Tekkiye Mosque complex in Damascus. After the fall of Constantinople in 1453, Hagia Sophia became the classic model for other great mosques of the Ottoman golden age, including the Süleymaniye. The greatest Turkish architect and mosque builder was the brilliant Sinan (1489–1588), who was born a Greek Christian and who learned his engineering skills while a janissary. A former Christian used a former Byzantine church as the model for the glorious mosques that awed visitors to Turkey and are today seen as the apex of Islamic civilization.[31]

Muslims and Christians

Within those mosques, too, Muslim worship and practice often recall older styles.[32] A modern Christian transported back in time to the Near East of the sixth or seventh century would be struck at the many resemblances between the Christianity of that time and the modern world of Islam. It is not always easy to tell whether Muslims were influenced by practices they witnessed in Ethiopia or the eastern Syriac world, because the two were so closely related, but somewhere they observed the Christian practice of fasting, which shaped the Islamic custom of Ramadan. Modern Christians are struck by the severity of Ramadan, which forbids believers to eat or drink during daylight hours for the space of a month, a severe discipline in hot climates. Yet this was in fact close to the oldest Christian practice of Lent. Here, for instance, is the Ethiopian practice as followed during the sixteenth century: "This fast follows the old law, for they do not eat at midday, and when the sun is setting they go to church and confess and communicate and then go to supper." Even when allowed to eat, "they eat nothing that has suffered death, nor milk, nor cheese, nor eggs, nor butter, nor honey, nor drink wine. Thus during the fast days they eat only bread of millet, wheat and pulse, all mixed together, spinach and herbs cooked with oil." A

Jesuit observer noted, "The severity of their fasts is equal to that of the primitive church. In Lent they never eat till after sunset."[33]

Another surprising continuity involves the prostrations, *rak'a,* that are so common a feature of Muslim prayers, and which to Western eyes surely denote characteristically "Oriental" behavior. Yet these, too, have undeniable Christian precedents. The earliest Christians prayed standing, but kneeling or prostration became increasingly common in the early centuries, especially for penitential prayer. Sinners approached God in the manner of a poor mortal abased before a king or emperor. As Saint Augustine recorded, "They who pray do with the members of their body that which befits suppliants; they fix their knees, stretch forth their hands, or even prostrate themselves on the ground." Early saints' lives boast how many prostrations their heroes would perform to show their love of God. Nestorian Christians genuflected often, especially during the penitential season of Lent. Far from prostration being a traditional Arabic practice, many Arabs saw the new practice both as humiliating and as a foreign import associated with protocol-fixated Christian courts and churches.[34]

Originally, Muslims saw prostration as eccentric Christian behavior, exactly as many modern Christians are puzzled by Muslim styles of prayer. In the eighth and ninth centuries, what divided Muslims and Christians was not whether they prostrated themselves, but whether this was appropriate behavior before an icon or holy image, as Christians believed, or solely before God, as Muslims advocated. As William Dalrymple observes, witnessing Christians prostrating themselves in the monastery of Mar Gabriel, "Islam and the Eastern Christians have retained the original early Christian convention: it is the Western Christians who have broken with sacred tradition."[35]

Nor would early Eastern Christians have been amazed by Muslim attitudes toward women. Now, scholars disagree on just how secluded early Muslim women were expected to be, and some quite conservative Muslim authorities challenge the idea that Muhammad demanded the extreme policies that are today found in a society like Saudi Arabia. But Muslims were not alone in expecting some form of veiling, or in keeping women secluded from the world, as had been expected in both classical Greece and ancient Persia. Early Christian women covered their heads in church, where men and women were segregated by sex and probably entered by separate doors. Eastern Christian societies also used forms of head covering and veiling, although it is not always easy to distinguish references to head covering—something like a modern Muslim headscarf—from descriptions of a facial veil. Byzantine women were supposed to remain in the *gynaeceum,* the women's quarters, until married, and even after marriage they wore a veil in public. One story from Mesopotamia tells how, around the year 770, authorities made extortionate tax demands, humiliating those who refused to pay. For the Christian chronicler recording the event, one of the worst official atrocities involved the violation of women's seclusion. Agents dragged respectable Christian women from their houses, so that "women who were never seen in the street. . . . became ignominious in the midst of men." As in other matters, later Muslim practice largely preserves the normal expectations of early Eastern Christianity.[36]

In their religious rhetoric, also, Muslims strove to present their faith as the true successor to older Christianity. This approach was critical when debating Near Eastern Christians, whose scriptures were familiar and venerated, yet somehow Muslims had both to assert the claims of Muhammad and to establish the Muslim view of Jesus. They accomplished this by reading prophecies retroactively into Christian texts, or by cultivating alternative scriptures. Often, they argued that the Christian Gospels would speak more directly to Muslim needs if they were the "real" Gospels, and had not been adulterated by devious churchmen. One weapon in such debates was the Gospel of Barnabas, a pseudo-Gospel originally constructed in the fourteenth century but probably using some ancient early sources, perhaps even the Diatessaron. The Gospel of

Barnabas as we have it is the life of Jesus retold from a Muslim perspective, culminating with Jesus prophesying the coming of Muhammad, while other texts told of the evil deceptions wrought by Saint Paul. ("Others preached, and yet preach, that Jesus is the Son of God, among whom is Paul deceived.") These ideas had a powerful impact in religious controversy and are regularly cited in accounts of conversion to Islam, especially in the Balkans. Even in the 1990s, Dalrymple still found Turkish Muslim leaders appalled that Christians clung on stubbornly to their false gospels rather than acknowledging the plain truth of Barnabas. If not in the Catholic sense, Muslims still care about claiming an authentic apostolic succession: Jesus matters.[37]

Mystics

When we talk about people accepting new religions or abandoning old ones, we are usually applying a particular idea of what constitutes a "religion." Western cultures commonly assume that religions are mutually exclusive packages of ideas and practices, so that one cannot simultaneously be a Christian and a Muslim, and, logically, conversion from one system to another should mean a wholesale transformation of religious life. But such an exclusive vision of religious loyalty is not universally held. In East Asian practice, it is quite common for a given individual to draw freely on the religious images and practices of a number of different faiths, whether Buddhist, Taoist, or Confucian. In the West, likewise, accepting a particular religious label does not always mean that an individual renounces everything that he or she believed from older systems. Older forms can remain alive for many years, and even come to form part of the newly dominant faith. Often, newly ascendant faiths make imaginative use of the older beliefs, incorporating them into their own systems. Across Latin America, older deities were transformed into the saints that became central to Catholic devotion.

Such informal continuities appear in the transition from Christianity to Islam. Quite apart from the issue of obstinate crypto-Christians, even communities that converted wholeheartedly to the new faith retained older customs, in ways that reshaped the practice of Islam. The most striking of these continuities involve the Sufi brotherhoods. What Westerners call the Middle Ages was to Muslims the golden age of their faith, and central to that era were the great Sufi brotherhoods, mystical orders that first appeared in the ninth and tenth centuries and spread over the whole of the Muslim world, *dar al-Islam,* between 1200 and 1500. The Sufis cultivated one of the world's greatest mystical traditions, and that religious devotion permeated the art and poetry for which they are legendary: the thirteenth-century mystic Rumi was a great Sufi. Since the Sufi orders (*tariqat*) led the expansion of Islam beyond the faith's original core in the Middle East, it is impossible to understand the Islam of North Africa or most of Asia without a grasp of Sufi tradition.[38]

Although scholars debate the origins of Sufism, some of the parallels to Eastern Christianity are overwhelming, particularly in terms of practices of mystical prayer and devotion. From the earliest Christian ages, Egypt and the Near East had flourishing mystical and ascetic traditions, which reached their height in the Syriac-speaking churches of late antiquity. Little effort is needed to trace these themes long after the rise of Islam, as Sufi mysticism used very similar concepts and practices, commonly in the same geographical settings and milieus.[39] Probably by the fourth or fifth century, Eastern Christian monks developed the technique of the Jesus Prayer or Prayer of the Heart, the repetition of a simple mantralike petition many thousands of times in order to create a trancelike state of devotion in which the prayer pervades one's very being. Through repeating this prayer, which in its usual form was "Jesus, have mercy on me a sinner," the believer really learns to "pray without ceasing," as Jesus instructed. This practice was recommended by famous Egyptian mystics and saints such as John Climacus in the sixth century and Hesychios in the eighth, but it was always a standard form of mystical devotion. Western Christians who know about the Prayer of the Heart usually encounter it through the nineteenth-century Russian spiritual classic *The Way of a Pilgrim*. (Modern Americans might also know it through J. D. Salinger's *Franny and Zooey*.)[40]

With this ancient tradition in mind, we recall that the most characteristic Sufi devotion involves the multiple recitation of the central proclamation *"La ilaha illa'llah"* ("There is no god but God"). In their *dhikr,* remembrance, Sufis recite these words, the *shahada,* thousands of times each day, exactly as Egyptian or Syrian monks recite the Prayer of the Heart. In both cases, the goal is to realize the falsity of the world and to draw closer to the ultimate reality or truth, which is God. Of course, practices are not identical, since the two faiths now have centuries of distinct evolution: Christians probably had no exact parallel to the organized ritual in which groups of Sufi devotees recite the *shahada* until they enter ecstatic states. But in so many ways, Sufi practices parallel those of the monks and hermits, in lands that had been overwhelmingly Christian. Even the name suggests continuity. *Sufi* derives from the Arabic word for "wool," the material of an ascetic's garment. This costume followed the practice of the Nestorian churches, whose bishops and higher clergy were expected to wear wool, rather than linen or silk, as a sign of simplicity and devotion. Both types of holiness, Muslim and Christian, were "wooly."[41]

One of the original Sufi centers was Basra, which was officially founded as an Arab military settlement in the 630s but stood on older Syriac roots. The original town was a bishopric by 225, and became the seat of a metropolitan in the fifth century. In the early eighth century, Basra was home to the pioneer Sufi thinker Hasan al-Basri, who is cited in most of the Sufi lineages; the city also produced the great woman Sufi mystic and poet Rabi'a. Another source of Sufi activism was Balkh in Turkestan, which was also a center for Nestorians, Manichaeans, and Buddhists: the Chinese Nestorian Tablet mentions a priest of Balkh. As a result of these many connections, Sufis would always have a special devotion to the ascetic master Jesus. The great martyr of Sufism is al-Hallaj, whose mystical utterances led him to identify himself with God, and who was duly martyred in 922. He repeatedly compared himself with Christ and saw his execution as a direct emulation of Christ's death, to the point of speaking about drinking the cup that he had been given. Like Jesus, he was, literally, crucified.[42]

Besides his Sufi successors, other movements claimed Hasan al-Basri as spiritual forefather, including the Mutazilites, who tried to apply rationalistic Greek thought to Islam. Their ideas generated ferocious debate in which their opponents certainly made them out to be more extreme and even heretical than they actually were. Yet at least some Mutazilites did hold startling ideas about the role of Jesus, placing him above Muhammad and seeing him as the firstborn of creation. Some were said to view Christ as the incarnate Word:

> The creation had two lords and two creators. One of them is from eternity and He is Allah, and the other is created, and he is Isa b. Maryam [Jesus son of Mary]. And they said that Christ was the Son of God in the sense of adoption and not of birth. And they also said that the Christ is He who will judge Creation at the last day.[43]

The Sufis were much more orthodox in their views but still held a high view of Jesus, whom they saw as the ultimate ascetic, "the monk of monks." Over the next two centuries, Sufi writing grew in volume and sophistication, culminating about 1100 in the classic *Revival of Religious Sciences (Ihya' 'ulum al-din)*, by al-Ghazali: Karen Armstrong calls this "the most-quoted Muslim text after the Quran and the hadith." The *Ihya'* "contains the largest number of sayings ascribed to Jesus in any Arabic Islamic text . . . Jesus was enshrined in Sufi sensibility as the prophet of the heart par excellence."[44]

Such thinkers compiled a body of sayings attributed to Jesus, scriptures that some have called the Muslim Gospel. Some of these texts are quoted, usually in free form, from the New Testament, but many others are rooted in Syriac Christianity. In some instances, Muslims inherited truly ancient sayings attributed to Jesus that date back to the first or second century, and which appear in apocryphal Gospels. Through the "Muslim Gospel," two sayings at least from the Gospel of Thomas continued to circulate widely in the Muslim world, including "Become passers by" and the call for the believer to bring forth what is inside him. Perhaps accurately, Muslims recalled that Jesus had taught his followers that "the world is a bridge. Pass over it, but do not build upon it." And quite plausibly, perhaps they heard these sayings originally from monks in Syria or Mesopotamia.[45]

Saints

Common origins need have no implications for later development: the millions of Muslims hearing a sermon from *minbars* know or care nothing about its Christian origins. Yet in the case of the Sufi orders, Christian parallels and contacts continued for centuries after their foundation, with potent implications for the growing hold of Islam on Middle Eastern countries. In their practice, these orders developed very much as Christian churches had before them, with a strong focus on holy individuals, great sheikhs and mystics, and the founders of the orders, who came to occupy a place in popular devotion exactly like that of the Christian monks and saints. Ordinary believers traveled to the tombs and other sites associated with these champions of faith, hoping to find some benefit from that contact with holiness, and often to obtain special blessings, especially in the form of healing. Christians and Muslims celebrated the *mulid,* or feast, of their particular sheikh or a saint, and to an outside observer the rituals are hard to distinguish.[46]

For Westerners accustomed to the harsh simplicity of the Islam of Saudi Arabia or the Taliban, it can be shocking to realize just how focused on saints and intermediaries much of Islam was in the past, and remains today in much of the world. Many of these saints resemble Christian predecessors, though none perhaps as strongly as Fatima, the daughter of the Prophet, whose role in Shiite Islam closely recalls that of the Virgin Mary in Catholic or Orthodox Christianity. She is the loving mother who bears the woes of the world, whom believers turn to in times of despair.[47] When we consider other aspects of Shiite tradition—the messianism, the ritual passion plays that reenact the bloody deaths of the great martyrs—it is tempting to seek parallels in the practice of older Mesopotamian Christianity. But in Sunni Islam also, the Sufi sheikhs would be venerated much like the Christian saints before them. Across what had been the Christian Middle East, common religious practice continued to be a matter of saints and shrines, healing and pilgrimage.

Now, the fact that this new spiritual world looks so much like the old does not necessarily indicate any direct influence, and all the great religions have independently evolved similar practices at different times. But the "catholic" character of Sufi practice certainly attracted former Christians living under Muslim rule, and made their transition to the new religious order much easier and more attractive. In turn, the more Christians who accepted Islam in this guise, the stronger the potential following for a devotional Sufi Islam.

The Sufi impact on Christians was evident in Asia Minor. As Muslim power established itself during the thirteenth century, the region became a major center for Sufi activity, led by mystics like Haji Bektash, founder of the Bektashi order. Haji Bektash became the subject of a popular hagiography, the *Vilayet-name,* which might be of limited value as sober history but does give the flavor of Muslim-Christian interactions. In these accounts, the Haji does exactly the same things that would have been reported of a great Christian saint, and often the miracles he accomplishes are for the benefit of Christians, who are duly led to accept Islam. Through his special powers, Haji Bektash ended famines, allowed the poor to sow rye and reap wheat, and aided those injured in falls. On occasion, we hear of Christian monks who were his secret followers.[48] In both Asia Minor and the Balkans, the Bektashi order had a particular appeal for crypto-Christians and covert members of other faiths. The Haji is the "main source" of the faith of the Alevis, a sect that claims the loyalty of 15 or 20 percent of the people of Turkey, and of Turkish migrants in contemporary Europe. Although theoretically Shiite Muslims, the Alevis follow virtually no Muslim practices and do not even respect prohibitions on pork and alcohol: their women go unveiled. Their ritual calendar includes a mix of old Persian and Christian festivals, including a New Year celebrated around Easter time, and Old Saint George's Day.[49]

Besides Haji Bektash, other Sufis commanded a broad following. Rumi was reputedly never happier than when communing with the Christian monks of the house of Saint Chariton, near Iconium (Konya). Rumi's followers founded the Mevlevi order, which won many adherents for Islam among the Christian populations of the battered Anatolian cities. Incidentally, many of the famous Sufi leaders of these years were driven out of central Asia by war and political crisis, and moved to Syria or Asia Minor: both Rumi and Haji Bektash were originally from Khurasan. Possibly, their good relations with Christians can be traced back to longstanding interactions with Nestorians and others in those Eastern regions.[50]

Shrines

From the completion of the Muslim conquest in the fifteenth century until the final purge of Christianity in the twentieth, Christians and Muslims not only coexisted in Asia Minor, but also shared many devotional practices and venerated the same holy men and women. Of course, both Christians and Muslims shared a common heritage of patriarchs and saints who appear in both the Bible and Quran, but later individuals also exercised their appeal. Christians venerated the shrine of Haji Bektash as the tomb of Saint Charalambos. In turn, the new Muslim majority showed devotion to the main saints of the Christian pantheon, albeit under new names.

The Muslim affinity for ancient Christian sites had different outcomes in various regions. In some cases, older sites became so Islamized that Christians were progressively excluded. One of Egypt's oldest Christian centers was Oxyrhynchus, where archaeologists in the early twentieth century found some of the most ancient manuscripts of the New Testament, together with other early Gospels. In later times, this became the site of al-Bahnasa, where Coptic pilgrims worshipped at the site where the Holy Family supposedly rested during the flight into Egypt. From the thirteenth century, though, the sanctuary was increasingly surrounded by the tombs of Muslim sheikhs and holy men, and the Christian presence dwindled. At Hebron in Palestine, at the tomb of Abraham, Christians and Jews were enthusiastic visitors until the fierce sultan Baybars formally excluded them, a prohibition that remained in force from 1266 until 1967.[51]

More commonly, different faiths shared their shrines. Up to modern times, one popular holy figure in Muslim Turkey, Syria, and Palestine was Khidr, reputedly a Quranic saint associated with Moses. In popular devotion, though, he is difficult to separate from older Orthodox wonder workers such as the Prophet Elijah (the Orthodox Saint Elias) and Saint George. Like them, Khidr helped travelers, and slew dragons. His name, "the Green One," suggests the distinctive color of Islam but also meshes well with older pagan gods, and Old Greeny's feast marked the beginning of spring. A century ago, a Western scholar reported that "Moslems who have made vows to Khidr frequently pay them to his Christian counterpart [Saint George]": his shrines were often sites formerly associated with crusaders. Even today, Muslim and Christian Arabs converge on the Orthodox church of Beit Jala near Jerusalem, where they pay homage to George/Khidr. Turkey's Alevis similarly make Khidr a central figure of their faith.[52]

Other shrines, too, attracted both Christian and Muslim visitors, whose religious practices overlapped in ways that baffled Western observers. Near Konya, the house of Saint Chariton stood in a complex that included a mosque and the ancient churches of Saint Amphilochius. Into the twentieth century, Turkish Muslims retained many folk customs that suggest an older inheritance, including the use of crosses and icons for healing purposes. In rural areas, Christian priests were often asked to baptize children to ensure their health and well-being. Even at the start of the twentieth century, Muslims requested Christians to parade the relics of their saints as a means of driving off an epidemic. In 1912, an American archaeologist told how, in greater Syria,

> Christians, Moslems, Jews and Nuseiriyeh [Alawites] visit each others' shrines. The Moslems take their insane, or "possessed" to get rid of their evil spirits in the cave of Saint Anthony, belonging to the Maronite convent of Qozhayya in the Lebanon. Christians go on a similar errand to the well at the shrine of Sheikh Hassan er Rai (the Shepherd) near Damascus. . . . During the procession on Good Friday, barren Moslem women pass under the cloth on which is stamped the figure of Christ, in hopes that they may bear children. Christian women in Hums consult Dervish diviners. The Nuseiriyeh observe Christmas, though they subordinate Jesus to Ali. . . . Instances of Moslems seeking baptism for their children as a sort of charm have been reported from all parts of Syria and Palestine.[53]

Dalrymple reported these crossovers as still very much alive in the 1990s. Muslims visited the famous church of the Virgin at Seidnaya in Syria. As a nun reported, "The Muslims come here because they want babies. Our Lady has shown her power and healed many of the Muslims. Those people started to talk about her and now more

Muslims come here than Christians. If they ask for her, she will be there."[54]

Reading accounts of the long struggles between Christianity and Islam, and the savagery each religion has wrought upon the other, it is easy to become discouraged, to see this history as the definitive clash of civilizations, which has no obvious ending except in an apocalyptic showdown. For each side, accounts of the destruction of communities add to the catalog of grievances: Muslims lament the loss of Spain, *al-Andalus*; Greek, Arab, and Armenian Christians recount in nostalgic detail the homelands from which their ancestors were expelled, or where their communities suffered collective martyrdom. Western conservatives parade stories of jihad and dhimmitude. None of these stories are necessarily false: throughout this history, great crimes have been committed. Yet for all this, the histories of Christianity and Islam remain quite inextricable, and repeatedly, even in dissolution, each faith has shaped the other. Underlying the struggle between Christians and Muslims is the fact that theirs is, ultimately, a conflict within a family, and no feud is more bitter.

7

How Faiths Die

May religions perish of disease or only by violence? If by disease, what are its symptoms and its causes? How many diseases are there which in the past have proved fatal to religions? Are the symptoms of any of these diseases to be found in any of the present religions of the world? Are they to be found in our own?

—James Bissett Pratt

Responding to a threat of persecution, sixteenth-century Protestant Theodore Beza urged a foe to "remember that the Church is an anvil that has worn out many a hammer." The history of all the great world faiths proves that religions are highly resilient, and difficult to eradicate. History is littered with false claims about the imminent deaths of religions, claims that in retrospect make almost comic reading. The first known contemporary reference to the Jewish people is an Egyptian inscription boasting that "Israel is laid waste: his seed is no more." Mark Twain remarked on how often the world had turned out for the burial of Roman Catholicism, only to find it postponed yet again, "on account of the weather or something. . . . Apparently one of the most uncertain things in the world is the funeral of a religion."[1]

Faiths are dynamic, and periods of difficulty or persecution can have the effect of forcing believers to delve into the rich diversity of traditions they have evolved over thousands of years. Usually, they find at least some ideas and practices that prove effective in adapting to the new world, and that can in fact provide the foundation for significant revival. In the 1790s, Europe's Catholic churches suffered a fearsome encounter with Enlightenment thought and revolutionary politics, a near-terminal crisis that was followed within a generation by the rise of an aggressively self-confident Catholic revival. Fifty years ago, most observers felt that the historical currents sweeping the Islamic world surely portended the rapid fading of that religion, at least as a relevant political force; and that seeming obliteration preceded the modern-day Islamic revival.

To varying degrees, all the great religions have scriptural resources that allow them to explain defeat, disaster, and persecution; catastrophe can even strengthen these religions in the long term. Moreover, although religions might weaken over time, and might drift toward secularism and indifference, such trends do not in themselves become sufficient to drive a religion out of existence. While some forms of faith, some denominations, might enter terminal crisis, their decline is compensated by the rise of other Christian traditions better able to adjust to changing circumstances. Even in a highly secular culture such as contemporary Europe, at least a minority will try to return to the fundamentals of the religion as they understand it, so that we see an upsurge of evangelical and charismatic groups and other neotraditional movements. Nothing so clearly indicates the imminent revival of a religion as a rising torrent of prophecies about its demise.[2]

On occasion, though, religions certainly do die, or at least vanish utterly from regions that they once dominated, and no great religion has proved immune from such localized disasters. As we have seen, all the world's religions have at some point been excluded from some once-cherished homeland, however abundant the phantoms they leave behind. If Christianity has suffered more frequently from such amputations than other faiths, that just reflects its more ambitious global reach: it usually had more to lose. The frequency of religious elimination is all the more impressive when we realize how sturdy faith traditions are, and how often they have defied seemingly deadly enemies. Why, then, should attempts at destruction succeed on some occasions rather than others? And how far do religions make blunders that contribute to their own demise? Are faiths killed, or do they die?

States and Nations

Based on the experiences of Christianity through history, we must stress the primary role of the state in the elimination of churches and communities. Alliances with states pose many dilemmas for religious traditions, especially those that, like Christianity, are suspicious of worldly authority; but such a political linkage might have been the only way of surviving through the long ages when all states had some religious affiliation, and did their best to promote particular faiths. Certainly by the sixteenth century, the overwhelming majority of the world's Christians lived in Christian states, and most of them on the European continent, where networks of Christian nations could provide mutual support and defense. Christians might bemoan the persistence of church-state affiliations, but without such alliances there might today be no Christians left to experience those regrets. Otherwise, Christianity might be a footnote in Islamic or Chinese history textbooks, alongside Manichaeanism. Conversely, lack of political power potentially posed a lethal danger when the state was in the hands of a rival determined to reshape culture to institutionalize its own ways of belief and practice. Powerlessness placed intolerable burdens upon the churches, forcing them to make daily compromises while offering rich rewards for apostasy.

This political element forced Christian churches to make difficult decisions. As state protection was so critical to the survival and influence of a faith, it was desirable to make political allies. Yet at the same time, a church that allied with the wrong nation or faction could make its own position much worse as it became identified with the wrong side. This is what happened with those Christians in Mesopotamia and China who came to be seen as tools of the Mongol conquerors. Japanese Christians were targeted as potential allies of European imperialism; Latin Christians in the Levant, as the advance guard of the crusader movement.

This emphasis on state power may seem surprising if only on the grounds of plausibility. At least before modern times, few states possessed the organized strength and willpower to mobilize the kind of long-term enterprise that could annihilate a minority religion. Also, as we have seen, all but the most intolerant Muslim societies had a notional commitment to tolerating the existence of Christian and Jewish populations. Yet somehow the old Christian world of the Middle East and North Africa become the core of *dar al-Islam*.

The severity of persecution or enforcement varied over time but was at its worst when an established religion faced a real or perceived danger to its own existence. When such threats did occur, even premodern states could mobilize significant resources against minorities that were seen as allies of external enemies: at least in their rhetoric, ethnic and religious persecutions are usually defensive in nature. The worst period for Middle Eastern Christians followed the social and religious revolution introduced by the Mongol regime in the thirteenth century; and the later Japanese state faced a genuine threat from predatory European colonial powers. In such circumstances, states launched brutal and enduring persecutions, which over decades or centuries could not fail to take their effect. The question of time frame is also important. Although Communist regimes devastated churches and other religious bodies, they had only a few decades to impose their will. In contrast, Christian communities suffered sporadic persecutions over many centuries. Rare indeed is the religion that can withstand a full thousand years of extreme maltreatment.

In considering the role of violence, we would not have to assume that massacres and pogroms need be frequent or regular, or indeed that they need occur more than once every generation or so. Although not necessarily frequent, such outbreaks leave memories that create a pervasive atmosphere of intimidation. These memories instruct the minority community about their inferior status and the vital necessity of not overstepping proper bounds. We might draw an analogy to the effects of race riots and lynchings in the American South before the civil rights era, when sporadic incidents combined to institutionalize fear and submission among African Americans. The difference, of course, between the racial example and the religious is that members of minority faiths always had the option of escaping their lot by conversion, and over time, an ever-greater number took this course.

We also see what we might call a ratchet effect, taking the name of the mechanical device that limits movement to only one direction. For Christians under Muslim rule (and for Jews in Christian Europe), the minority community could expect to exist for decades or even centuries without the outbreak of major violence or persecution, even though petty restrictions and insults were commonplace. On occasion, though, large-scale persecution erupted in response to some natural cataclysm, or to the rise of a particularly zealous regime. Following such an event, the minority community would be reduced or scattered still further, and the survivors of the shrinking minority could then expect peace until the next cycle of intolerance began. The ratchet turned another notch, and the minority moved closer to ultimate elimination or exile.

Beyond Persecution

Even more important than individual acts of intimidation was the long-term process of demographic restructuring and population transfer that states could and did organize. Throughout history, demography has played a crucial role in the rise and fall of religions, and in modern times differential birthrates do much to explain the shift of Christian numbers to the global South. In the Middle East also, higher education and better access to contraception have resulted in Christian communities having much lower birthrates than Muslim neighbors, so that Christians have progressively lost their share of population. Even in the contemporary United States, some believe that differential birthrates go far to explaining the decline of liberal mainline denominations and the growth of evangelical churches.

In earlier times, migration played a much greater role than birthrates in altering the balance between religions, and governments did much to manipulate migration trends. In some cases, as in twelfth-century Spain, this involved population transfers deliberately aimed at undermining religious minorities, and Muslim rulers were particularly anxious to remove Christian populations from the Arabian Peninsula. Over time, though, immigration proved at least as important to religious change as was deportation. Successive governments brought in Muslims to outnumber Christians, and imported Berbers to use against restive Arabs. From the earliest days of the Muslim expansion, new regimes sponsored the migration of Arab and Muslim peoples into what had been Coptic or Syriac territories, reducing the relative power of older-stock populations and their cultures—and their faiths. Over time, intermarriage with these newer groups helped push older families toward accepting Islam. While many native Egyptians did accept Islam on its merits, the presence of these new populations contributed mightily to giving Egypt the strongly Muslim coloring that we find by the late Middle Ages. Between the ninth century and the eleventh, Sicily was another recipient of heavy Arab and Berber immigration.[3]

In Asia Minor, too, Islam grew after 1200 by means of the immigration of new Turkish populations with their different social and economic structures, not dependent on the traditional urban systems. Often, they moved into lands vacated by older-stock people (mainly Greeks) fleeing the constant warfare. As in Egypt or Mesopotamia, Asia Minor gained a Muslim majority less by forcing existing residents to convert than by importing Muslim populations. As

Turkish populations reached a critical mass, the remaining old-stock communities no longer needed to conduct their dealings in Greek and to keep up Greek lifestyles and aspirations. Christianity became marginalized. So successful were these policies in Asia Minor that the Turks used a similar immigration strategy to remodel the Balkans in the Muslim image. Inevitably, the Greek counterattack against Turkish Muslim influence during the 1820s brutally targeted these imported communities.[4]

The fact that a particular faith enjoyed established status also permitted it to withstand disasters that annihilated subordinate religions. Premodern societies occasionally suffered disasters on a scale that modern observers find difficult to contemplate. We think of the destruction wrought by warfare in medieval Asia Minor, the catastrophic impact of the Mongol or Timurid invasions, or the great plagues of the fourteenth century. To find modern parallels, we would have to look to the destruction and social dislocation experienced by Europe by 1945, with the difference that medieval societies could expect no assistance from benevolent external powers: there would be no Marshall Plan.

War and plague would have a similar impact on all religious communities, but only the dominant faith could expect official assistance in reconstructing, in rebuilding structures, reestablishing networks of clergy and charitable institutions. Consider, for instance, the devastation that plague wrought in the structures of the Christian churches of France and England, which suffered long vacancies in bishoprics and other offices. These effects were not repaired for decades, but at least the Christian state and Christian patrons were ultimately there to rebuild, which was not the case for Nestorians in Mesopotamia or Copts in Egypt. Subordinate faiths were all the more likely to be crippled by general disasters if, as so often happened, minority believers had been blamed for the catastrophes, if they were punished as allies of the external attackers or as agents spreading plague.[5]

Over time, the fact that a given religion held power in a particular state was likely to mean an ever-growing numerical majority for that faith, due in part to population changes, voluntary or otherwise. And when states following rival ideologies came into conflict, they made life ever more difficult for minorities by penalizing internal dissenters. Dominance reinforces dominance.

The Power of Islam

Throughout history, Christianity has found Islam to be its most persistent and, often, most successful rival. Quite setting aside the issue of violence and coercion, Muslim regimes over the centuries succeeded wonderfully in creating societies and cultures that exercised overwhelming pressures toward religious conformity, in establishing the faith of Muhammad as the natural default religion, which permeated the whole of culture. Full membership of society was open only to Muslims, while all others faced burdens of varying intensity. Islamic regimes first created a society in which being Muslim was natural, meant being part of the social and cultural mainstream; and then built a world in which being a Christian or Jew consigned one to the status of a despised outsider.

In understanding the appeal of Islam, we should not focus just on the negative burdens imposed on unbelievers. In any society, powerful forces draw subject peoples to assimilate to the ways of their masters. As the fourteenth-century scholar Ibn Khaldun observed, "The vanquished always want to imitate the victor in his distinctive marks, his dress, his occupation, and all his other conditions and customs." Yet the cost was potentially immense, as "a nation that has been defeated and comes under the rule of another nation will quickly perish."[6] The Muslim message was all the stronger because of its profoundly attractive theme of brotherhood, of bringing all believers together into a new human family. This message carried special weight during times of social turmoil, when existing structures were under severe stress.

Outside this family, though, nonmembers faced real difficulties. Even under fairly tolerant regimes, rival religions were strictly limited in their activities, in ways that had a painful impact on Christians who had enjoyed preferential status for several centuries. Clarence Darrow famously noted that the great lesson he had learned in his life was that "[e]very advantage in the world goes with power." Historically, much of that advantage involved the control of the built environment, of the cityscape. Under Muslim rule, churches were tightly constrained in their ability to project their presence physically into the landscape, by the public display of icons and images or statuary, by bell ringing or public processions. It was no longer possible to use the liturgy and the spectacular external decoration of church buildings to offer believers a taste of the ultimate. Even today, the lack of prominent structures or pageantry contributes to the Western neglect of Christian traditions in the Middle East: when painters or photographers or filmmakers wish to portray the region's cities, they focus on dominant Islamic imagery—mosques and minarets. By implication, any Christian presence must be extraneous.[7]

Far from dominating and sanctifying the public landscape, as they might have done in Mediterranean countries a century ago, Christian structures and rituals were forced into varying degrees of concealment, which grew all the more discreet following waves of riot or violence. Over the centuries, for instance, Nestorians abandoned what had once been their common use of icons, and had few opportunities to use the wooden clappers they employed in place of bells. Nor, of course, could Christians do anything that might be interpreted as evangelizing among Muslims. Progressively reducing the conspicuous display of signs of faith reduced the number of reasons for minority believers to maintain their stubborn dissidence, and encouraged conformity.[8]

Just how thoroughly the different faiths internalized these restrictions is suggested by an almost comic incident narrated by the traveler Ibn Battuta, visiting a Genoese settlement in the Crimea about 1330. "We stayed at Kaffa in the mosque of the Muslims. An hour after our arrival we heard bells ringing on all sides. As I had never heard bells before, I was alarmed and made my companions ascend the minaret and read the Koran and issue the call to prayer." They were stopped only by the intervention of fellow Muslims, who feared a religious civil war. But the initial statement is astonishing: in all his vast travels, Ibn Battuta had never heard church bells. The affair had clear symbolic implications. Cities could have a sound-scape based on the Muslim muezzin or Christian bells, but not both. Several times a day, the call to prayer sent a straightforward message about who held political power. In 1378, Egyptian authorities de-stroyed a church at the behest of a man who "had heard the sound of the wooden gongs with which, on the Friday night, announce-ment was made in that church": the old church thereupon became the site of a mosque. When Al-Maqrizi described the crusader cap-ture of coastal Palestinian towns in 1243, he particularly mentions their attempt to annex the sound waves: "They expelled Muslims from the mosque Aksa, made a church of it, and hung bells in the minaret." So emotive was the battle between bells and muezzin that, when Greece was liberated in 1829, the first targets for destruction were the minarets that proclaimed Muslim hegemony every few hours.[9]

Control of the landscape involved positive steps as well as mere restrictions, as the official faith of a state decided who would receive the patronage needed to erect fine buildings and foster great art. In the first century after the Arab conquest, Muslims in Syria and Egypt lived in cities dominated visually by Christianity. Only gradu-ally did wealth pour into the construction of mosques and minarets, great Muslim palaces and libraries. The need to challenge the Chris-tian landscape was the explicit reason for building the Dome of the Rock, and other Muslim states soon followed suit. Egypt's Ibn Tulun Mosque, completed in 879, covers a seven-acre complex. As the cathedrals and temples of Roman Africa decayed, there emerged a new sacred landscape centered on the splendid new mosque of Kairouan. These were the glories that struck the traveler approach-

ing a city, not the discreet churches or synagogues. We can appreciate the power of such landmarks if we think of the prominent older
features that strike us in a European medieval city, whether architec-
tural or artistic—virtually all of which suggest a Christian background. In Islamic countries, by contrast, the city was just as
assuredly Muslim space. Sacred buildings were still more dominant
in smaller communities: again, think of the churches around which
medieval villages clustered.[10]

Also over time, the dominant faith placed its imprint on the historical landscape beyond the cities. The Arab invaders entered a
countryside signposted everywhere by churches and monasteries, by
Roman and Byzantine remains. Many of these places were celebrated for the spiritual power believed to reside there, and became
centers of pilgrimage that tied a particular locality into much wider
webs of regional and international connections. Over the centuries,
Muslims created their own landmarks, their own pilgrim shrines and
historical monuments, which were scattered across all Muslim lands.
The Mamluk dynasty (1250–1517), which so persecuted Christians,
made heroic efforts to create a whole new landscape of Muslim devotion and pilgrimage, aimed especially perhaps at new converts.
Everywhere, they built or restored many shrines, mosques, and ma-
drassas. Just in and around Damascus,

> one could visit a variety of shrines, many revered by Muslims
> and Christians alike: the Mosque of Moses' Footprints, the
> birthplace of Abraham, the Cave of [Abel's] Blood, Adam's
> Cave, the Hunger Cave, the refuge of Mary and Jesus, Elias'
> oratory, and the Cemetery of the Prophets. Within four miles
> of the city were the cemeteries of holy men and women and
> numerous mausolea of multifarious venerables, such as the
> founder of the Umayyad caliphate, Mu'awiyya, and his sister,
> Umm Habiba; various Companions of the Prophet . . . and
> "People of the House" of the Prophet (Umm Kulthum, Ali

Talib's daughter; the children of Hasan and Husayn, the sons of 'Ali, son-in-law of the Prophet); the "Martyrs" . . .; Seth, Noah, and Moses; and numerous other luminaries.[11]

Nor were such centers exclusively religious in nature. Once, Christians knew Tikrit as the site of a great monastery and fine churches. From the twelfth century, though, it was famous as the birthplace of Saladin, and the modern city stands in Salah-ad-Din Province, which was named for him. In the thirteenth century, a mosque was built over the remains of the monastery.

Religious emblems also marked the coins that were the main tokens of official power that most people ever saw. From the end of the seventh century, Umayyad rulers began striking their own Islamic coins, marked with the Muslim profession of faith, while Byzantine coins were strictly proscribed. Public transactions involved these Muslim symbols, and never the cross-marked coins of Eastern Rome.

Muslim societies restructured everyday life so that at every point, the so-called Umaric code made ordinary lay unbelievers conscious of their inferior status, and of the severe limits imposed on their life-chances. Restraints became steadily tighter after the fourteenth century, and by the eighteenth and nineteenth centuries were the source of horrifying injustice. One eighteenth-century Egyptian sheikh comprehensively listed the burdens that should be enforced upon non-Muslims:

They should not be allowed to clothe themselves in costly fabrics which have been cut in the modes which are forbidden to them, in order that they may not offend the sensibilities of poor Muslims. . . . They should not be permitted to employ mounts like the Muslims. They must use neither saddles, nor iron-stirrups, in order to be distinguished from the true believers. They must under no circumstance ride horses because of the noble character of this animal. . . . They are forbidden while going through the streets to ape the manners of the Muslims, and still less those of the cities of the religion. They shall only walk single-file, and in narrow lanes they must withdraw even more into the most cramped part of the road. . . . The absence of every mark of consideration toward them is obligatory for us; we ought never to give them the place of honor in an assembly when a Muslim is present. This is in order to humble them and to honor the true believers. . . . It is no longer permitted them to put themselves, with respect to their houses, on an equal footing with the dwellings of their Muslim neighbors, and still less to build their buildings higher.

Systematic discrimination limited the rights of non-Muslims in all their interactions with Muslims. In legal disputes, unbelievers could not testify against believers. One wrenching restriction involved the basic right of retaliation against insult, which was the basis of enforcement within a society founded on honor. The fact that non-Muslims were forbidden from responding accordingly against Muslims made life extraordinarily difficult. Persistent reminders of inferiority extended into everyday speech, where non-Muslims were forbidden from using the forms of speech reserved for the majority. Depending on the time and place, a Christian who used the greeting "Salaam aleikum" risked getting a beating or worse. Peace was reserved for brothers, for Muslim believers.[12]

These rules were not enforced universally, but they were certainly imposed at particular times and places. "As late as 1820, no Christian in Damascus could wear anything but black, or could ride a horse." A nineteenth-century visitor to northwest Persia remarked that

[t]he Nestorian is not allowed a place in the bazaar; he cannot engage in commerce. And in the mechanic arts, he cannot aspire higher than the position of a mason or carpenter; which, of course, is not to be compared to the standing of the same

trades among us. When our missionaries went to Urumia, a decent garment on a Nestorian was safe only as it had an outer covering of rags to hide it.[13]

Without an organized police force, Islamic states varied greatly in their enforcement of the various rules, but the idea of religious superiority became deeply ingrained within the Muslim community, so that clergy and ordinary believers often felt impelled to enforce proper standards. The obvious presence of deviants—of wealthy Christians riding horses, for example, or speaking and living like Muslims—always offered the potential for popular rabble-rousing. At such times, even tolerant states might feel the need to support persecution as a means of defending their power.

Over time, the pressures on Christian communities grew ever stronger as their faith moved ever closer to marginal status—a creed for the old and politically irrelevant. Such a perception would be all the stronger for the younger generation, who always had the ability to escape their disabilities by conversion.

The Language of Faith

Language was critically important to the religious transition. The rise of Islam meant not just the eclipse of Christianity but the near annihilation of what had hitherto been the commonly spoken vernaculars of the Middle East and the Mediterranean world: of Syriac, Coptic, Greek, and Berber. Already in the eighth century, Arabic was the language of politics and administration from Spain into central Asia, although Persian and Turkish would both become critical vehicles for Islamic thought and culture.

From the earliest years of the Muslim era, the Arabic language and its attendant culture exercised a magnetic pull for non-Muslims, even for church leaders. As early as 800, Christians like Theodore Abu Qurrah, a Melkite bishop born in Edessa, were publishing their treatises in Arabic. The greatest Eastern Christian philosopher of the tenth century, Yahya ibn 'Adi, wrote in Arabic and lived in a thoroughly Arabized intellectual world. Even in the self-confident world of Syriac literature, ninth-century hymn writers began introducing the Arabic poetic device of rhyme.[14]

In ninth-century Mesopotamia, Muslim exclusivist al-Jahiz denounced the Christians not just for their worldly success, but for their immersion in Arabic culture, even to the point of taking familiar Arabic names: "They are called Hasan and Husain and Abbas and Fadl and Ali, and they take all these as surnames; and there is nothing left but that they should be called Muhammad and be surnamed Abu 'l-Qasim!"[15] Such wholesale absorption allowed wealthy and successful minorities to parade their success without any obvious sign of their religious taint, any hint of inferiority, and such overassimilation in all matters except the religious provoked Muslim regimes to enforce the symbolic badges of the Umaric code. But such cultural boundaries did not limit the spread of Arabic, and an Arabic-speaking world had already made a massive leap toward the possible adoption of Islam. As Peter Brown remarks, "[U]ltimately, it was the victory of Arabic which opened the doors to Islamization."[16]

The older languages of the subject peoples fell increasingly into disuse, sometimes because Muslim regimes limited their use in the public sphere. At the start of the eighth century, the caliph Walid I took the historic step of replacing Greek by Arabic in the language of official documents at his court at Damascus. Muslim acquaintance with Greek declined still further when the caliphate moved to Baghdad. Greek also faded early in Egypt, its disappearance made easier by its association with unpopular Byzantine power.[17]

Yet even when such languages did not face direct official sanction, speakers of older tongues knew that they had little chance of getting on in an Arabic world. By the eleventh century, Coptic and Syriac were declining as major languages, and the compiler of the

History of the Patriarchs of Alexandria translated the work into Arabic because "today Arabic is the language that the people of Egypt know . . . most of them being ignorant of Coptic and Greek."[18] Vernacular Coptic faded steadily until it was almost entirely replaced by Egyptian Arabic, probably around the seventeenth century. Today, it is spoken by just two or three families. Syriac lasted rather longer as a mainstream language, but the transition was accelerated by the horrors of the Mongol invasions, and Arabic largely replaced it during the fourteenth century.

In Muslim-dominated Spain, the condemned minority language was the Latin spoken by the Visigoths and the old Roman peoples, and this swiftly fell out of fashion. A ninth-century Spanish Christian lamented,

> Alas, the Christians are ignorant of their own tongue, and Latins neglect their language, so that in all the College of Christ there is scarcely to be found one who can write an address of welcome to his brother intelligibly in Latin, while numbers can be found competent to mouth the flowery rhetoric of the Chaldeans [i.e., Arabs].

The Mozarabs who at their height constituted perhaps 30 percent of *al-Andalus* were Arabic-speaking Christians, who succeeded the older Latinate generations.[19] Reinforcing such cultural trends were the long-term demographic effects of immigration, as newcomers everywhere reinforced the Muslim presence.

The long-term religious consequences for Christianity were grim. The texts and liturgy of the faith were all available in languages that, though venerable, were clearly associated with fading cultures— literally, the words of the very old. Worse, when members of a faith are unable to express their ideas except in a language that is primarily associated with a rival religious system—can use only the words and intellectual categories of another creed—that minority religion is en route to oblivion.

Success Succeeds

In a Muslim-dominated world, it was difficult to avoid the sense that Islam had triumphed, and that that victory was irreversible. Until modern times, the vast majority of people in the Muslim world had limited access to information about life in other cultures, and knew little about advances in Western societies. For much of the history of Islam, moreover, the Christian world was not noticeably ahead in political or economic power, or in culture. When Muslims recalled the crusading era, they remembered a series of wars that they had won, decisively. At least until the eighteenth century, there was little reason to question the assumption that the Muslim world was the heart of civilization, that Islam had won globally and was continuing to win.

Worldly success was a potent force in the growth of Islam, and in the shriveling of Christianity. That fact may be troubling to Christians, whose faith so often extols the triumph of the meek and humble while rejecting worldly success, and who are so familiar with the concept of defeat as the root of long-term victory. In practice, though, Christians often had used material successes as proofs of their faith. As we have seen, church writers pointed to miracles and healings to vouch for the power of Christ, and such events often explained important conversions. Though such claims continued to be made, they were increasingly outweighed by the obvious successes of Muslim states and armies. At several critical moments, Muslim victories proved enormously damaging to the Christian cause, from the early triumphs over the Byzantine Empire onward. As the early Islamic convert 'Ali Tabari explained, "[Muhammad's] victory over the nations is also by necessity and by undeniable arguments a manifest sign of the prophetic office."[20] If God had not been on his side, how could Muhammad's followers possibly have won such stunning victories over ancient empires?

Another turning point just as ruinous for Christians occurred in 1291, at a time when the Mongol rulers of much of the Middle

East were subject to several competing influences—Christian, Muslim, and Buddhist—and elite families were divided between representatives of the rival faiths. Victory might easily have gone in other directions, but the decisive point in Islam's favor was the capture in that year of the Christian fortress of Acre, which ended the crusading venture that had begun with such messianic hopes two centuries earlier. The defeat ended any serious chance that the Western powers might use Acre as a bridgehead to launch new assaults on the Levant. As we have seen, other factors certainly contributed to the more intolerant religious atmosphere of these years, but Acre ensured that in much of the Middle East, it was the Christians who would be the recipients of official persecution. As a Muslim author crowed a few years afterward, Christianity was self-evidently the religion of losers: "[Islam] has blotted out their strong and well defended kingdoms, and their lofty and towering fortifications, and has turned them into refugees in hiding." When Latin Christians invited Kublai Khan to convert, he scoffed: "How do you wish me to make myself a Christian? You see Christians in these parts are so ignorant that they do nothing and have no power."[21]

Other Muslim contemporaries noted that the greatest military victories went to those Islamic states that most rigorously enforced the laws against unbelievers, and recommended that all future rulers emulate them. After the fall of Acre, the long sequence of Ottoman victories meant that it would be over four centuries before Muslims ceased extending their power over new groups of Christians, or until Christian states and forces once more gained the upper hand in their struggles against Muslim forces. Any acquaintance with recent history made nonsense of any claim that God was on the side of Christian states. As one scholar suggests, what turned Christians to Islam was "the common acceptance by Muslim and Christian alike of the error that the favor of God is shown by worldly success."[22]

Self-evidently, Islam represented growth, expansion, and success, in contrast to the tattered shreds of Christianity. Any traveler could see the splendid mosques rising amid the landscape of ruined churches and deserted monasteries. The heart-breaking consistency of defeats, generation after generation, carried a deadly message.[23]

8

The Mystery of Survival

Look in the mirror, and don't be tempted to equate transient domination with either intrinsic superiority or prospects for extended survival.
—Stephen Jay Gould

So potent were the forces mounted against them that it might seem incredible that Christian communities lasted as long as they did, or that at least some groups still survive as sturdy minorities. Instead of trying to understand why religions perish, we should perhaps be asking why they survive at all under such difficult circumstances. What gave some churches the flexibility and fortitude to endure for so long—in some cases, for over a millennium? In trying to answer this question, we can see that some groups developed much more successful strategies than others in terms of coping with minority status, and with persecution, while a few made mistakes that proved lethally self-destructive. These differences are important to recall when we consider charges about the intolerant nature of Islam. Persecution and discrimination could indeed destroy Christianity, but decisions by Christian churches themselves contributed to the outcome.

Survival and Ruin

To take an extreme contrast, we can compare the fate of Christianity in two regions that in different ways had been critical to the development of the early church. Muslim forces occupied Egypt in the middle of the seventh century, and North Africa (roughly, Algeria and Tunisia) over the following fifty years or so. In Egypt, the Coptic Christians coped impressively with the new regime. Coptic Christianity flourishes today, in stark contrast to the faith of North Africa, which was all but extinct within a hundred years of the coming of the Arabs. The Copts are not the only example of extreme Christian resilience over long ages—witness also the Maronites and Armenians—but numerically they are the most significant.

In its day, the African church had been one of the wonders of the Christian world. The great classicist Theodor Mommsen wrote: "In the development of Christianity, Africa plays the first part. If it arose in Syria, it was in and through Africa that it became the religion of the world." Latin Christian traditions developed in Carthage rather than Rome, and Africa was the home of such great early leaders as Tertullian, Cyprian, and Augustine. By the late fifth century, North Africa had five or six hundred bishoprics, while monasteries were a familiar part of the local social landscape. Even after long struggles between rival Christian sects, North Africa in the century after 560 was a potent center of spiritual, literary, and cultural activity: "in no part of the West were the clergy and people so orthodox as in Africa."[1]

Yet within fifty years of the completion of the Arab conquest in 698, local Muslim rulers were apologizing to the caliphs that they could no longer supply Christian slaves, since Christians were now so scarce. Most sequences of bishops end suddenly, and even in the few surviving sees, we find gaps of decades or centuries at a time. Long centuries of darkness are illuminated only briefly. A tenth-century pope consecrated a new archbishop of Carthage, but it is far from clear how many bishops survived within his province. And although isolated Christian communities of African Christians (*Afariqa*) do appear in the eleventh and twelfth centuries, there is little evidence of a semitolerated Christian presence continuing away in the boondocks. What little remained by the twelfth century was ended by the fiercely pious Almohad rulers. For all intents and purposes, though, North African Christianity had largely perished centuries before. The geographical scale of the change must be stressed, as Christianity soon had virtually no visible presence from the western boundaries of Egypt clear across to the Atlantic—over fifteen hundred miles of the southern coastline of the Mediterranean. European Christian powers lacked the faintest hope of a fifth column across the Mediterranean.[2]

Some of the reasons that a modern observer might identify for the church's decline need not necessarily have been fatal. Over the previous century, African Christians had suffered appalling sectarian divisions between various groups, each denouncing the others as heretics. Orthodox Catholics faced puritanical Donatists, Vandal Arians, and insurgent peasant Circumcelliones, and dominant factions were not shy about enforcing their rule through blood and terror. Yet such a statement could equally well be made about most other regions of the late Roman world, including those in Syria and Mesopotamia, where some churches at least took the coming of Islam in their stride. Indeed, we might take the depth of partisanship as a measure of the passion that believers felt about their religion, making it unlikely that they would renounce it overnight. In their day, Egyptian monks had been quite as fanatical and intolerant, occasionally as violent, as the church factions of North Africa.

Where the African church failed was in not carrying Christianity beyond the Romanized inhabitants of the cities and the great estates, and not sinking roots into the world of the native peoples. Like most regions of the Western empire, such as Gaul and Spain, Africa was divided between Latin-speaking provincials and old-stock natives, who spoke their ancient languages—in this case, varieties of Berber. Unlike these other provinces, though, the African church had made next to no progress in taking the faith to the villages and the neighboring tribes, nor, critically, had they tried to evangelize in local languages. This would not have been an unrealistic expectation, in that already by the fourth century missionaries elsewhere were translating the scriptures into Gothic, and Hunnic languages followed by the sixth century. Evidence of the neglect of the countryside can be found in the letters of Saint Augustine, by far the best known of African bishops, whose vision was sharply focused on the cities of Rome and Carthage; he expressed no interest in the rural areas or peoples of his diocese.[3]

Christianity in this region remained as much a colonists' religion as it would be once again during the French Empire of the twentieth century, and, just as in that later period, when the colonists left, so did the religion. Long wars during the sixth and seventh centuries forced many Romanized Africans to flee to other parts of the Mediterranean, and the Arab conquest virtually completed this process. As a Victorian scholar noted, "[T]he African churches were destroyed not because they were corrupt but because they failed to reach the hearts of the true natives of the province. . . . They fell because they were the churches of a party and not of a people."[4] Muslims did not have to eradicate African Christianity, because its believers had already fled.

The Coptic Achievement

In vivid contrast, the Egyptian churches certainly did reach the hearts of their natives, and from early times. Even the name Copt is a corruption of *Aigyptos*—that is, native Egyptians, whose language descends from the tongue of the pyramid builders. (The word *Aigyptos* derives from the name of ancient Memphis, the city of Ptah.) When nineteenth-century scholars translated the hieroglyphics on the Rosetta Stone, they did so by using the language they found spoken in the liturgies of the Coptic church. Though Alexandrians wrote and thought in Greek, Coptic was from the earliest years a sophisticated language of Christian literature and theology, making it easy to spread the faith among ordinary Egyptians. The famous Nag Hammadi collection of alternative scriptures, probably written in the fourth century, is in Coptic.

One measure of the Coptic achievement is the *Life* of Saint Antony, who was born around 270 and who became the founder of Christian monasticism. His biographer Athanasius depicts a native Coptic-speaking Egyptian of respectable stock, living in a small village of the Fayum region, in which Christianity is already the familiar faith of the community. And for all his fame, Antony never learned Greek. Nor did many of the early monks and hermits, who used Coptic Gospels, Psalters, and liturgies. The monks in themselves reinforced popular devotion, because they differed so obviously from the higher clergy who might be seen as tools of distant authority. The monks were very much of the people, far removed from the world of wealth and luxury, and their deep piety and asceticism showed them to be heroic warriors against the forces threatening the community. Peasants, no less than city dwellers, united to support their spiritual troops.[5]

Already by 300, Christianity was firmly rooted among ordinary Egyptians, too deeply to be affected very badly by most disasters that might befall, whether by the loss of the Greek language, of all the great cities, or of their elites. When we also realize that after Antony's time Egyptian Christianity would still have another 350 years of development and tradition before the coming of Islam—at least twelve generations—we can understand just how knotty a task Muslims would have in challenging the older faith.[6]

Even when Coptic itself gave way to Arabic, Christianity was too thoroughly naturalized to vanish without a lengthy struggle. Not all the disasters of the fourteenth century could eliminate this absolute association between Christianity and Egyptian-ness. At the end of the fourteenth century, a Muslim chronicler complained that

> [t]he Copts declare that this country still belongs to them, and that the Muslims evicted them from it unlawfully. Then they often steal as much as they can from the state treasury in the belief that they are not doing wrong. As to the possibility of confiscation and punishment, torture, they hold that the chances of these happening to them are about equal to that of falling sick; that is to say, sickness does sometimes come upon a man, but is not likely to be frequent.[7]

Once a practice is confined to a stigmatized hard core, further elimination is very difficult.

For all the abundant scholarly literature dedicated to Coptic Christianity, one of the richest depictions of its continuing power comes in the 1991 novel *Aunt Safiyya and the Monastery,* by Egyptian writer Bahaa' Taher. The book offers a lyrical portrait of Muslim-Coptic coexistence and friendship in twentieth-century Upper Egypt, where an ancient Christian monastery is integral to the life of the village and region. Even the wildest Muslim bandits respect its sacred quality. Just as in medieval Europe, hunted criminals can safely take sanctuary within the inviolable monastic boundaries.[8]

The Fate of Europe?

The African-Egyptian contrast raises intriguing counterfactual questions as to what might have happened if Muslims had occupied large sections of Europe, as could easily have occurred. Recent historians stress that the notorious Arab incursions were not full-fledged invasion attempts designed for conquest, and Muslim attacks like that defeated at Poitiers in 732 should better be seen as large-scale raiding expeditions, or reconnaissances in force. Yet on repeated occasions in this era, the accidents of warfare transformed raids into missions of conquest, and Islam could easily have projected its power over Gaul, Germany, and beyond. In Spain, after all, the Muslims were invited in by a dissident Christian faction, and the Franks and other nations had their own rebellious minorities, who could easily have sought Arab help. Let us suppose that Muslims secured control over much of western Europe, say in the 730s or 740s. Can we realistically speculate whether European Christianity would have shared the fate of its counterpart in North Africa, or in Egypt?

In all probability, European Christianity would have faced a grim future. Although the faith was very well established in Italy, Gaul, and the Rhineland, where people looked to local shrines and monasteries, it looked more colonial and "African" farther to the north and east, in the sense that the religion was strongly associated with foreigners, whether rulers or missionaries. By 730, Christianity had made only slight incursions into much of Germany and the Netherlands, and as late as 754, Frisian pagans lynched English missionaries. The major evangelization of Saxony began in the 770s, and missions among the Slavs and Scandinavians had made even slighter progress.[9]

In much of western Europe, any successes the missionaries had achieved would have fallen apart once Christian officials and clergy departed. A suggestive story written around 700 tells of English peasants happily watching an imminent shipwreck that was about to claim the lives of some monks. When a clergyman rebuked them for their glee, the rustics

> fumed against him with boorish minds and boorish words and said "Let no man pray for them, and may God have no mercy on any one of them, for they have robbed men of their old ways of worship, and how the new worship is to be conducted, nobody knows."[10]

Such comments make it quite plausible to imagine that, had the Muslims established themselves, the church in large sections of

Europe would have, in the words of the Victorian scholar quoted in chapter 1, "perished so completely that the very causes of its ruin have disappeared."

Adapting

Comparing African and Egyptian circumstances also points to other reasons why churches survived in some regions and failed in others. From earliest times, Christianity had developed in the particular social and economic world of the Mediterranean and the Near East, and networks of church organization and mission followed the familiar routes of trade and travel. Also, this social world was founded upon cities, which were the undisputed centers of the institutionalized church. Mediterranean Christianity was founded upon a hierarchical system of metropolitans and bishops based in cities: even the name *metropolitan* suggests a fundamentally urban system. Over time, though, trade routes changed and some cities lost power or vanished altogether. Between the fifth century and the ninth, these changes had a special effect on the Mediterranean, as sea routes declined in importance and states tended to look more inland, to transcontinental routes within Asia and Africa. This process was accelerated by the impact of plague, particularly during the 540s, and perhaps of climate change. Cities like Carthage and Antioch shrank to nothing, while Damascus and Alexandria lost influence before the new rising stars of Baghdad and Cairo.[11]

These changes coincided with the coming of Islam rather than being caused by that event, but they had immense religious consequences. Churches that remained wedded to the old social order found themselves in growing difficulty, while more flexible or adaptable organizations succeeded. Nestorians and Jacobites coped well for centuries with an Eastern world centered in Baghdad and looking east into Asia. Initially, too, the old urban framework adapted successfully to the Arab conquest, and Christian bishops made their peace quite easily. Matters were very different, though, when the cities themselves were faced with destruction. By the seventh century, the decline of Carthage and its dependent cities undermined the whole basis of the North African church, and accelerated the collapse of the colonial social order. Once the cities were gone, no village Christians remained to take up the slack. The Coptic Church flourished because its network of monasteries and village churches allowed it to withstand changes in the urban system.[12]

One extreme example of this social collapse occurred in Asia Minor, where four hundred years of war, massacre, and enslavement utterly destroyed a society, including the cities on which the whole economy depended. Outside Constantinople, next to nothing remained of the old urban hierarchy, and with the cities there perished the ancient network of bishops and dioceses. Certainly, they had some flexibility, so that dioceses that were destroyed or conquered could be merged with other, more thriving entities, but that worked only as long as some parts of the region were under strong Christian control. Without dioceses, local parishes and village churches could barely continue, even if the villages themselves could have long survived the constant turmoil and bloodshed. And as we have seen, monasteries and shrines could not last for long in an environment of prolonged warfare. The strength of early and medieval Christianity was that it created a sanctified landscape in which Christian institutions were visible everywhere. The weakness of being so heavily invested in real estate was that it left an almost infinite abundance of tempting targets for plunder and destruction, and once these were gone, so were many of the forces that kept believers attached to the faith.

The question must arise as to whether some other kind of organization might have offered a better chance of resisting decline. In theory, we can imagine church structures less dependent on monks and clergy, and lacking the tight hierarchy dependent on the empire's cities. Retroactively, we could even think of a Christianity that looked more Protestant, in the sense of placing more control and initiative in the hands of ordinary believers, whose decentralized church life would depend less on institutions than on direct access to the scriptures. But such an alternative is difficult to conceive realistically, as monasticism and episcopacy were so deeply engrained in Eastern tradition, while the Protestant idea of access to the Bible assumes forms of printing technology that would not be feasible until centuries afterward. And the annihilation of European heretics like the Cathars suggests that even quite imaginative forms of clandestine organization could not withstand unrelenting persecution.

The Geography of Survival

Whatever their beliefs or structures, the fate of religious and cultural minorities owes an immense amount to geography, and thus to conditions beyond human control. In most respects, the churches of Egypt and Mesopotamia had an immense amount in common: both developed flourishing institutional structures and presented their teachings in the language of the ordinary people—namely, Coptic and Syriac. Geography, however, helps explain why the Coptic Church flourishes today whereas its Mesopotamian counterparts shriveled to a pathetic remnant of former glories.

Asian Christians—the communities of Syria, Mesopotamia, and Persia—had the immense benefit of an open door to central Asia and beyond, and as we have seen, their missionary activities built splendidly upon these opportunities. But the other side of that good fortune was the deadly danger of invasion from the barbarous nomadic communities of those regions, from successive waves of Turks and Mongols. Between the eleventh century and the fifteenth, the wars resulting from these invasions destroyed the Christian world of Asia Minor and crushed the churches of Mesopotamia. In contrast, Egypt's protected geographical position helped keep it immune from these conflicts, and Egyptian dynasties largely fought their wars in Syria. Even Timur never invaded, although he did secure the submission of the country's sultan. The survival of

Egyptian Christianity owes much to the land bottleneck joining Egypt and Palestine, Africa and Asia.

In other ways, too, understanding the geography of survival helps us understand the history of Christianity beyond Europe. Quite apart from the large national churches like the Egyptian, many smaller communities continued to exist for centuries after the rise of Islam, while others that seemed comparable in most ways vanished altogether. The crucial distinction was the presence or absence of effective government, which owed much to geography. Before modern times, few governments were able to control every inch of their territory, and minorities found their best refuge in regions where central authority was weakest. An old story tells of the rabbi asked whether an appropriate blessing could be found for the czar at a time when the Russian government was notoriously oppressive and anti-Semitic. The rabbi replied that such a blessing certainly existed: God keep the czar—far away from us.

Natural features created redoubts for unpopular minorities, where the czar (or sultan) was comfortably remote. A geographer who knows nothing about the history of a society can tell from a good map just where we are most likely to find areas of religious dissidence, together with other manifestations of cultural difference such as the survival of minority languages. We would look first for those regions where major cities are rare, with only the minimum number of roads. Often, these areas are marked by difficult physical features—by inaccessible hills, or by swamps and marshes—and it is here we find communities that would be quickly snuffed out in easier terrain. When Fernand Braudel wrote his classic account of the Mediterranean world, he began with the mountains, "a world apart from civilization, which is an urban and lowland achievement. Their history is to have none. . . . In the mountains, then, civilization is never very stable."[13]

Across Europe and the Middle East, minority faiths flourish best in upland settings, where dissidents can take refuge in the hills in time of trouble and, in extreme circumstances, can organize effective resistance. Even modern armies rarely find it easy to suppress irregular warfare in this sort of country, and earlier forces found it next to impossible without nearly exterminating the population. Pastoral and nomadic communities also find it easier to take their wealth with them as they flee, an option not available to landowners and peasants in arable country. Farmers' lives may be more prosperous and stable than those of hill people, but they are also much easier for governments to control. An eighteenth-century traveler in the Levant wrote that "the steepest places have been at all times the asylum of liberty. In traveling along the coast of Syria, we see despotism extending itself all over the flat country and its progress stopped towards the mountains." Another described the Maronites of Mount Lebanon, where "everyone, whether shaikh or peasant, walks continually armed with a fusil and poniards [i.e., a musket and daggers]. This is perhaps an inconvenience but this advantage results from it that they have no novices in the use of arms among them when it is necessary to employ them against the Turks."[14]

That observation about remote refuges applies widely. It is true for proscribed Catholics in Protestant England, for Protestant dissenters in Catholic France and Italy, and for Christians in Mesopotamia. (It also applies to other religions: the Buddhism that we today associate with mountainous Tibet preserves the faith that would once have been practiced throughout lowland India.) The longest-enduring communities of northern Mesopotamia survived in regions at two or three thousand feet. The Christian kingdoms of Armenia and Georgia flourished in the Caucasus, and no part of Armenia is below thirteen hundred feet. In Africa, low-lying Christian Nubia succumbed to Muslim assaults. Ethiopia survived, but only after relocating its capital and main territories into its mountainous heartland. When Muslims conquered most of Spain, the defeated Christian forces created the sturdy kingdom of Asturias in the Cantabrian Mountains of the northwest. From that base, Christian forces began the long process of reconquest.

Often, such inaccessible areas provide refuge for multiple groups of dissidents. Mountainous Lebanon, for example, is home not just to Maronite Christians but also to Shiites and Druze, both of which suffered severely at the hands of orthodox Sunni Muslim regimes. Besides long providing a refuge for Christians, northern Iraq is also the last home for the Yezidis, a sect that inherits many beliefs and practices from the ancient Zoroastrians. Once ensconced in such regions, dissidents were hard to pry out, at least before modern times, and they faced their greatest danger not from states but from rival mountain peoples. Thus at many points the Druze and Shiites have posed the deadliest threat to the Maronites. The states recognized the potential of having such possible allies, and deliberately mobilized selected hill peoples against their neighbors, sometimes by appeals to religion. Through such means, Mesopotamia's Christians were progressively dislodged and largely destroyed by another group of mountain tribes—namely, the Kurds. If we look at a map of the hilly Kurdistan that modern-day activists seek to carve out of several Middle Eastern nations, we can see an accurate portrayal of the lost Christian Mesopotamia.

Unlike these geographical features, other factors protecting dissidents were more temporary but nonetheless important. Just as some minorities could flee into inaccessible hills or badlands, others found comfort in being located in borderlands, from which they could easily seek the protection of neighboring states.[15] The importance of borders and disputed jurisdictions explains the rich tradition of dissidence along the lands that once separated the Roman and Persian empires and that later divided Byzantines from the caliphate. Armenia, northern Syria, and Mesopotamia were successively home to several sects of Christian dissidents, as well as to dualist heretics and the remnants of ancient Gnostic sects. Harran, near Edessa, maintained its overt paganism through centuries of Christian rule, and succumbed to Muslim pressure only in the ninth century; even then, it was far from certain that Harran's conversion was anything more than nominal. (The city also had a thoroughly illegal Manichaean monastery.) In time of crisis, Christians in Upper Egypt could flee over the border to Nubia. Dissidents also took advantage of sympathetic local lords or governors, who might have personal or family ties to an unpopular religion, making them reluctant to carry out draconian orders from the central government.[16]

The End of Survival

Under these various circumstances, Christianity might have survived indefinitely, but two lethal problems arose. The first concerned the character of the faith in these bunker conditions, so focused on mere survival. As the Nestorians demonstrated, Christianity lost most of its vigor, and became the cultural badge of yet another hill tribe. It was insular and radically sectarian, and had little sense of connection to the wider Christian world, except insofar as transnational churches were seen as predatory rivals bent on annexation. When churches did form wider links, as the Maronites and Chaldeans did with the Roman Catholics, these new ties threatened to submerge the distinctive practices that had been essential to their identity.

Also, precisely the conditions that allowed Christian survival proved deadly dangerous with the emergence of modern states that sought to control their entire territory, and had no patience for the tolerance previously granted to dissident regions. Early modern states could tolerate minorities only within remote enclaves where the writ of government barely ran; but exactly those features made the existence of those enclaves intolerable to modern nation-states. Around the world, nineteenth- and twentieth-century states expanded their authority through military conscription, through censuses, and through compulsory education, making it ever harder to hide from authority. Railroads and newspapers, telegraphs and telephones, carried national standards into the farthest reaches of the land. In practice, the czar or sultan never could be kept away, and that development would be critical for minority survival. With a growing sense of national identity, reinforced by grave external dangers, the Ottoman and later Turkish regimes were deeply sensitive to minority regions that might well seek to break away.

In these circumstances, enclaves located near borders looked dangerously inviting for potential invaders. Furthermore, once the decision had been made to eliminate a troublesome community, the new technologies made it easier to send orders to local authorities, to ensure they were obeyed, and to supply the means for mass murder. Although not as central as they would later be in the Nazi genocide, railroads were an important weapon for the Turkish ethnic cleansings after 1915. New forms of transportation contributed to the spread of Muslim militancy by allowing Muslims to travel widely by train and steamship, to share ideas: the multimillion-strong crowds of pilgrims flocking to Mecca are a strictly modern phenomenon. Such wide travel encourages the creation of Pan-Islamic ideologies. Moreover, a fire-breathing sermon preached in Cairo or Constantinople could within days have grim practical consequences for Christians hundreds of miles away. In this new world, not only did the factors that once protected Christians cease to matter; they even invited official intervention. There was no place left to hide.

Such considerations guided the new states that succeeded the Ottoman world, which based their claims to national identity on their ability to defend the nation's territory and to evict both foreign aggressors and their domestic puppets. Kemal Atatürk's regime in Turkey founded its legitimacy on the successes in the war of liberation, which was also the period of ethnic and religious cleansing. Yet, far from ruling as the Islamic hero who defeated the infidels, Kemal himself was a radical secularist who emphasized national loyalties above all.[17] In Iraq, too, although the Assyrian massacres of 1933 horrified the European world, they won wide sympathy in the Middle East and boosted the nascent national identity of an Iraq that had formally come into existence only in the previous year. The immediate consequence of the affair was the passage of a law permitting mass military conscription. The Assyrian campaign also made the career of the Kurdish general responsible, Bakr Sidqi, who was portrayed as both an Iraqi and an Islamic hero, the nemesis of the British. In 1936, he built on this fame to launch the first military coup in modern Iraqi (and Arab) history. If Christians were traitors, then punishing them was patriotic.

Lessons

Observing the decline and ruin of Christian communities offers many lessons for modern Western societies, although not in the directions commonly favored by the far Right—namely, as a deadly warning against the Islamic threat. Historically, all major religions have produced multiple instances of intolerance and persecution, and the scriptures of Islam include considerably fewer calls to blood-curdling violence than do their Christian and Jewish counterparts: witness Joshua's conquest of the land of Canaan, or the ethnic purges associated with Ezra and Nehemiah. Nor, of course, has any Muslim regime ever approached the sophisticated annihilation campaigns of modern ultrasecular regimes, under Hitler and Stalin, Mao and Pol Pot. At various times, some Muslim regimes have been inconceivably brutal, others mild and accommodating. That diversity suggests that episodes of persecution and violence derive not from anything inherent in the faith of Islam, but from circumstances in particular times and places.

In some parts of the modern world, particularly in Africa and Asia, past encounters between Christianity and Islam can seem all too relevant. In such regions, the potential power of an Islamic state and social order is much more than merely a historical question, in that many Muslims today strive to create such entities, and it remains an open question how far these aspirations can be reconciled with the rights of minorities, or even with their existence. As such challenges grow, contemporary Christians can indeed learn lessons from past experience. One involves the idea of success in a society in which religions use worldly prosperity to prove spiritual claims. Many successful global-South churches teach a gospel of prosperity, telling believers that their faith will bring worldly success. Such a doctrine might well be dangerous if Muslim regimes and forces won conspicuous victories while Western influence declined. Global-South Christians are also acutely aware of the danger that they will be seen as puppets or agents of external, Western forces, to be blamed for the sins of Western society. Most such churches strive to put as much symbolic distance as possible between themselves and Euro-American culture, and the policies of Western states.

Even if the perils they face are much less immediate, churches elsewhere can learn from persecutions in bygone eras, and particularly from the very diverse outcomes of various attempts to destroy Christianity. In particular, churches today should discover what some failed entities did to hasten their demise. For churches as for businesses, failure often results from a lack of diversification, from attaching one's fortunes too closely to one particular set of circumstances, political or social. Churches might, for instance, try to secure their position by allying with a particular nation or political cause, but that is a gamble, and in the worst scenario, such a linkage could draw down the wrath of political rivals. Better than anyone else, churches should understand the concept of transience—the fact that political arrangements and allegiances are seldom lasting, however permanent they may seem at a given time.

This observation also applies to social and economic matters. Churches often make the mistake of imitating what seems at the time to be the natural and inevitable shape of secular society, and allocate resources accordingly. In the sixth century, it was difficult to contemplate a future world that might not always be based on a flourishing Mediterranean trade and the cities it sustained, just as later generations of Christians believed that society would always be founded on agriculture and village life. Matters do, of course, change, in ways that can leave once-great churches struggling badly.

When serious challenges arise, either from hostile governments or, more likely, rival faiths, churches are ill prepared to respond.

Such failure is also likely when churches find virtually all their members among one particular ethnic or linguistic group while neglecting others. Christianity then becomes a badge of class or race rather than an open invitation to the whole society. Such a formula can work well for long periods, but if that narrow group declines— or indeed vanishes, as in the African case—churches face disaster. Conversely, churches succeed when they reach broadly across sections of society and make their religion part of the ordinary lived reality of a diverse range of communities. The effects become apparent in times of stress or persecution. While an individual might agree under duress to change a lightly worn religious label, such a transition is very unlikely when religious loyalties are intimately bound up with the traditions and thought-world of the wider community.

Churches also survive best when they diversify in global terms, so that they are not dependent on just one region of the world, however significant that region might appear at a given time. For all its most energetic efforts, the great Nestorian Church accomplished little outside Asia, where it was destroyed by the twin dangers of Islamic expansion and resurgent Chinese nationalism. Losses in one area could not be counterbalanced by gains elsewhere. And although the analogy might not seem fair, in that we are dealing with a denomination that is anything but dead, consider the fate of the modern Orthodox churches. In 1900, the Orthodox represented 21 percent of the world's Christian population, while Catholics made up 48 percent. Over time, though, Catholics benefited enormously from their presence in growing sections of the global South, while Orthodox missions enjoyed limited success, and Catholics were much more likely than Orthodox to carry their faith with them to new parts of the world. Catholics, in other words, invested in emerging markets, while the Orthodox did not. After 1917, Orthodox believers suffered enormously under Communist persecution. When European birthrates declined steeply in the late twentieth century, this trend hit the Orthodox world very severely while affecting only that portion of Catholic Christianity that lived in Europe. Today, Catholics account for 52 percent of Christians, but the Orthodox just 11 percent.[18]

Churches must adapt, but they face the grave dilemma of just how far to take such accommodation. This is critical when churches are confronted with a powerful and hostile hegemonic culture, creating a society with many temptations to accommodate. Historically, Christians faced the issue of whether to speak and think in the language of their anti-Christian rulers. If they refused to accommodate, they were accepting utter marginality, and cutting themselves off from any participation in a thriving society. Yet accepting the dominant language and culture accelerated the already strong tendency to assimilate to the ruling culture, even if the process took generations. Although a comparable linguistic gulf does not separate modern Western churches from the secular world, Christians still face the dilemma of speaking the languages of power, of presenting their ideas in the conceptual framework of modern physics and biology, of social and behavioral science. To take one example, when churches view sin as dysfunction, an issue for therapy rather than prayer, Christians are indeed able to participate in national discourse, but they do not necessarily have anything to offer that is distinctive. Nor is there any obvious reason why believers should retain their attachment to a religious body that in its language and thought differs not at all from the secular mainstream. Too little adaptation means irrelevance; too much leads to assimilation and, often, disappearance.

In addition to such practical lessons, historical experience can teach modern Western Christian communities to put threats or controversies in context. Modern states may do things that churches criticize heartily, to the point that clergy could conceivably find themselves jailed for opposing government policies: we think of conservative European Christians who face hate-crime charges for denouncing homosexuality as sinful. Realistically, though, no foreseeable Western regime is going to attempt a true persecution of Christianity. Such circumstances could in theory arise—of a government that began not just restricting church activities, but seeking to replace Christianity with a whole all-compassing rival ideology, whether secular or religious—but we are a long way from any such scenario. Persecution has been one of the constant facts of Christian history, and we should not trivialize it. When we know the authentic history of anti-Christian persecution and discrimination, we realize how sparing we should be in deploying such terminology today.

9

Endings and Beginnings

The beginning of Christendom is, strictly, at a point out of time.
—Charles Williams

Shusaku Endo's novel *Silence* has as its central character Father Sebastian Rodrigues, the last serving priest of the seventeenth-century mission to Japan. Although Father Sebastian has been trained to expect persecution and martyrdom, the anti-Christian campaign he witnesses appalls him less because of its extreme ferocity than for its apparent lack of meaning. Why, he asks, are Christians willing to die for an endeavor that is so conspicuously failing? And why, amid all the persecution, does God offer no signs of hope? Already, twenty years have passed since the start of the great inquisition:

> The black soil of Japan has been filled with the lament of so many Christians; the red blood of priests has flowed profusely; the walls of the churches have fallen down; and in the face of this terrible and merciless sacrifice offered up to him, God has remained silent.[1]

Knowing that churches are born in blood, he is initially willing to suffer the torment or death that might prove to be the labor pains of a future Japanese Catholicism; but he has no intellectual framework to cope with the death of a church. Encountering only a divine silence, he is driven to ask whether God exists, and if so, whether God takes any interest whatever in human affairs.

Contemplating the extinction of Christian communities, others might also be moved to consider profound issues of meaning, which recall the agonized dilemmas of Jewish thinkers seeking to reconcile the fact of the Holocaust with the existence of a just God. In the presence of such horrors, why did the skies not darken? One might even see the failure of churches as a potent argument against the truth of Christianity. If in fact the religion is true, if God intends his church to carry a message to the utmost ends of the earth, why would he ever allow that church to die? Is God silent, or nonexistent? Christians have always believed that God guides all earthly affairs. An ancient hymn prays to Christ as incarnate Wisdom:

> O come, Thou Wisdom from on high,
> Who orderest all things mightily.

But did that mighty "ordering" include the annihilation of many of the world's churches, the persecution or defection of their believers?

So often, too, it is difficult to see in this story the workings of providence, as opposed to blind chance. The survival or eclipse of churches seems to depend on the decisions of particular individuals, on the outcome of battles, or indeed of geographical factors. If not for the defensible land bridge separating Egypt from Western Asia, would the Coptic Church be with us today? Persecuted churches could endure for centuries above the two-thousand-foot contour, but succumbed nearer to sea level. From a secular standpoint, such stories just remind us yet again of the role of political factors, and indeed of chance, in shaping the history of religions. If matters had worked out differently, Manichaean Uygurs or Christian Keraits might have transformed the history of the Middle East, rather than Muslim Turks. In terms of better-known historical events, if Henry VIII's first queen had borne a son, perhaps England would have remained loyal to the popes and to the Roman Catholic Church, with all that would have implied for the later history of North America and the wider world.

For Christians, or for other believers, the apparent role of chance or randomness raises difficult questions. If the history of Christianity is at its heart a tale of the chance survival of particular forms of faith, how is it possible to speak of any meaning or purpose in that process? Even if we imagine the workings of subtler forms of divine intervention that we cannot immediately understand, the historical process still seems bizarre and puzzling. In fact, the search for meaning is not as hopeless as it may appear, but the questions raised must be addressed. Besides the missionary theology cultivated by many churches, we also need a theology of extinction.

Explaining Disaster

The ruin of Christianity in a particular region might confound Christians who have long been accustomed to seeing the expansion of their faith as a fundamental expectation. Missionaries through the ages have been inspired by the Great Commission that Jesus gives his followers at the end of the Gospel of Matthew: go and make disciples of all nations. Certainly for the last five centuries, the trajectory of Christian history seems to have been one of constant growth beyond the confines of Europe. That pattern has never been more true than in our own time, as Christianity has spread so rapidly in Africa and Asia. In the triumphant words of a hymn composed a century ago, at the climax of the Western missionary boom:

> Lift high the cross, the love of Christ proclaim
> Till all the world adore his sacred Name.

God, it seems, wants to spread the news of his truth to the whole world, and that mission is coming daily closer to fruition.

But how then to explain the failures? What if Christians *do* make disciples of all nations, but subsequently lose them or their descendants? How can we account for such devastating reversals as the annihilation of the church in North Africa, the crushing of Catholic missions in Asia, and, above all, the strangulation of the faith in the Middle East? Presumably, each of these failures happened regardless of countless fervent but unanswered prayers. In terms of its global reach, only in very modern times has Christianity resumed the span that it had achieved a thousand years ago. Christianization, obviously, is not an inevitable process, nor a one-way road.

In trying to understand the death of churches, several possible explanations come to mind, some much less convincing to modern ears than others. Throughout Christian history, observers seeking to understand catastrophe have turned to the Bible. They have looked in particular at the many cases in the Old Testament in which Israelite kingdoms fell to massacre and exile, leaving only a tiny righteous remnant as the basis for later building. These disasters are generally explained in terms of the failings of those societies, their refusal to obey divine laws, especially to enforce strict monotheism. When the Turks sacked Edessa in the 1140s, Michael the Syrian described how

> the city of Abgar, the friend of Christ, was trampled underfoot *because of our iniquity.* . . . Some aged priests . . . recited the words of the prophet, "I will endure the Lord's wrath, because I have sinned against Him and angered Him." And they did not take flight, nor did they cease praying until the sword rendered them mute.[2]

Such punishments could be understood as a form of correction from which the society would learn lessons for the future, and from which it would emerge stronger. This was, after all, a society in which fathers were expected to apply strict corporal punishment to erring children.

For centuries after the Arab conquest, Christians explored the scriptures to understand the scourging they were enduring. In the tenth century, Bishop John of Córdoba described the compromises that Spanish Christians had to make under Muslim rule, which he delicately described as "the great calamity that we suffered for our sins." The Syriac-speaking churches often favored this interpretation. Solomon of Basra in the 1220s traced the history of Muslim victories in the form of a retroactive prophecy:

> [T]here shall the fat ones of the kingdom of the Greeks, who destroyed the kingdoms of the Hebrews and the Persians, be destroyed by Ishmael, the wild ass of the desert; for in wrath shall he be sent against the whole earth, against man and beast and trees, and it shall be a merciless chastisement. It is not because God loves them that He has allowed them to enter into the kingdoms of the Christians, but by reason of the iniquity and sin which is wrought by the Christians, the like of which has never been wrought in any one of the former generations.

And such an analysis is by no means confined to medieval thinkers: we think of modern-day evangelicals like Jerry Falwell and Pat Robertson blaming the horrors of September 11 on the immorality and sinfulness of contemporary America. God might be chastening his people, or perhaps the explanation was even more fundamental: sin had become so rampant that he had determined to destroy the society utterly, and to begin again, by forming a whole new community. Some early Eastern writers thought the Arab victories might be an apocalyptic sign, the overthrow of worldly rulers that presaged the end of things.[3]

A modern reader of literal inclinations might also see the destruction of the historic churches of Africa and Asia as a form of punishment. Perhaps they had failed in theological or moral terms, leading God to withdraw his favor from them, or else God was punishing them actively, using them as an object lesson for other Christians. The English Victorian editor of the works of historian John of Ephesus explicitly adopted such an Old Testament perspective when he wrote that

> the young Mahomet, repelled in his first inquiries by the idolatrous aspect which Christianity outwardly bore, was rising to be the instrument of God's just anger against the Eastern Church. For the picture which John has drawn for us . . . of the narrowness and bigotry, the fierce strifes, the want of self-restraint, the injustice and cruelty and utter absence of Christian charity, which characterized all parties in his days alike, makes us feel that the times were ripe for punishment.[4]

Many of the vanished African and Asian churches were, after all, heretical by the standards of the Catholic/Orthodox tradition—largely Monophysite, but also Nestorian.

Obviously, such opinions carry little weight for most mainstream Christians today. Few would contemplate a God so rigid in his devotion for precise orthodoxy, as laid down in the fifth-century councils, that he would allow his mildly erring servants to suffer massacre, rape, and oppression. And Orthodox and Catholic believers have repeatedly been the worst sufferers from persecution and ethnic cleansing, especially in medieval Asia Minor. Nor do we have any evidence that the uprooted churches were any more sinful or lacking in faith than those anywhere else in the world. Some of the main victims included such missionary powerhouses as the Nestorian churches of the high Middle Ages.

It is no less repellent to think of God discarding portions of the Christian world that do not fit in with a long-term process of sculpting or shaping. Can we imagine a deity permitting churches to be slaughtered because they do not mesh with a particular vision of the Christian future—for instance, that the destiny of the church was to be in Europe, so that the older centers no longer mattered? Creative destruction is a controversial enough theory in economics, and is still more dubious when applied to theology.

Like a Watch in the Night

Other possible approaches demand more respect. For one thing, we must be careful in describing a religion as extinct, either entirely, or in a particular area; churches end, but The Church goes on. A conservative Catholic once criticized my statement that the North African church had ceased to exist. Of course it had not, he argued. True, the dioceses in question happened, at present, to have no clergy, no members or lay believers, and no buildings. But regardless of the number of people it included, the church never ceased to exist as a body at once mystical and institutional. Diocesan names and identities survived, and the Catholic Church still used them as honorary titles. A modern cleric might be given the honorary title of an African or Asian see that ceased to exist as a functioning body a thousand years ago and was now *in partibus infidelium,* in the lands of unbelievers. At various times, such phantom bishops have been quite numerous in the Roman church.

At the time, I thought my colleague's views sounded absurdly legalistic: if Christianity had lost all its living and breathing followers in Tunisia (say), what did it matter if the institutional minutiae survived? But on reflection, I think he was making a worthwhile point about the time span of human history. The scriptures of many religions remind us that the divine does not necessarily work according to our concepts of time. As the Psalmist declares, "[A] thousand years in your sight are just like yesterday when it is past, like a watch in the night." Perhaps only our limited awareness of time leads us to think that the ruin of a church has happened "forever," when all we mean is that, by our mortal standards, we can see no chance of it being reversed. In fact, religions are like biological organisms, which do not become extinct just because they are driven from a particular environment. Provided they continue to exist elsewhere, they might well return someday to recolonize. And often, in the human context, memories of that historical precedent help shape the new settlement.

Other religious traditions offer powerful examples of how historical memory shapes the return to old habitats. The best-known example of this process is the return of the Jews to the land of Palestine, from which they seemed to have been definitively expelled in the second century. For many centuries, most outside observers thought that the uprooting of the Jews was a clear sign of divine wrath, an eternal judgment, yet this verdict was utterly reversed some eighteen hundred years after the original catastrophe.

Other final exits have proved less terminal than they might once have seemed. In Spain, Muslim political power was broken in 1492, and Muslims as a community lingered on only into the early seventeenth century, when they were altogether driven out. After a 350-year gap, however, Muslim immigration resumed as the Spanish economy boomed, and today Spain has perhaps a million Muslims, the new *Moros.* As a proportion of the population, Muslims will undoubtedly grow in importance over time, because of the difficulties of regulating migration into Europe, and also because of the historically low birthrates of old-stock Spaniards. Of course, the mainly poor North African migrants who flooded into Spain did not choose that destination because of vague memories of the lost splendors of *al-Andalus,* but educated Muslims are anxious to reestablish old ties. An evocative symbol of the new presence came in 2003 when the Spanish Muslim community dedicated the new mosque at the historic capital of Granada, near the ancient Alhambra palace. However totally eradicated Islam seemed, it came back.

Christianity offers similar stories, and the global Christianity that perished in the late Middle Ages has revived in the past century. China offers an amazing example of long-term continuity. The Christian faith has established itself in that nation on at least four occasions, and the first three missions ended in ruin. This was the case with the first Nestorian mission, which operated from the seventh century through the ninth; their second attempt in the thirteenth and fourteenth centuries; and the Roman Catholic venture of the sixteenth and seventeenth. This last mission collapsed after 1700, when the Vatican prohibited Jesuit attempts to accommodate Chinese customs and language in the liturgy, provoking the Chinese government to persecute Christians as agents of a foreign power. The last remnants of that particular underground church disappeared in the mid–eighteenth century. The fourth Christian incursion began with Protestant and Catholic missionary ventures in the nineteenth century, although this, too, seemingly suffered total defeat when the Communists took over in 1949. Since that date, however, China's Christian community has flourished, growing in number from perhaps 5 million in 1949 to anywhere between 50 and 90 million today. Although estimates vary widely, even the lower figures would already give China one of the world's largest Christian populations. And China's revived churches have a potent missionary dynamic, rooted firmly in memories of Asia's Christian roots. The country's Back to Jerusalem movement aims to send thousands of Chinese missionaries across central Asia into the Middle East so that Asian missionaries will re-evangelize what is now the Muslim world. They plan in effect to restore the Silk Road as a highway for Christian missions.[5]

Knowing this subsequent history must affect how we judge the earlier ventures. In the late tenth century, for instance, an Arabian Nestorian monk reported the horrible discovery he had made on a visit to China. "Christianity had become quite extinct in China," he found. "The Christians had perished in various ways; their church been destroyed; and but one Christian remained in the land."[6] Perhaps the Nestorians were tempted to write off their Chinese missions as having failed forever, but as we have seen, *forever* can be a risky term to apply to human affairs, and so can *extinction*. And even if particular denominations or churches perish, Christian believers do in fact return, and flourish. Nestorians planted, Catholics watered, and many churches ultimately benefited. To return to Endo's example, any thought of Christianity returning in force to Japan seems absurd today, but who can speak with confidence of matters in a hundred years, or a thousand?

Also, while it is far from clear whether different phases of such missions have any connection with each other, we should not presume that just because we cannot see such linkages, they do not exist. In some cases, even failed missions leave memories that guide later ventures, while mystics discern spiritual connections that cannot be approached through the techniques of conventional history. As the historian Leopold von Ranke once remarked, all ages are equidistant from eternity, and just as immediately accessible to God's presence. Catholic doctrine includes the idea of the Communion of Saints, in which the holy and redeemed of all generations and all eras stand equally before God, and are equally accessible to those who invoke them.

Alongside Endo's *Silence,* we might read another great Christian novel—namely, Charles Williams's *Descent into Hell,* which also deals with themes of martyrdom and, in worldly terms, failure. One of the book's characters is a sixteenth-century Protestant about to be executed for his faith, but his fear of suffering and pain means that he dreads giving in to his persecutors. He draws courage from a mystical linkage with his descendant, a woman in the twentieth century. The lives of both individuals find meaning and purpose across long centuries that for us demarcate separate worlds, but which have no existence in the mind of God. Such a connection is absurd in terms of secular thought, as God does a miserably poor job of respecting human precision about time and space. But such a story reminds us that long ages of Christian absence that we might clumsily term an "eternity" might in reality be no such thing.

God in History

Similarly, in terms of our limited perceptions, we should be careful about speaking of "blind chance," or assuming that the rise or fall of Christian communities is solely a matter of political and social circumstances. Deeply ingrained in the Christian tradition, as in the Jewish and Muslim faiths, is the concept of a God who intervenes in history, through many and diverse ways. In the Bible, we hear of God guiding history through determining the outcome of battles, through granting or withholding children, through shortening or extending lives. Often, God permits his chosen people to suffer defeat and dispersal, for reasons no mortal can discern at the time. The book of Isaiah presents the pagan king Cyrus as the agent fulfilling God's will in this world, whether or not the Persian ruler had any inkling of the fact. To paraphrase an earlier remark, the fact that we cannot discern purpose or guidance in earthly events does not mean that none exists. To the contrary, we might argue that a purpose that can be easily traced—for instance, God always granting victory to his Catholic servants, or his Muslim followers—would be evidence of a simple deity of brute strength more like those of pagan Greece or Rome, rather than the complex God of history presented by later faiths.

For Christians, the destruction of churches also focuses attention on the role of other religions in the divine plan, assuming that such exists. If we assume for the sake of argument that Christianity's claims are genuine, why did God permit that religion to suffer so many severe setbacks at the hands of Islam, and in fact to be replaced by Islam over so large an area of the world? How might Islam be fitted within that Christian worldview?

Through much of the Old Testament, outside peoples like the Assyrians and Babylonians feature chiefly for their relevance to the fate of Israel, and serve as walk-on characters only in that particular drama: their story has no interest in its own right. In much Christian history, too, other religions—especially Islam—play a comparable role. Islam is commonly seen as the alien force that God, for whatever mysterious reasons, permits to scourge or destroy his church. Little thought is given to those Christians, individuals or communities, who accept other religions: they just drop off the map of faith. They become immaterial to the main story, except as possible future targets for reconversion. When in 1933 Laurence Browne published his innovative and wide-ranging work *The Eclipse of Christianity in Asia,* he concluded with a brusquely dismissive chapter titled "The Empty Triumph of Islam." Although Islam triumphed across the Middle East, largely eliminating Christianity, this scarcely mattered because the victors inherited a dying society, and anyway, he continued, their own faith was bankrupt:

> Lest any suppose that the eclipse of Christianity was in any sense a real triumph for Islam, it is well to remember that this very period marks the turn of the tide for Islam. . . . From the fifteenth century Islam had no religious contribution to give to the world, unless one includes its effect in modern times on the primitive races of Africa.[7]

While we can see here an element of sour grapes, Browne was accurately reflecting a then-common Western view of Islam as a spiritual and cultural dead end.

Although they still might not know exactly what to make of it, many modern Christians would reject the assumption that Islam represented either the dark side of the force or, perhaps even more insultingly, an irrelevant state of nonbeing. If Islam is not understood as the scourge that God applies to faithless Christians—and nor is it, as Muslims believe, the only true faith—then how exactly should it be seen? Might Christians someday accept that Islam fulfils a positive role, and that its growth in history represents another form of divine revelation, one that complements but does not replace the Christian message? The linkage between the two religions goes far beyond an ultimate grounding in Abrahamic tradition, for as we have seen, the development of Islam can scarcely be understood except in the context of centuries of close contact with Eastern Christianity.

However difficult such a reappraisal might be, we recall how fundamentally Christian views of Judaism have changed over the past few decades. Not long ago, the common Christian approach was one of supersession, the idea that the Christian covenant replaced and invalidated the older Jewish covenant. More recently, many contemporary Christian theologies accept the eternal value of God's covenant with Israel, with the implication that Christian evangelism of Jews is unnecessary and unacceptable. On the same grounds, even to speak of the "Old Testament" has unacceptable implications of supersession, and many prefer to use the term *Hebrew Bible*.

Determining the proper relationship between Christianity and Islam appeared much less critical when Muslims were not a common presence in Western societies, but of course they are today, particularly in Europe.[8] And international conflicts give special urgency to such a rethinking. Christian theologians must of necessity give thought to the nature of Islam, whether they see it as a global adversary in a spiritual cold war, as a Christian heresy, or as an equally valid path to God. That rethinking has obvious implications for understanding the closely linked history of the two faiths through the centuries. Do churches simply die? Or does something positive rise from their ruins?

Winning the World

Perhaps theological attempts to explain the destruction of churches or of "Christian nations" are asking the wrong question, if they judge success and failure by the standards of the secular world. When, for instance, a Christian community loses political or cultural hegemony, historians might conventionally think of it as having failed, as if the faith must of necessity be allied to political power,

and even military victory. Although such a linkage to worldly success was commonplace in earlier times, it has fewer adherents today.
Instead of seeking explanations for the loss of divine favor, Christians should rather stress the deep suspicion about the secular order
that runs through the New Testament, where the faithful are repeatedly warned that they will live in a hostile world, and a transient one.
Nowhere in that scripture are Christians offered any assurance that
they will hold political power, or indeed that salvation is promised
to descendants or to later members of a particular community. Perhaps the real mystery of Christianity is not in explaining failure or
eclipse at particular times, but rather in accounting for the successes
elsewhere.

Indeed, someone from the Anabaptist tradition might argue that
minority status and persecution are the natural and predictable outcome of attempting to live a Christian life, and it is the communities
that coexist comfortably with state power that have departed from
the norm. What matters is not the size or numbers claimed by
churches, but rather the quality of witness demonstrated by Christians in their particular circumstances. Of course, Christians were
persecuted in seventeenth-century Japan, and in many other places
before and since. And just as evidently, Christians have often experienced the status of being persecuted minorities, or, commonly, persecuted majorities, sometimes in societies they had once dominated.
Why should any historically informed observer expect matters to be
different? As the letter to the Hebrews declares, here, we have no
abiding city.

Looking at the sweep of Christian history, we are often reminded
of this message of the transience of human affairs, and, based on
that, of the foolishness of associating faith with any particular state
or social order. Even the Roman Empire was not to exist forever.
Yet while Christian states have come and gone, not all the apparent
disasters that afflicted particular communities have prevented the
growth of what is today the world's most numerous religion, and
which will remain so for the foreseeable future. Although he was

describing the Roman Catholic papacy, the nineteenth-century Lord Macaulay might well have been writing of the wider church that spans denominations:

> She saw the commencement of all the governments and of all the ecclesiastical establishments that now exist in the world; and we feel no assurance that she is not destined to see the end of them all. She was great and respected before the Saxon had set foot on Britain, before the Frank had passed the Rhine, when Grecian eloquence still flourished at Antioch, when idols were still worshipped in the temple of Mecca. And she may still exist in undiminished vigour when some traveller from New Zealand shall, in the midst of a vast solitude, take his stand on a broken arch of London Bridge to sketch the ruins of St. Paul's.[9]

The more we study the catastrophes and endings that befell individual churches in particular eras, the better we appreciate the surprising new births that Christianity achieves in these very years, in odd and surprising contexts. Just as Turkish power was reaching its height in the traditional Christian lands of the Middle East and the Balkans, so the seafaring Christian powers were bringing their faith to the New World and the Pacific. And while the 1915–25 period in the Middle East marked the extinction or ruin of ancient Christian communities, this was exactly the era in which the religion began its epochal growth in black Africa, arguably the most important event in Christian history since the Reformation. But the history can be appreciated in its fullness only by acknowledging the defeats and disasters alongside the triumphs and expansions.

The fictional Father Rodrigues could find no explanation for the divine silence in the face of the annihilation of churches. Yet perhaps, the silence is not as baffling as it seems. Silence, after all, comes in two very different forms. Sometimes, indeed, nobody is speaking; but on other occasions, people are unable or unwilling to listen to what is being said. Christians believe that God speaks through history; and only by knowing that history can we hope to interpret momentous events like the Japanese persecutions and the fall of the Asian churches. Yet Christians have systematically forgotten or ignored so very much of their history that it is scarcely surprising that they encounter only a deafening silence. Losing the ancient churches is one thing, but losing their memory and experience so utterly is a disaster scarcely less damaging. To break the silence, we need to recover those memories, to restore that history. To borrow the title of one of Charles Olson's great poems: the chain of memory is resurrection.

Notes

A NOTE ON NAMES AND -ISMS

1. Raphaël J. Bidawid, ed., *Les lettres du patriarche nestorien Timothée I* (Vatican City: Biblioteca Apostolica Vaticana, 1956), 27–28.

1. THE END OF GLOBAL CHRISTIANITY

1. James Bissett Pratt, *Why Religions Die* (Berkeley and Los Angeles: Univ. of California Press, 1940). For the obliteration of Indian Buddhism, see Charles Allen, *The Buddha and the Sahibs* (London: John Murray, 2002). For Zoroastrianism, see Jamsheed K. Choksy, *Conflict and Cooperation* (New York: Columbia Univ. Press, 1997).

2. Michael Burleigh, *Sacred Causes* (New York: HarperCollins, 2007).

3. C. R. Boxer, *The Christian Century in Japan, 1549–1650* (Berkeley: Univ. of California Press, 1967; first published 1951); Andrew C. Ross, *A Vision Betrayed* (Maryknoll, NY: Orbis, 1994).

4. Philip Jenkins, *The Next Christendom* (New York: Oxford Univ. Press, 2002); Lamin Sanneh, *Disciples of All Nations* (New York: Oxford Univ. Press, 2007). In recent years, a number of writers have attempted truly global histories of Christianity. See, for instance, Adrian Hastings, ed., *A World History of Christianity* (Grand Rapids, MI: W. B. Eerdmans, 1999); David Chidester, *Christianity: A Global History* (San Francisco: HarperOne, 2000); Dale T. Irvin and Scott W. Sunquist, *History of the World Christian Movement: Earliest Christianity to 1453* (Maryknoll, NY: Orbis Books, 2001); Paul R. Spickard and Kevin M. Cragg, *A Global History of Christians* (Grand Rapids, MI: Baker Book House, 2001); John W. Coakley and

Andrea Sterk, eds., *Readings in World Christian History,* vol. 1 (Maryknoll, NY: Orbis Books, 2004); and Martin E. Marty, *The Christian World* (New York: Modern Library, 2008).

5. Estimates of Christian numbers are from David B. Barrett, *World Christian Encyclopedia,* 1st ed. (Nairobi, Kenya: Oxford Univ. Press, 1982). Scholars have long known of these Asian churches and their missions. After the Eastern churches fell into decline, they became the focus of a whole genre of academic study of the "Christian Orient." The foundation work was the *Oriens Christianus in Quatuor Patriarchatus Digestus* of Michel Le Quien, published posthumously in 1740. This particular subset of Orientalism was a booming field in the nineteenth century, as Euro-American travelers clambered over Syriac and Coptic monasteries, often in search of manuscripts. Typical titles include Asahel Grant, *The Nestorians; or, The Lost Tribes* (New York: Harper, 1841); and George Percy Badger, *The Nestorians and Their Rituals* (London: J. Masters, 1852). See also Thomas Laurie, *Dr. Grant and the Mountain Nestorians* (Piscataway, NJ: Gorgias Press, 2005); and William Taylor, *Antioch and Canterbury* (Piscataway, NJ: Gorgias Press, 2006). For the discovery of Egypt, see Somers Clarke, *Christian Antiquities in the Nile Valley* (Oxford: Clarendon Press, 1912). The Asian missions were thoroughly familiar to Edward Gibbon in the eighteenth century, and in the 1920s and 1930s Kenneth S. Latourette presented the story to a general audience. Latourette was one of the most influential modern church historians, whose works became standard texts for seminaries and history departments. Yet despite all these efforts, the story is barely known to the vast majority of Euro-American Christians. Kenneth Scott Latourette, *A History of Christian Missions in China* (New York: Russell and Russell, 1967; first published 1929). Kenneth Scott Latourette, *A History of the Expansion of Christianity,* 7 vols. (New York: Harper and Brothers, 1937–45); vol. 2 is titled *The Thousand Years of Uncertainty, A.D. 500–A.D. 1500.*

6. Bidawid, *Lettres.* Seleucia formed a twin city with the old Parthian capital of Ctesiphon, and the patriarchal see is sometimes called Seleucia-Ctesiphon. For surveys of the "Oriental" churches, see Walter F. Adeney, *The Greek and Eastern Churches* (New York: C. Scribner's Sons, 1908); Adrian Fortescue, *The Lesser Eastern Churches* (London: Catholic Truth Society, 1913); Beresford James Kidd, *The Churches of Eastern Christendom from A. D. 451 to the Present Time* (London: Faith Press, 1927); Donald Attwater,

The Christian Churches of the East, 2 vols. (Milwaukee: Bruce Pub. Co., 1947–48); Aziz S. Atiya, *A History of Eastern Christianity* (Notre Dame, IN: Univ. of Notre Dame Press, 1967); Ken Parry, *Eastern Christianity* (New York: Routledge, 2006); Ken Parry, David J. Melling, Dimitri Brady, Sidney H. Griffith, and John F. Healey, eds., *The Blackwell Dictionary of Eastern Christianity* (Oxford: Blackwell, 2000).

7. John Strugnell, "Notes on the Text and Transmission of the Apocryphal Psalms," *Harvard Theological Review* 59 (1966): 258.

8. Bidawid, *Lettres,* 37.

9. For Origenism, see G. Widengren, "Researches in Syrian Mysticism," *Numen* 8, no. 3 (1961): 161–98. Margaret Smith, *Studies in Early Mysticism in the Near and Middle East* (London: Sheldon Press, 1931); Paul Harb and François Graffin, eds., *Lettre sur les trois étapes de la vie monastique* (Turnhout, Belgium: Brepols, 1992); Mary Hansbury, *The Letters of John of Dalyatha* (Piscataway, NJ: Gorgias Press, 2006).

10. For the elephant, see Samuel Hugh Moffett, *A History of Christianity in Asia,* vol. 1, *Beginnings to 1500,* 2nd rev. ed. (Maryknoll, NY: Orbis, 1998), 498. John Stewart, *Nestorian Missionary Enterprise* (Edinburgh: T. and T. Clark, 1928); Aubrey R. Vine, *The Nestorian Churches* (London: Independent Press, 1937); Edward R. Hardy, Jr., *Militant in Earth* (New York: Oxford Univ. Press, 1940).

11. Bidawid, *Lettres,* 37. "In these days" is quoted from Alphonse Mingana, *The Early Spread of Christianity in Central Asia and the Far East* (New York: Longmans, Green, 1925), 12. "The countries of the sunrise" is from Alphonse Mingana, *The Early Spread of Christianity in India* (Manchester, UK: Manchester Univ. Press, 1926), 34. Compare Barrett, *World Christian Encyclopedia,* 1st ed. 796; Ian Gillman and Hans-Joachim Klimkeit, *Christians in Asia Before 1500* (Ann Arbor: Univ. of Michigan Press, 1999). See also Samuel Hugh Moffett, *A History of Christianity in Asia,* vol. 2, *1500 to 1900* (Maryknoll, NY: Orbis, 2005).

12. Bidawid, *Lettres,* 27–28. For the geographical perceptions of late antiquity, see J. W. McCrindle, ed., *The Christian Topography of Cosmas* (London: Hakluyt Society, 1897).

13. Charles F. Horne, ed., *The Sacred Books and Early Literature of the East* (New York: Parke, Austin, & Lipscomb, 1917), 12: 381–92.

14. Moffett, *History of Christianity in Asia,* 1:301–2.

15. Bidawid, *Lettres,* 25.

16. Alphonse Mingana, ed., *Timothy's Apology for Christianity,* Woodbrooke Studies, vol. 2 (Cambridge: W. Heffer and Sons, 1928), 41.

17. For the discovery of Indian numbers, see Severus Sebokht, "On the Constellations," http://www.tertullian.org/fathers/severus_sebokht_constellations_01_intro.htm. Peter Brown, *The Rise of Western Christendom,* rev. ed. (Oxford: Blackwell, 2003), 275. For Aristotle, see Bidawid, *Lettres,* 35.

18. Moffett, *History of Christianity in Asia,* 1:354–55. De Lacy O'Leary, *How Greek Science Passed to the Arabs* (London: Kegan Paul, 2001); Richard E. Rubenstein, *Aristotle's Children* (Orlando, FL: Harcourt, 2003). For the Muslim inheritance, see Michael Hamilton Morgan, *Lost History* (Washington, DC: National Geographic, 2007).

19. The Victorian scholar was John Mason Neale. Moffett, *History of Christianity in Asia* 1:380.

20. Klaus Koschorke, Frieder Ludwig, and Marian Delgado, eds., *History of Christianity in Asia, Africa, and Latin America, 1450–1990* (Grand Rapids, MI: Eerdmans, 2007), 3.

21. The sixth-century Christian writer Cosmas Indicopleustes was struck that "[t]he pagans even, availing themselves of what Moses has thus revealed, divide the whole earth into three parts: Asia, Libya and Europe, designating Asia the east, Libya the south, extending to the west; Europe the north, also extending to all the west." McCrindle, *Christian Topography,* book 2.

22. Evelyn Edson, *The World Map, 1300–1492* (Baltimore: Johns Hopkins Univ. Press, 2007); Andrew F. Walls, "Eusebius Tries Again," *International Bulletin of Missionary Research* 24, no. 3 (2000): 105–11.

23. Speros Vryonis, *The Decline of Medieval Hellenism in Asia Minor* (Berkeley: Univ. of California Press, 1971). For numbers of Christians, see Barrett, *World Christian Encyclopedia,* 1st ed., 796.

24. "A miserable community" is quoted from Mingana, *Christianity in Central Asia,* 20.

25. David B. Barrett, George T. Kurian, and Todd M. Johnson, *World Christian Encyclopedia,* 2nd ed. (New York: Oxford Univ. Press, 2001).

26. Walls, "Eusebius Tries Again."

27. The absence is not total, and a number of historians have explored the catastrophic destruction of the Catholic missions in seventeenth-century Japan. Also drawing on this experience is the fictional narrative of Shusaku Endo's 1967 novel *Silence,* which raises critical theological questions about how to interpret the failure of a doomed church. But with the exception of Japan, we find few such analyses, particularly for the vast regions that would one day become the core of the Muslim world. From the vast modern literature on the history of Christianity, I know of just three books specifically dedicated to the disappearance of these Christian communities, all impressive pieces of scholarship, but all quite dated: Leonard Ralph Holme, *The Extinction of the Christian Churches in North Africa* (New York: B. Franklin, 1969; first published 1898); Laurence Edward Browne, *The Eclipse of Christianity in Asia* (Cambridge: Cambridge Univ. Press, 1933); Vryonis, *Decline of Medieval Hellenism.* The dates alone (Vryonis's book was published in 1971) suggest that this is anything but a thriving field of scholarly inquiry. Other books have studied the decline of particular religions but not their final destruction: Bat Ye'or, *The Decline of Eastern Christianity Under Islam* (Madison, NJ: Fairleigh Dickinson Univ. Press, 1996).

28. Euan Cameron, *Interpreting Christian History* (Oxford: Blackwell, 2005).

29. Holme, *Christian Churches in North Africa,* 3.

30. Vivian B. Mann, Jerrilynn D. Dodds, and Thomas F. Glick, eds., *Convivencia* (New York: G. Braziller in association with the Jewish Museum, 1992).

31. *Catholic Encyclopedia,* s.v. "Early African Church," by H. Leclercq, http://www.newadvent.org/cathen/01191a.htm.

32. Colin H. Roberts, *Manuscript, Society, and Belief in Early Christian Egypt* (London: Published for the British Academy by Oxford Univ. Press, 1979); Birger A. Pearson and James E. Goehring, eds., *The Roots of Egyptian Christianity* (Philadelphia: Fortress Press, 1986); C. Wilfred Griggs, *Early Egyptian Christianity* (Leiden: E. J. Brill, 1990); Douglas Burton-Christie, *The Word in the Desert* (New York: Oxford Univ. Press, 1993); Birger A. Pearson, *Gnosticism and Christianity in Roman and Coptic Egypt* (New York: T. and T. Clark International, 2004).

33. The prayer is quoted from "Japan's Crypto-Christians," *Time,* January 11, 1982, http://www.time.com/time/magazine/article/0,9171,925197,00.html. Ann Harrington, *Japan's Hidden Christians* (Chicago: Loyola Univ.

Press, 1992); Stephen Turnbull, *The Kakure Kirishitan of Japan* (Richmond, UK: Curzon/Japan Library, 1998).

34. Barrett, Kurian, and Johnson, *World Christian Encyclopedia.*, 2nd ed.

35. Vryonis, *Decline of Medieval Hellenism.*

36. Philip Jenkins, *God's Continent* (New York: Oxford Univ. Press, 2007).

37. For dhimmitude, see Bat Ye'or, *Decline of Eastern Christianity.*

38. Deborah Solomon, "Questions for Katharine Jefferts Schori," *New York Times,* November 19, 2006; Gina Piccalo, "Devout Catholic Answers a Call to Challenge Church," *Los Angeles Times,* June 22, 2007. Compare James Carroll, *Constantine's Sword* (New York: Houghton Mifflin, 2001).

2. CHURCHES OF THE EAST

1. Georgina Herrmann and Hugh N. Kennedy, *Monuments of Merv* (London: Society of Antiquaries, 1999); Edmund O'Donovan, *The Merv Oasis* (New York: G. P. Putnam's Sons, 1883).

2. For scholarship at Merv, see Brown, *Rise of Western Christendom,* 275. Margaret Dunlop Gibson, ed., *The Commentaries on the New Testament of Isho'dad of Merv,* 6 vols. (Piscataway, NJ: Gorgias Press, 2005; first published 1903); Clemens Leonhard, *Ishodad of Merw's Exegesis of the Psalms 119 and 139–147* (Louvain, Belgium: Peeters, 2001).

3. W. H. C. Frend, *The Rise of Christianity* (Philadelphia: Fortress Press, 1984).

4. Peter Llewellyn, *Rome in the Dark Ages* (New York: Praeger, 1970); Chris Wickham, *Framing the Early Middle Ages* (New York: Oxford Univ. Press, 2005); Julia M. H. Smith, *Europe After Rome* (New York: Oxford Univ. Press, 2005).

5. R. N. Swanson, ed., *The Church and Mary* (Woodbridge, UK: Boydell Press, 2004).

6. "The earliest Christian hymnbook" is quoted from Moffett, *History of Christianity in Asia,* 1:52. For the history of music, see William Dalrymple, *From the Holy Mountain* (New York: Henry Holt, 1997), 175–78. John Meyendorff, ed., *Ephrem the Syrian* (New York: Paulist Press, 1989); Javier Teixidor, *Bardesane d'Édesse* (Paris: Le Cerf, 1992); R. J. Schork, *Sacred Song from the Byzantine Pulpit* (Gainesville: Univ. Press of Florida, 1995).

7. Bede, *Ecclesiastical History,* book 4, chap. 2, http://www.ccel.org/ccel/bede/history.v.iv.ii.html; Geoffrey Wainwright and Karen Westerfield

Tucker, eds., *The Oxford History of Christian Worship* (New York: Oxford Univ. Press, 2006).

8. Vryonis, *Decline of Medieval Hellenism,* 304.

9. Richard C. Foltz, *Religions of the Silk Road* (New York: St. Martin's Press, 1999).

10. Peter Green, *Alexander to Actium* (Berkeley: Univ. of California Press, 1990).

11. McCrindle, *Christian Topography,* 149–52.

12. Frances Wood, *The Silk Road* (Berkeley: Univ. of California Press, 2002); Susan Whitfield and Ursula Sims-Williams, eds., *The Silk Road* (Chicago: Serindia Publications, 2004).

13. Richard L. Kalmin, *Jewish Babylonia Between Persia and Roman Palestine* (New York: Oxford Univ. Press, 2006).

14. For Egypt's role as a hub of trade and communication, see Roger S. Bagnall, *Egypt in Late Antiquity* (Princeton, NJ: Princeton Univ. Press, 1993); Christopher Haas, *Alexandria in Late Antiquity* (Baltimore: Johns Hopkins Univ. Press, 1997).

15. Judah B. Segal, *Edessa "The Blessed City"* (Oxford: Clarendon Press, 1970); Steven K. Ross, *Roman Edessa* (London: Routledge, 2001); Robert Doran, *Stewards of the Poor* (Collegeville, MN: Liturgical Press, 2006).

16. Brown, *Rise of Western Christendom,* 277. Nina G. Garsoïan, Thomas F. Mathews, and Robert W. Thomson, eds., *East of Byzantium* (Washington, DC: Dumbarton Oaks, Center for Byzantine Studies, 1982); Thomas J. Samuelian and Michael E. Stone, eds., *Medieval Armenian Culture* (Chico, CA: Scholars Press, 1984); Nina G. Garsoïan, *Church and Culture in Early Medieval Armenia* (Brookfield, VT: Ashgate, 1999); Vrej Nersessian, *Treasures from the Ark* (Los Angeles: J. Paul Getty Museum, 2001).

17. Adriano Alpago-Novello, Vahtang Beridze, and Jacqueline Lafontaine-Dosogne, *Art and Architecture in Medieval Georgia* (Louvain-la-Neuve, Belgium: Institut Supérieur d'Archéologie et d'Histoire de l'Art, Collège Érasme, 1980); Antony Eastmond, *Royal Imagery in Medieval Georgia* (University Park: Pennsylvania State Univ. Press, 1998). For Adiabene, see Joel Thomas Walker, *The Legend of Mar Qardagh* (Berkeley: Univ. of California Press, 2006).

18. The quote about Cyriacus is from B. T. A. Evetts, ed., *History of the Patriarchs of the Coptic Church of Alexandria* (first published 1907–15), http://

www.tertullian.org/fathers/severus_hermopolis_hist_alex_patr_03_
part3.htm. For the power of the see of Alexandria, see http://www
.tertullian.org/fathers/severus_hermopolis_hist_alex_patr_04_part4
.htm. P. L. Shinnie, *Medieval Nubia* (1954), http://rumkatkilise.org/nubia
.htm. Elizabeth Isichei, *A History of Christianity in Africa* (Grand Rapids,
MI: Eerdmans, 1995); Bengt Sundkler and Christopher Steed, *A History
of the Church in Africa* (Cambridge: Cambridge Univ. Press, 2000); Sir
Laurence Kirwin, *Studies on the History of Late Antique and Christian Nubia*
(Aldershot, UK: Ashgate Variorum, 2002); Derek A. Welsby, *The Medieval
Kingdoms of Nubia* (London: British Museum, 2002). For the influence of
Alexandria, see Stephen J. Davis, *The Early Coptic Papacy* (Cairo and New
York: American Univ. in Cairo Press, 2005).

19. Donald Crummey, "The Ethiopian Orthodox Tawahedo Church," in *Cambridge History of Christianity: Eastern Christianity*, ed. Michael Angold (Cambridge: Cambridge Univ. Press, 2006), 457–62. Isichei, *History of Christianity
in Africa*; Sundkler and Steed, *History of the Church in Africa*.

20. "No country in the world" is from Father Jeronimo Lobo, "Voyage to
Abyssinia," http://lobo.thefreelibrary.com/Voyage-to-Abyssinia/3–4. See
also Isichei, *History of Christianity in Africa*, 52.

21. Sir E. A. Wallis Budge, *The Queen of Sheba and Her Only Son Menyelek*, 2nd
ed. (London: Oxford Univ. Press, 1932); Taddesse Tamrat, *Church and
State in Ethiopia, 1270–1527* (Oxford: Clarendon Press, 1972).

22. Koschorke, Ludwig, and Delgado, *History of Christianity*, 141. For the
threat to the Nile, see Browne, *Eclipse of Christianity in Asia*.

23. Walls, "Eusebius Tries Again." W. A. Wigram, *An Introduction to the History of the Assyrian Church* (Piscataway, NJ: Gorgias Press, 2004; first
published 1909).

24. W. H. C. Frend, *The Rise of the Monophysite Movement* (Cambridge: Cambridge
Univ. Press, 1972); Cornelia B. Horn, *Asceticism and Christological Controversy
in Fifth-Century Palestine* (New York: Oxford Univ. Press, 2006).

25. Patrick T. R. Gray, *The Defense of Chalcedon in the East* (Leiden: E. J. Brill,
1979); E. W. Brooks, ed., *A Collection of Letters of Severus of Antioch*, 2 vols.
(Turnhout, Belgium: Brepols, 1985–2003); Jan-Eric Steppa, *John Rufus and
the World Vision of Anti-Chalcedonian Culture* (Piscataway, NJ: Gorgias
Press, 2002); Ramsay MacMullen, *Voting About God in Early Church Councils* (New Haven, CT: Yale Univ. Press, 2006).

26. Mark Dickens, "The Church of the East" (1999), http://www.oxuscom.com/ch-of-east.htm; Wilhelm Baum and Dietmar W. Winkler, *The Church of the East* (London: RoutledgeCurzon, 2003); Christoph Baumer, *The Church of the East* (New York: I. B. Tauris, 2006).

27. Stephen Gero, *Barsauma of Nisibis and Persian Christianity in the Fifth Century* (Louvain, Belgium: Peeters, 1981).

28. McCrindle, *Christian Topography*.

29. For the Christian landscape of Palestine in the Byzantine and early Muslim period, see Yoram Tsafrir, ed., *Ancient Churches Revealed* (Jerusalem: Israel Exploration Society, 1993). Compare Brouria Bitton-Ashkelony and Aryeh Kofsky, *The Monastic School of Gaza* (Leiden and Boston: E. J. Brill, 2006).

30. For Egypt's Christian landscape around 1200, see B. T. A. Evetts, ed., *The Churches and Monasteries of Egypt and Some Neighbouring Countries* (Oxford: Clarendon Press, 1895). Gawdat Gabra, *Coptic Monasteries* (Cairo: American Univ. in Cairo Press, 2002). Massimo Capuani, with Otto F. A. Meinardus and Marie-Helene Rutschowscaya, *Christian Egypt* (Cairo: American Univ. in Cairo Press, 2002). For Saint Antony, see Elizabeth S. Bolman, ed., *Monastic Visions* (New Haven, CT: Yale Univ. Press, 2002). Otto F. A. Meinardus, *Two Thousand Years of Coptic Christianity* (Cairo: American University in Cairo Press, 2007).

31. For Saint Catherine's, see Thomas F. Mathews, David Jacoby, Justin Sinaites, Robert S. Nelson, and Kristen M. Collins, *Holy Image, Hallowed Ground* (Los Angeles: J. Paul Getty Museum, 2006). Françoise Micheau, "Copts, Melkites, Nestorians and Jacobites," in Angold, *Cambridge History of Christianity,* 399.

32. Andrew Palmer, *Monk and Mason on the Tigris Frontier* (New York: Cambridge Univ. Press, 1990).

33. Quoted from "The School of Nisibis," http://www.nestorian.org/the_school_of_nisibis.html.

34. Other metropolitan sees included Arbela, Kirkuk, Basra, and Jundaisapur (Gundeshapur). The catholicos had his main residence in Seleucia-Ctesiphon. Browne, *Eclipse of Christianity in Asia.*

35. *Catholic Encyclopedia,* s.v. "Melitene," http://www.newadvent.org/cathen/10166a.htm. For Amida, see Susan Ashbrook Harvey, *Asceticism and Society in Crisis* (Berkeley: Univ. of California Press, 1990).

36. Dalrymple, *From the Holy Mountain,* 100.

37. Oswald H. Parry, *Six Months in a Syrian Monastery, Being a Record of the Visit to the Head Quarters of the Syrian Church in Mesopotamia, with Some Account of the Yazidis or Devil Worshippers of Mosul and el Jilwah, Their Sacred Book* (Piscataway, NJ: Gorgias Press, 2002; first published 1895). For the monasteries as they exist today, see, for instance, http://www.morgabriel.org; https://www.deirmarmusa.org/; and Stephen Griffith, "The Situation in Tur Abdin" (2001), http://sor.cua.edu/Pub/StephenGriffith/Visit SETurkeyNov2001.html.

38. E. A. Wallis Budge, ed., *The Book of Governors* (London: Kegan Paul, 2003; first published 1893).

39. For the Hunnish translation, see Zachariah of Mitylene, "Syriac Chronicle," http://www.tertullian.org/fathers/zachariah12.htm. The story of the tattoos is from Brown, *Rise of Western Christendom,* 267.

40. Mingana, *Christianity in Central Asia,* 11–12; and 73–74 for the church in 650.

41. For "merchants," see Foltz, *Silk Road,* 62. For *nom,* see Brown, *Rise of Western Christendom,* 284. Christopher Dawson, *The Mongol Mission* (New York: Sheed and Ward, 1955); Wassilios Klein, *Das nestorianische Christentum an den Handelswegen durch Kyrgyzstan bis zum 14 Jahrhunderts* (Turnhout, Belgium: Brepols, 2000); Mark Dickens, "Nestorian Christianity in Central Asia" (2001), www.oxuscom.com/Nestorian_Christianity_in_CA .pdf. Zsuzsanna Gulácsi, *Mediaeval Manichaean Book Art* (Leiden: E. J. Brill, 2005); Roman Malek and Peter Hofrichter, eds., *Jingjiao: The Church of the East in China and Central Asia* (Sankt Augustin, Germany: Institut Monumenta Serica, 2006). "The Work of the Academy Project: Turfan Studies," http://www.bbaw.de/bbaw/Forschung/Forschungsprojekte/turfan forschung/en/blanko.2005–03–02.3373813525.

42. Mingana, *Christianity in Central Asia,* 13; Wallis Budge, *Book of Governors.*

43. Procopius *History of the Wars* 8.17.1–7.

44. Mingana, *Christianity in Central Asia;* Frits Holm, *My Nestorian Adventure in China* (Piscataway, NJ: Gorgias Press, 2001).

45. Quoted by T. V. Philip, "East of the Euphrates," http://www.religion-online.org/show chapter.asp?title=1553&C=1363.

46. Moffett, *History of Christianity in Asia,* vol. 1. Stephen G. Haw, *Marco Polo's China* (London: Routledge, 2006). James D. Ryan, "Conversion vs. Baptism?" in *Varieties of Religious Conversion in the Middle Ages,* ed. James

Muldoon (Gainesville: Univ. Press of Florida, 1997), 146–70. Herbert Franke and Denis Twitchett, eds., *The Cambridge History of China*, vol. 6 (Cambridge: Cambridge Univ. Press, 1994). For the Franciscan missions, see Lauren Arnold, *Princely Gifts and Papal Treasures* (San Francisco: Desiderata Press, 1999).

47. Mingana, *Christianity in India,* 6, and 27 for the Indian priest. McCrindle, *Christian Topography.*

48. Leslie Brown, *The Indian Christians of St. Thomas* (Cambridge: Cambridge Univ. Press, 1982); Stephen Neill, *A History of Christianity in India* (Cambridge: Cambridge Univ. Press, 1984); Leonard Fernando and George Gispert-Sauch, *Christianity in India* (New Delhi: Penguin India, 2004).

49. The "thirty thousand families" quotation is from Koschorke, Ludwig, and Delgado, *History of Christianity,* 4. Moffett, *History of Christianity in Asia,* 1:302 ("the islands . . . inside Java"), 1:459–62. Susan Visvanathan, *The Christians of Kerala* (New York: Oxford Univ. Press, 1993); Antony Kariyil, *Church and Society in Kerala* (New Delhi, India: Intercultural Press, 1995).

50. For the Jacobites, see Ian Gillman and Hans-Joachim Klimkeit, *Christians in Asia Before 1500* (Ann Arbor: Univ. of Michigan Press, 1999), 71.

51. Samuel N. C. Lieu, *Manichaeism in Mesopotamia and the Roman East* (Leiden and New York: E. J. Brill, 1994); Yuri Stoyanov, *The Other God* (New Haven, CT: Yale Nota Bene, 2000); Lilla Russell-Smith, *Uygur Patronage in Dunhuang* (Leiden: E. J. Brill, 2005).

52. Mingana, *Christianity in Central Asia,* 15–16; Moffett, *History of Christianity in Asia,* vol. 1.

53. Elaine Sanceau, *The Land of Prester John* (New York: Knopf, 1944).

54. David B. Barrett, *World Christian Encyclopedia,* 796. Muldoon, *Varieties of Religious Conversion;* Richard Fletcher, *The Barbarian Conversion* (Berkeley: Univ. of California Press, 1999); Martin Carver, ed., *The Cross Goes North* (York, England: York Medieval Press, 2004).

3. ANOTHER WORLD

1. Dalrymple, *From the Holy Mountain,* 141. "The sweet aroma" is from "The Order of the Hallowing of the Apostles," http://www.cired .org/liturgy/apostles.html. Compare Susan Ashbrook Harvey, *Scenting Salvation* (Berkeley: Univ. of California Press, 2006); Christine Chaillot, "The Ancient Oriental Churches," in Wainwright and Tucker, *Christian*

Worship; and F. E. Brightman, *Eastern Liturgies* (Piscataway, NJ: Gorgias Press, 2004).

2. Wallis Budge, *Book of Governors,* 27. Arthur Vööbus, *History of Asceticism in the Syrian Orient,* 3 vols. (Louvain, Belgium: Secrétariat du Corpus SCO, 1958–88); Theodoret of Cyrrhus, *History of the Monks of Syria* (Collegeville, MN: Cistercian Publications, 1985); Peter Brown, *Society and the Holy in Late Antiquity* (Berkeley: Univ. of California Press, 1989); James E. Goehring, *Ascetics, Society, and the Desert* (Harrisburg, PA: Trinity Press International, 1999); David Brakke, *Demons and the Making of the Monk* (Cambridge, MA: Harvard Univ. Press, 2006).

3. For stylites, see Amir Harrak, ed., *The Chronicle of Zuqnīn, A.D. 488–775* (Toronto: Pontifical Institute of Mediaeval Studies, 1999), 294. "A religion of intense moral seriousness" is from Walls, "Eusebius Tries Again." The passage about Bar Sauma is from E. A. Wallis Budge, *The Monks of Kûblâi Khân, Emperor of China* (London: Religious Tract Society, 1928). Susanna Elm, *Virgins of God* (New York: Oxford Univ. Press, 1994).

4. For Mother Sara, see E. A. Wallis Budge, ed., *The Laughable Stories* (New York: AMS Press, 1976), 40; and 136 for the two women. For Shirin, see Sebastian P. Brock and Susan Ashbrook Harvey, *Holy Women of the Syrian Orient* (Berkeley: Univ. of California Press, 1987), 177–81. Pieternella Van Doorn-Harder, *Contemporary Coptic Nuns* (Columbia: Univ. of South Carolina Press, 1995); Lynda L. Coon, *Sacred Fictions* (Philadelphia: Univ. of Pennsylvania Press, 1997); Alice-Mary Talbot, ed., *Holy Women of Byzantium* (Washington, DC: Dumbarton Oaks Research Library and Collection, 1996). Laura Swan, *The Forgotten Desert Mothers* (New York: Paulist Press, 2001); Rebecca Krawiec, *Shenoute and the Women of the White Monastery* (New York: Oxford Univ. Press, 2002).

5. Elaine Pagels, *The Gnostic Gospels* (New York: Random House, 1999); Elaine Pagels, *Beyond Belief* (New York: Random House, 2003); Karen King, *What Is Gnosticism?* (Cambridge, MA: Belknap Press of Harvard Univ. Press, 2003).

6. G. E. H. Palmer, Philip Sherrard, and Kallistos Ware, eds., *The Philokalia,* 4 vols. (London: Faber and Faber, 1983–95). For Ephraem, see Smith, *Early Mysticism,* 86.

7. Norman Russell, *The Doctrine of Deification in the Greek Patristic Tradition,* new ed. (New York: Oxford Univ. Press, 2006).

8. Alphonse Mingana, ed., *Early Christian Mystics* (Cambridge: W. Heffer and Sons, 1934); John Chryssavgis, *John Climacus* (Aldershot, England: Ashgate, 2004).

9. For Cosmas, see Harrak, *Chronicle of Zuqnīn,* 156. "I find the proof" and "they do not accept" are from Browne, *Eclipse of Christianity in Asia,* 82; "is only received and believed" is from 81.

10. Amanda Porterfield, *Healing in the History of Christianity* (New York: Oxford Univ. Press, 2005).

11. William Wright, *A Short History of Syriac Literature* (London: Adam and Charles Black, 1894); Ignatius Aphram I. Barsoum, *The Scattered Pearls,* 2nd rev. ed. (Piscataway, NJ: Gorgias Press, 2003).

12. Adam H. Becker, *Fear of God and the Beginning of Wisdom* (Philadelphia: Univ. of Pennsylvania Press, 2006). For Cassiodorus, see Brown, *Rise of Western Christendom,* 574. For the 1026 debate, see Herman Teule, "La renaissance syriaque (1026–1318)," *Irenikon* 75, nos. 2 and 3 (2002): 174–94.

13. The quotes from Severus Seboukt are from http://www.tertullian.org/fathers/severus_sebokht_constellations_01_intro.htm. Brown, *Rise of Western Christendom,* 275.

14. Moffett, *History of Christianity in Asia,* 1:354–55. O'Leary, *Greek Science;* Rubenstein, *Aristotle's Children;* Matti Moosa, *The Maronites in History,* 2nd ed. (Piscataway, NJ: Gorgias Press, 2005).

15. Richard J. Saley, *The Samuel Manuscript of Jacob of Edessa* (Leiden: E. J. Brill, 1998); Sidney H. Griffith, ed., *Yahya ibn 'Adi: The Reformation of Morals* (Provo, UT: Brigham Young Univ. Press, 2002); Gibson, *Commentaries.*

16. Badger, *Nestorians and Their Rituals,* 2:361–79.

17. Abdulmesih BarAbrahem, "Patriarch Michael the Great," *Journal of Assyrian Academic Studies* 12, no. 2 (1998), www.jaas.org/edocs/v12n2/BarAbrahem.pdf. Brown, *Rise of Western Christendom,* 313.

18. Quoted in Badger, *Nestorians and Their Rituals,* 2:361–79.

19. The remark about Bar-Hebraeus's accomplishments is from *Catholic Encyclopedia,* s.v. "Bar Hebræus," http://www.newadvent.org/cathen02294a.htm. Arent Jan Wensinck, ed., *Bar Hebraeus's Book of the Dove* (Leiden: E. J. Brill, 1919); Ján Bakos, ed., *Le candélabre des sanctuaires de Gregoire Aboulfaradj dit Bar Hebraeus* (Paris: Firmin-Didot, 1930). Ernest A. Wallis Budge, ed., *The Chronography of Gregory Abū'l Faraj, the Son of Aaron, the*

Hebrew Physician, Commonly Known as Bar Hebraeus (London: Oxford Univ. Press, 1932). Wallis Budge, *Laughable Stories.*

20. Elise Antreassian, ed., *The Fables of Mkhitar Gosh* (New York: Ashod Press, 1987).

21. Sidney H. Griffith, "Christians and Christianity," in *The Cambridge Companion to the Qur'ān,* ed. Jane Dammen McAuliffe (Cambridge: Cambridge Univ. Press, 2001), 307–15.

22. E. A. Wallis Budge, *The Book of the Bee* (Oxford: Clarendon Press, 1886), http://www.sacred-texts.com/chr/bb/bb48.htm.

23. "The Doctrine of Addai" (1876), http://www.tertullian.org/fathers/addai_2_text.htm. Amir Harrak, ed., *The Acts of Mār Māri the Apostle* (Leiden: E. J. Brill, 2005).

24. Wallis Budge, *Book of the Bee.*

25. Walther Bauer, *Orthodoxy and Heresy in Earliest Christianity* (London: SCM Press, 1972), 20. Bauer was one of many modern scholars to reject the Nestorian succession story.

26. Richard Bauckham, *Jude and the Relatives of Jesus in the Early Church* (Edinburgh: T. and T. Clark, 1990).

27. Badger, *Nestorians and Their Rituals.* Sébastien de Courtois, *Forgotten Genocide* (Piscataway, NJ: Gorgias Press, 2004), 10.

28. Mingana, *Christianity in Central Asia,* 41–42.

29. Moffett, *History of Christianity in Asia,* 1:74. William L. Petersen, *Tatian's Diatessaron* (Leiden: E. J. Brill, 1994); Sebastian Brock, *The Bible in the Syriac Tradition* (Piscataway, NJ: Gorgias Press, 2006).

30. Philip Jenkins, *Hidden Gospels* (New York: Oxford Univ. Press, 2001).

31. Gibson, *Commentaries.*

32. Michael E. Stone, ed., *Armenian Apocrypha Relating to Adam and Eve* (Leiden and New York: E. J. Brill, 1996). Michael E. Stone, *Adam's Contract with Satan* (Bloomington: Indiana Univ. Press, 2002); Margaret Dunlop Gibson, ed., *Apocrypha Sinaitica* (London: C. J. Clay, 1896); E. A. Wallis Budge, ed., *Legends of Our Lady Mary, the Perpetual Virgin and Her Mother Hanna* (London: Oxford Univ. Press, 1933).

33. Gibson, *Commentaries,* 1:xxix.

34. Bar-Hebraeus is quoted from George Lane, "An Account of Gregory Bar Hebraeus, Abu al-Faraj, and His Relations with the Mongols of

Persia." *Hugoye* 2, no. 2 (1999), http://syrcom.cua.edu/Hugoye/Vol2No2/ HV2N2GLane.html. For Solomon, see Wallis Budge, *Book of the Bee,* http://www.sacred-texts.com/chr/bb/bb58.htm.

35. Wallis Budge, *Book of Governors,* 26; Robert C. Hill, *Reading the Old Testament in Antioch* (Leiden and Boston: E. J. Brill, 2005).

36. E. A. Wallis Budge, *The Book of the Cave of Treasures* (London: Religious Tract Society, 1927).

37. Gibson *Commentaries.*

38. James C. Russell, *The Germanization of Early Medieval Christianity* (New York: Oxford Univ. Press, 1996).

39. For "all the Buddhas" see Moffett, *History of Christianity in Asia,* 1:310. Ralph R. Covell, *Confucius, the Buddha, and Christ* (Maryknoll, NY: Orbis Books, 1986); Irene Eber, Sze-Kar Wan, Knut Walf, and Roman Malek, eds., *The Bible in Modern China* (Sankt Augustin, Germany: Institut Monumenta Serica, 1999); Martin Palmer, *The Jesus Sutras* (London: Piatkus, 2001); Ray Riegert and Thomas Moore, eds., *The Lost Sutras of Jesus* (Berkeley, CA: Seastone, 2003); Russell-Smith, *Uygur Patronage in Dunhuang;* Malek and Hofrichter, *Jingjiao.*

40. John Damascene [pseud.], *Barlaam and Ioasaph,* trans. G. R. Woodward and Harold Mattingly, Loeb Classical Library 34 (Cambridge, MA: Harvard Univ. Press, 1914). D. A. Scott, "Medieval Christian Responses to Buddhism," *Journal of Religious History* 15 (1988): 165–84.

41. Moffett, *History of Christianity in Asia,* 1:430–34. Wallis Budge, *Monks of Kûblâi Khân;* James A. Montgomery, *The History of Yaballaha III and of His Vicar Bar Sauma* (New York: Columbia Univ. Press, 1927); Paul Bedjan, *The History of Mar Jab-Alaha and Rabban Sauma* (Piscataway, NJ: Gorgias Press 2007). Stephen Andrew Missick, "The Assyrian Church in the Mongolian Empire as Observed by World Travelers in the Late 13th and Early 14th Centuries," *Journal of Assyrian Academic Studies* 13, no. 2 (1999): 85–104, http://www.jaas.org/edocs/v13n2/missick.pdf .

42. Budge, *Monks of Kûblâi Khân.*

43. Budge, *Monks of Kûblâi Khân.*

44. "Exercised ecclesiastical sovereignty" is from Moffett, *History of Christianity in Asia,* 1:434. For Maragha, see Micheau, "Copts, Melkites, Nestorians and Jacobites," 387.

4. THE GREAT TRIBULATION

1. Quoted in Donald P. Little, "Coptic Conversion to Islam Under the Bahri Mamluks, 692–755/1293–1354," *Bulletin of the School of Oriental and African Studies* 39 (1976): 568. For Al-Maqrizi's fifteenth-century account of earlier persecutions, see Evetts, *Churches and Monasteries*, 328–40.

2. Karen Armstrong, *Muhammad* (San Francisco: HarperOne, 1992), 22. Compare Karen Armstrong, *Holy War*, 2nd ed. (New York: Anchor Books, 2001).

3. Bat Ye'or, *Decline of Eastern Christianity*; Andrew G. Bostom, ed., *The Legacy of Jihad* (Amherst, NY: Prometheus, 2005).

4. Andrew Wheatcroft, *Infidels* (New York: Penguin Putnam, 2003); Richard Fletcher, *The Cross and the Crescent* (New York: Allen Lane, 2003); A. G. Jamieson, *Faith and Sword* (London: Reaktion, 2006); Hugh Kennedy, *The Great Arab Conquests* (London: Weidenfeld & Nicolson, 2007).

5. Holme, *Christian Churches in North Africa.*

6. David M. Olster, *Roman Defeat, Christian Response, and the Literary Construction of the Jew* (Philadelphia: Univ. of Pennsylvania Press, 1994); Walter E. Kaegi, *Heraclius* (Cambridge: Cambridge Univ. Press, 2003).

7. Brown, *Rise of Western Christendom,* 297. Walter E. Kaegi, *Byzantium and the Early Islamic Conquests* (Cambridge: Cambridge Univ. Press, 1992); Michael D. Bonner, *Aristocratic Violence and Holy War* (New Haven, CT: American Oriental Society, 1996); Michael D. Bonner, ed., *Arab-Byzantine Relations in Early Islamic Times* (Aldershot, UK: Ashgate/Variorum, 2004); Nadia Maria El Cheikh, *Byzantium Viewed by the Arabs* (Cambridge, MA: Harvard Univ. Press, 2004). For the tenth-century campaigns, see Alice-Mary Talbot and Denis F. Sullivan, eds., *The History of Leo the Deacon* (Washington, DC: Dumbarton Oaks Research Library and Collection, 2005).

8. For Arabs and Syrians, see Harrak, *Chronicle of Zuqnin.* Robert G. Hoyland, *Seeing Islam as Others Saw It* (Princeton, NJ: Darwin Press, 1997).

9. For violence between Christian sects, see Michael Gaddis, *There Is No Crime for Those Who Have Christ* (Berkeley: Univ. of California Press, 2005). Ira M. Lapidus, *A History of Islamic Societies,* 2nd ed. (Cambridge: Cambridge Univ. Press, 2002).

10. Choksy, *Conflict and Cooperation.*

11. Sidney H. Griffith, *The Church in the Shadow of the Mosque* (Princeton Univ. Press, 2007); "The Arabs to whom God has given" is from Browne, *Eclipse of Christianity in Asia,* 41; "Justice flourished" is from Brown, *Rise of Western Christendom,* 299; "the hearts of Christians" is from Moffett, *History of Christianity in Asia,* 1:325. G. J. Reinink, *Syriac Christianity Under Late Sasanian and Early Islamic Rule* (Aldershot, UK: Ashgate Publishing, 2005). See also the valuable essays collected in Emmanouela Grypeou, Mark Swanson, and David Thomas, eds., *The Encounter of Eastern Christianity with Early Islam* (Leiden: E. J. Brill, 2006). Barnaby Rogerson, *The Heirs of Muhammad* (New York: Overlook, 2007).

12. "And the Lord abandoned" is from Evetts, *History of the Patriarchs.* "The God of vengeance" is from Browne, *Eclipse of Christianity in Asia,* 39–40. "Employed for the administration" is from Micheau, "Copts, Melkites, Nestorians and Jacobites," 382. Nick Ford, *Jerusalem Under Muslim Rule in the Eleventh Century* (New York: Rosen, 2004).

13. For *Sarakenophron,* see Dalrymple, *From the Holy Mountain,* 299; Andrew Louth, *St. John Damascene* (New York: Oxford Univ. Press, 2002); and Frederic H. Chase, Jr., ed., *Joannes of Damascus: Writings* (Washington, DC: Catholic Univ. of America Press, 1970). "They are just" is from Browne, *Eclipse of Christianity in Asia,* 48.

14. Harrak, *Chronicle of Zuqnin,* 147–48; and 150–52 for the campaign of 717–18. Nehemia Levtzion, "Conversion to Islam in Syria and Palestine, and the Survival of Christian Communities," in *Conversion and Continuity,* ed. Michael Gervers and Ramzi Jibran Bikhazi (Toronto: Pontifical Institute of Medieval Studies, 1990), 289–312. For issues of conversion and interfaith relations in the early centuries of Islam, see Robert Hoyland, introduction to *Muslims and Others in Early Islamic Society,* ed. Robert Hoyland (Burlington, VT: Ashgate, 2004), xiii–xxx.

15. For Egyptian persecutions, see Evetts, *History of the Patriarchs,* which is the source for the decree in which Muslim authorities "commanded the monks." Hugh Kennedy, "Egypt as a Province in the Islamic Caliphate," in *The Cambridge History of Egypt,* ed. Carl F. Petry (New York: Cambridge Univ. Press, 1998), 1:62–85; Walter Beltz, ed., *Die koptische Kirche in den ersten drei islamischen Jahrhunderten* (Halle: Institut für Orientalistik, Martin-Luther-Universität, 2003); Jill Kamil, *Christianity in the Land of the Pharaohs* (New York: Routledge, 2002).

16. For the fates of the holy desert, see Evetts, ed., *History of the Patriarchs.*. Terry G. Wilfong, "The Non-Muslim Communities," in Petry, *Cambridge History of Egypt,* 1:175–97.

17. For tax protests, see Harrak, *Chronicle of Zuqnīn,* 273–74. For martyrs, see Mark Swanson, "The Martyrdom of 'Abd al-Masih," in *Syrian Christians Under Islam,* ed. David Thomas (Leiden: E. J. Brill, 2001), 107–20. Kenneth Baxter Wolf, *Christian Martyrs in Muslim Spain* (Cambridge: Cambridge Univ. Press, 1988); Jessica A. Coope, *The Martyrs of Córdoba* (Lincoln: Univ. of Nebraska Press, 1995).

18. Anthony O'Mahony, "Coptic Christianity in Modern Egypt," in Angold, *Cambridge History of Christianity,* 489 n. 9; Browne, *Eclipse of Christianity in Asia,* 46–47; Youssef Courbage and Philippe Fargues, *Christians and Jews Under Islam* (London and New York: Tauris, 1997). Anne-Marie Eddé, Françoise Micheau, and Christophe Picard, *Communautés chrétiennes au pays d'Islam du debut de VIIe siècle au milieu du XIe siècle* (Paris: SEDES, 1997). For debates over the origin of Umaric codes, see Albrecht Noth, "Problems of Differentiation Between Muslims and Non-Muslims," in Hoyland, *Muslims and Others,* 103–24.

19. Micheau, "Copts, Melkites, Nestorians and Jacobites," 381–82.

20. Griffith, *Church in the Shadow of the Mosque*; For legal autonomy, see Hoyland, introduction to *Muslims and Others,* xv–xvi; Michael G. Morony, "Religious Communities in Late Sasanian and Early Muslim Iraq," in Hoyland, *Muslims and Others,* 1–24; and Néophyte Edelby, "The Legislative Autonomy of Christians in the Islamic World," in Hoyland, *Muslims and Others,* 37–82. For "Islam rested as lightly as a mist" and "local Christian elites," see Brown, *Rise of Western Christendom,* 306. For the new Christ figure, see Harrak, *Chronicle of Zuqnīn,* 248–52. Michael G. Morony, *Iraq After the Muslim Conquest* (Princeton, NJ: Princeton Univ. Press, 1984); Robert Schick, *The Christian Communities of Palestine from Byzantine to Islamic Rule* (Princeton, NJ: Darwin Press, 1995); Chase F. Robinson, *Empire and Elites After the Muslim Conquest* (Cambridge: Cambridge Univ. Press, 2000). For the fluidity of social and religious arrangements, see Steven A. Epstein, *Purity Lost* (Baltimore: Johns Hopkins Univ. Press, 2006).

21. The quote about Christian primates is from Wolf, *Christian Martyrs in Muslim Spain.* "May God—praised be He" is from Micheau, "Copts, Melkites, Nestorians and Jacobites," 375–76.

22. Mingana, *Timothy's Apology for Christianity*; "thou art empowered" is quoted from Alphonse Mingana, ed., *A Charter of Protection Granted to the Nestorian Church in AD 1138* (Manchester, UK: Manchester Univ. Press, 1925).

23. Brown, *Rise of Western Christendom*, 316; Browne, *Eclipse of Christianity in Asia;* David Thomas, ed., *Syrian Christians Under Islam* (Leiden: E. J. Brill, 2001); David Thomas, ed., *Christians at the Heart of Islamic Rule* (Leiden: E. J. Brill, 2003). "Hunt down what is contradictory" is quoted from Hoyland, introduction to *Muslims and Others,* xviii.

24. Harrak, *Chronicle of Zuqnīn,* 322–24. For the caliphate, see Hugh N. Kennedy, *The Prophet and the Age of the Caliphates,* 2nd ed. (New York: Pearson/Longman, 2004); and Hugh N. Kennedy, *When Baghdad Ruled the Muslim World* (Cambridge, MA: Da Capo Press, 2005).

25. Richard Bulliet, *Conversion to Islam in the Medieval Period* (Cambridge, MA: Harvard University Press, 1979), 131. Michael Morony, "The Age of Conversions," in Gervers and Bikhazi, *Conversion and Continuity,* 135–50. Kennedy, *The Great Arab Conquests,* also suggests that Islamization and Arabization were "a gradual, almost entirely peaceful result of the fact that more and more people wanted to identify with and participate in the dominant culture of their time" (376).

26. Stephen O'Shea, *Sea of Faith* (New York: Walker and Company, 2006).

27. What follows draws heavily on Vryonis, *Decline of Medieval Hellenism*. For the older world of Anatolia, see Ramsay MacMullen, *Christianizing the Roman Empire A.D. 100–400* (New Haven, CT: Yale Univ. Press, 1986); and Raymond Van Dam, *Becoming Christian* (Philadelphia: Univ. of Pennsylvania Press, 2003).

28. The sack of Melitene is quoted from Mark Dickens, "Medieval Syriac Historians' Perceptions of the Turks" (MPhil diss., Aramaic and Syriac Studies, Faculty of Oriental Studies, University of Cambridge, 2004), 22. "Everywhere the Christians" is from Vryonis, *Decline of Medieval Hellenism,* 172.

29. Michael the Syrian is quoted from Vryonis, *Decline of Medieval Hellenism,* 157. Joseph Tarzi, "Edessa in the Era of Patriarch Michael the Syrian," *Hugoye* 3, no. 2 (2000), http://syrcom.cua.edu/Hugoye/Vol3No2/HV3N2 Tarzi.html.

30. Ernest A. Wallis Budge, introduction to *Chronography of Gregory Abū'l Faraj.* For the Muslims and the monasteries, see Elizabeth A. Zachariadou, "The

Great Church in Captivity," in Angold, *Cambridge History of Christianity,* 155. Rosemary Morris, *Monks and Laymen in Byzantium, 843–1118* (New York: Cambridge Univ. Press, 1995); Michael Angold, *Church and Society in Byzantium Under the Comneni, 1081–1261,* new ed. (Cambridge: Cambridge Univ. Press, 2000).

31. Vryonis, *Decline of Medieval Hellenism,* 195.

32. For the church's tradition of charitable activities, see Susan R. Holman, *The Hungry Are Dying* (New York: Oxford Univ. Press, 2001); and Richard Finn, *Almsgiving in the Later Roman Empire* (Oxford: Oxford Univ. Press, 2006).

33. Vryonis, *Decline of Medieval Hellenism,* 177–78.

34. Christopher Tyerman, *Fighting for Christendom* (New York: Oxford Univ. Press, 2004); Christopher Tyerman, *God's War* (New York: Allen Lane, 2006). See also James M. Powell, ed., *Muslims Under Latin Rule, 1100–1300* (Princeton, NJ: Princeton Univ. Press, 1990); Janet Shirley, ed., *Crusader Syria in the Thirteenth Century* (Aldershot, UK, and Brookfield, VT: Ashgate, 1999); Michael Gervers and James M. Powell, eds., *Tolerance and Intolerance* (Syracuse, NY: Syracuse Univ. Press, 2001); and Christopher MacEvitt, *The Crusades and the Christian World of the East* (Univ. of Pennsylvania Press, 2007). For mob action in Egypt around 1200, see Evetts, *Churches and Monasteries,* 116–18.

35. The deportations are described in Reinhart Dozy, *Spanish Islam* (London: Chatto & Windus, 1913). See also Charles Reginald Haines, *Christianity and Islam in Spain* (London: Kegan Paul, Trench, 1889); Bernard F. Reilly, *The Contest of Christian and Muslim Spain* (Cambridge, MA: Blackwell, 1992); and Brian A. Catlos, *The Victors and the Vanquished* (New York: Cambridge Univ. Press, 2004). For the supposed tolerance of Islamic Spain, see, for instance, Maria Rosa Menocal, *The Ornament of the World* (New York: Little, Brown, 2002); and Chris Lowney, *A Vanished World* (New York: Free Press, 2005).

36. Browne, *Eclipse of Christianity in Asia,* 181; Michael Prawdin, *The Mongol Empire* (New Brunswick, NJ: AldineTransaction, 2006; first published 1940).

37. Lane, "Account of Gregory Bar Hebraeus." Hulegu's wife is quoted from Browne, *Eclipse of Christianity in Asia,* 151–55. Mingana, *Christianity in Central Asia,* 18–19; Dawson, *Mongol Mission;* Isenbike Togan, *Flexibility and Limitation in Steppe Formations* (Leiden: E. J. Brill, 1998).

38. Solomon is quoted from E. A. Wallis Budge, *Book of the Bee*. Browne, *Eclipse of Christianity in Asia*, 159, 151. Reuven Amitai-Preiss, *Mongols and Mamluks* (Cambridge: Cambridge Univ. Press, 1995). Peter Jackson, "The Crisis in the Holy Land in 1260," *English Historical Review* 95 (1980): 481–513.

39. Browne, *Eclipse of Christianity in Asia*, 147–55; Moffett, *History of Christianity in Asia,* 1:424.

40. Dickens, "Nestorian Christianity in Central Asia," 16. Devin A. DeWeese, *Islamization and Native Religion in the Golden Horde* (University Park: Pennsylvania State Univ. Press, 1994).

41. Micheau, "Copts, Melkites, Nestorians and Jacobites," 386; Peter Thorau, *The Lion of Egypt* (London: Longman, 1992); Thomas F. Madden, *The New Concise History of the Crusades* (Rowan & Littlefield, 2005), 181–82.

42. Little, "Coptic Conversion to Islam"; Browne, *Eclipse of Christianity in Asia.*

43. Evetts, *Churches and Monasteries,* 329–31, and 340 for "at Suyut. . . ." Browne, *Eclipse of Christianity in Asia,* 177.

44. M. Perlmann, "Notes on Anti-Christian Propaganda in the Mamluk Empire," *Bulletin of the School of Oriental and African Studies* 10 (1942): 843–61.

45. For "hibernation," see O'Mahony, "Coptic Christianity in Modern Egypt," 490.

46. The account by Al-Maqrizi can be found in Evetts, *Churches and Monasteries,* 305–25.

47. Browne, *Eclipse of Christianity in Asia*, 163–66.

48. Browne, *Eclipse of Christianity in Asia,* 169–70.

49. Browne, *Eclipse of Christianity in Asia,* 163–71; for "The persecutions and disgrace," see Moffett, *History of Christianity in Asia,* 1:476, 1:487.

50. Browne, *Eclipse of Christianity in Asia*, 172; for Persia, see Micheau, "Copts, Melkites, Nestorians and Jacobites," 387–88.

51. Vryonis, *Decline of Medieval Hellenism,* 297–98, 344–48. H. A. R. Gibb, ed., *Ibn Battuta, Travels in Asia and Africa 1325–1354* (London: Broadway House, 1929), 133–34.

52. Vryonis, *Decline of Medieval Hellenism.*

53. Vryonis, *Decline of Medieval Hellenism,* 445.

54. The historian quoted is Dickran Kouymjian, "Armenia from the Fall of the Cilician Kingdom (1375) to the Forced Emigration Under Shah Abbas (1604)," in *The Armenian People from Ancient to Modern Times,* ed. Richard

Hovannisian (New York: St. Martin's Press, 1997), 2:1–50. Angus Stewart, *The Armenian Kingdom and the Mamluks* (Leiden: E. J. Brill, 2002); Razmik Panossian, *The Armenians* (New York: Columbia Univ. Press, 2006).

55. Moffett, *History of Christianity in Asia,* 1:478.

56. Koschorke, Ludwig, and Delgado, *History of Christianity,* 142–154; Shinnie, *Medieval Nubia;* Peter Grossmann, "Christian Nubia and Its Churches," http://www.numibia.net/nubia/christian.htm.

57. "A systematic campaign" is from Adrian Hastings, *The Church in Africa, 1450–1950* (Oxford: Clarendon Press, 1996), 137; Harold G. Marcus, *A History of Ethiopia,* new ed. (Berkeley: Univ. of California Press, 2002).

58. Browne, *Eclipse of Christianity in Asia.*

59. Janet L. Abu-Lughod, *Before European Hegemony* (Oxford: Oxford Univ. Press, 1989). For Aragon, see David Nirenberg, *Communities of Violence* (Princeton, NJ: Princeton Univ. Press, 1996). Michael D. Bailey, *Battling Demons* (University Park: Pennsylvania State Univ. Press, 2003).

60. Browne, *Eclipse of Christianity in Asia,* 180. Ross E. Dunn, *The Adventures of Ibn Battuta,* rev. ed. (Berkeley: Univ. of California Press, 2005). Adolf Reifenberg, *The Struggle Between the Desert and the Sown* (Jerusalem: Hebrew Univ. Press, 1955); Arie S. Issar and Mattanyah Zohar, *Climate Change: Environment and History of the Near East* (New York: Springer, 2007).

61. Stuart J. Borsch, *The Black Death in Egypt and England* (Austin: Univ. of Texas Press, 2005).

62. Justin Marozzi, *Tamerlane* (Cambridge, MA: Da Capo Press, 2006).

63. Dale A. Johnson, "Tamerlane: The Mongol Raider of Mor Gabriel Monastery," http://www.socdigest.org/articles/02jan06.html; Dickens, "Nestorian Christianity in Central Asia," 17.

5. THE LAST CHRISTIANS

1. "An Appeal from Mar Eshai Shimun XXI, Catholicos Patriarch of the Assyrians, to All the Christian Churches" (1933), http://www.edessa.com/histdocs/appeal1933.htm.

2. R. S. Stafford, *The Tragedy of the Assyrians* (Piscataway, NJ: Gorgias Press, 2006).

3. Raphael Lemkin, "Acts Constituting a General (Transnational) Danger Considered as Offences Against the Law of Nations," http://www.preventgenocide.org/lemkin/madrid1933-english.htm. Raphael Lemkin,

Axis Rule in Occupied Europe (Washington, DC: Carnegie Endowment for International Peace, Division of International Law, 1944).

4. Caroline Finkel, *Osman's Dream* (New York: Perseus Books, 2006); Lapidus, *History of Islamic Societies.*

5. Dennis P. Hupchick, *The Bulgarians in the Seventeenth Century* (Jefferson, NC: McFarland, 1993).

6. Wheatcroft, *Infidels.* O'Shea, *Sea of Faith.* For Muslim slaving ventures in the West, see Robert C. Davis, *Christian Slaves, Muslim Masters* (New York: Palgrave Macmillan, 2004); and Giles Milton, *White Gold* (New York: Farrar, Straus and Giroux, 2005).

7. For the *rayah*, see Bostom, *Legacy of Jihad,* 66. Anton Minkov, *Conversion to Islam in the Balkans* (Leiden: E. J. Brill, 2004). Hupchick, *Bulgarians in the Seventeenth Century.* Some accounts of forced conversion are controversial and may be based on bogus documents: Maria Todorova, "Conversion to Islam as a Trope in Bulgarian Historiography, Fiction and Film," *Eurozine* (2003), http://www.eurozine.com/articles/2003–11–04-todorova-en.html. Suphan Kirmizialtin, "Conversion in Ottoman Balkans," *History Compass* 5, no. 2 (2007): 646–57.

8. H. T. Norris, *Islam in the Balkans* (Columbia: Univ. of South Carolina Press, 1993); Mark Pinson, ed., *The Muslims of Bosnia-Herzegovina,* 2nd ed. (Cambridge, MA: Harvard Univ. Press, 1996).

9. Stephen C. Neill, *A History of Christian Missions,* rev. ed. (London: Penguin, 1990); R. Po-chia Hsia, ed., *Cambridge History of Christianity: Reform and Expansion 1500–1660* (Cambridge: Cambridge Univ. Press, 2006); and MacEvitt, *Crusades and the Christian World of the East.*

10. Chidester, *Christianity,* 332.

11. Koschorke, Ludwig, and Delgado, *History of Christianity,* 169; Alastair Hamilton, *The Copts and the West, 1439–1822* (New York: Oxford Univ. Press, 2006).

12. Lobo, "Voyage to Abyssinia." Koschorke, Ludwig, and Delgado, *History of Christianity,* 159.

13. Koschorke, Ludwig, and Delgado, *History of Christianity,* 28.

14. John Joseph, *Muslim-Christian Relations and Inter-Christian Rivalries in the Middle East* (Albany: State Univ. of New York Press, 1983); John Joseph, *The Modern Assyrians of the Middle East* (Leiden: E. J. Brill, 2000); Hastings, *Church in Africa.*

15. K. S. Mathew, ed., *Maritime Malabar and the Europeans, 1500–1962* (London: Greenwich Millennium, 2003); Ines G. Zupanov, *Missionary Tropics* (Ann Arbor: Univ. of Michigan Press, 2005). For a depressing list of some of the works lost, see Mingana, *Christianity in India,* 68.

16. Courbage and Fargues, *Christians and Jews Under Islam;* Edhem Eldem, Daniel Goffman, and Bruce Masters, *The Ottoman City Between East and West* (New York: Cambridge Univ. Press, 1999).

17. Benjamin Braude and Bernard Lewis, *Christians and Jews in the Ottoman Empire* (New York: Holmes and Meier, 1982); Speros Vryonis, "The Experience of Christians Under Seljuk and Ottoman Domination," in Gervers and Bikhazi, *Conversion and Continuity,* 185–216; Bruce Masters, *Christians and Jews in the Ottoman Arab World* (Cambridge: Cambridge Univ. Press, 2001); Zachary Karabell, *People of the Book* (London: John Murray, 2007).

18. Zachariadou, "Great Church in Captivity," 183–84; Finkel, *Osman's Dream,* 310; Oded Peri, *Christianity Under Islam in Jerusalem* (Leiden: E. J. Brill, 2001); Mark Mazower, *Salonica, City of Ghosts* (New York: Random House, 2005). For the traveler, see George A. Bournoutian, ed., *The Travel Accounts of Simeon of Poland* (Costa Mesa, CA: Mazda, 2007).

19. Daniel Goffman, *The Ottoman Empire and Early Modern Europe* (New York: Cambridge Univ. Press, 2002), 85; Avedis K. Sanjian, *The Armenian Communities in Syria Under Ottoman Dominion* (Cambridge: Harvard Univ. Press, 1965).

20. Nomikos Michael Vaporis, *Witnesses for Christ* (Crestwood, NY: St. Vladimir's Seminary Press, 2000); Zachariadou, "Great Church in Captivity," 182.

21. "God perpetuate the empire" is from Timothy Ware, *The Orthodox Church* (London: Penguin, 1964), 105–6. Stefano Carboni, *Venice and the Islamic World, 828–1797* (New Haven, CT: Yale Univ. Press, 2007); Benjamin Arbel, Bernard Hamilton, and David Jacoby, eds., *Latins and Greeks in the Eastern Mediterranean After 1204* (London: Frank Cass, 1989).

22. Quoted in Ware, *Orthodox Church,* 96.

23. Dalrymple, *From the Holy Mountain,* 141. For spells and folk magic, see Hermann Gollancz, ed., *The Book of Protection* (London: Henry Frowde/ Oxford Univ. Press, 1912). For the Catholic comment, see *Catholic Encyclopedia,* s.v. "Syriac Language and Literature," http://www.newadvent. org/cathen/14408a.htm. Sir Austen Henry Layard, *Nineveh and Its Remains:*

With an Account of a Visit to the Chaldæan Christians af Kurdistan, and the Yezidis, or Devil-Worshippers (New York: G. P. Putnam, 1849); Badger, *Nestorians and Their Rituals;* Parry, *Six Months in a Syrian Monastery.*

24. These remarks are drawn from articles in the *Catholic Encyclopedia,* http://www.newadvent.org/cathen/index.html; and from Eldem, Goffman, and Masters, *Ottoman City.*

25. *Catholic Encyclopedia,* s.v. "Diocese of Amida," http://www.newadvent.org/cathen/01429c.htm.

26. Barrett, Kurian, and Johnson, *World Christian Encyclopedia.*

27. The British traveler was Robert Curzon, *Visits to Monasteries in the Levant* (London: John Murray, 1850), liii. Efraim Karsh and Inari Karsh, *Empires of the Sand* (Cambridge, MA: Harvard Univ. Press, 1999).

28. Finkel, *Osman's Dream,* 460.

29. Efraim Karsh, *Islamic Imperialism* (New Haven, CT: Yale Univ. Press, 2006), 97; Leila Tarazi Fawaz, *An Occasion for War* (Berkeley: Univ. of California Press, 1994); Leila Tarazi Fawaz, *Merchants and Migrants in Nineteenth-Century Beirut* (Cambridge, MA: Harvard Univ. Press, 1983); Ussama Makdisi, *The Culture of Sectarianism* (Berkeley: Univ. of California Press, 2000).

30. Finkel, *Osman's Dream;* John Joseph, *The Nestorians and Their Muslim Neighbors* (Princeton, NJ: Princeton Univ. Press, 1961).

31. The account of the Armenian massacres is from Lord Kinross, *The Ottoman Centuries* (New York: Morrow Quill, 1977), 457–60, which includes the quote about "the murderous winter." Sébastien de Courtois, *Forgotten Genocide* (Piscataway, NJ: Gorgias Press, 2004), 106; Gökhan Çetinsaya, *Ottoman Administration of Iraq, 1890–1908* (London: Routledge, 2006).

32. Jonathan Frankel, *The Damascus Affair* (Cambridge: Cambridge Univ. Press, 1996). Ronald Florence, *Blood Libel* (Madison: Univ. of Wisconsin Press, 2004). Salo Baron, "The Jews and the Syrian Massacres of 1860," *Proceedings of the American Academy for Jewish Research* 4 (1932–33): 3–31.

33. Karsh and Karsh, *Empires of the Sand.*

34. The account of Diyarbakir is from Dalrymple, *From the Holy Mountain,* 81. Karsh, *Islamic Imperialism,* 113–18; Peter Balakian, *The Burning Tigris* (New York: HarperCollins, 2003); Donald Bloxham, *The Great Game of Genocide* (Oxford: Oxford Univ. Press, 2005); David Gaunt, *Massacres, Resistance, Protectors* (Piscataway, NJ: Gorgias Press, 2006).

35. Lord Bryce is quoted from Joseph Naayem, *Shall This Nation Die?* (New York: Chaldean Rescue, 1920), http://www.aina.org/books/stnd.htm. Yonan Shahbaz, *The Rage of Islam* (Piscataway, NJ: Gorgias Press, 2006).

36. Bernard Lewis, *The Emergence of Modern Turkey,* 3rd ed. (New York: Oxford Univ. Press, 2001); Bruce Clark, *Twice a Stranger* (Cambridge, MA: Harvard Univ. Press, 2006).

37. "Appeal from Mar Eshai Shimun." (see Chap. 5, note 1.)

38. Speros Vryonis, *The Mechanism of Catastrophe* (New York: Greekworks. com, 2005). For Edessa's Christian population, see Tarzi, "Edessa."

39. Dalrymple, *From the Holy Mountain,* 84.

40. Dalrymple, *From the Holy Mountain,* 81–82 for Lucine; 91.

41. This account of contemporary Middle Eastern Christians is drawn from several sources: Robert Brenton Betts, *Christians in the Arab East,* rev. ed. (Atlanta: John Knox Press, 1978); Kenneth Cragg, *The Arab Christian* (Louisville, KY: Westminster/John Knox Press, 1991); Andrea Pacini, ed., *Christian Communities in the Arab World* (New York: Oxford Univ. Press, 1998); and Anthony O'Mahony, "Syriac Christianity in the Modern Middle East," in Angold, *Cambridge History of Christianity,* 511–35.

42. Sami Zubaida, "Contested Nations," *Nations and Nationalism* 6, no. 3 (2000): 363–82; Phebe Marr, *The Modern History of Iraq,* 2nd ed. (Boulder, CO: Westview Press, 2004); Reeva S. Simon and Eleanor H. Tejirian, eds., *The Creation of Iraq, 1914–1921* (New York: Columbia Univ. Press, 2004).

43. Robert M. Haddad, *Syrian Christians in Muslim Society* (Princeton, NJ: Princeton Univ. Press, 1970); Dalrymple, *From the Holy Mountain,* 154. Barbara L. Carter, *The Copts in Egyptian Politics* (London: Croom Helm, 1986); Sana Hasan, *Christians Versus Muslims in Modern Egypt* (New York: Oxford Univ. Press, 2003); Maya Shatzmiller, ed., *Nationalism and Minority Identities in Islamic Societies* (Montreal: McGill-Queens Univ. Press, 2005). For Armenian contributions to modernizing and national movements in Iran, see Cosroe Chaqueri, ed., *The Armenians of Iran* (Cambridge, MA: Harvard Univ. Press, 1998).

44. Samih K. Farsoun and Naseer H. Aruri, *Palestine and the Palestinians,* 2nd ed. (Boulder, CO: Westview Press, 2006). Dalrymple, *From the Holy Mountain,* 317.

45. For more recent relations between the faiths, see Chad F. Emmett, *Beyond the Basilica* (Chicago: Univ. of Chicago Press, 1995); Charles M. Sennott,

The Body and the Blood (New York: Public Affairs, 2001); and Raphael Israeli, *Green Crescent over Nazareth* (London: Frank Cass, 2002).

46. Jenkins, *God's Continent.*
47. John H. Watson, *Among the Copts* (Eastbourne, UK: Sussex Academic Press, 2000); Pieternella van Doorn-Harder and Karl Vogt, eds., *Between Desert and City* (Eugene, OR: Wipf and Stock, 2004); O'Mahony, "Coptic Christianity in Modern Egypt," 488–510.
48. Suha Rassam, *Christianity in Iraq* (Leominster, England: Gracewing Publishing, 2005).
49. Sandro Magister, "The Last Mass of Father Ragheed, a Martyr of the Chaldean Church," http://chiesa.espresso.repubblica.it/dettaglio.jsp?id= 145921&eng=y.

6. GHOSTS OF A FAITH

1. For the peasants visiting the priest, see Koschorke, Ludwig, and Delgado, *History of Christianity,* 78–79. Harrington, *Japan's Hidden Christians;* Turnbull, *Kakure Kirishitan.*
2. Gretchen D. Starr-LeBeau, *In the Shadow of the Virgin* (Princeton, NJ: Princeton Univ. Press, 2003); David Coleman, *Creating Christian Granada* (Ithaca, NY: Cornell Univ. Press, 2003); L. P. Harvey, *Muslims in Spain, 1500 to 1614* (Chicago: Univ. of Chicago Press, 2005); Benjamin Ehlers, *Between Christians and Moriscos* (Baltimore: Johns Hopkins Univ. Press, 2006). For crypto-Jews, see Jonathan I. Israel, *Diasporas Within a Diaspora* (Boston, MA: E. J. Brill, 2002); Janet L. Jacobs, *Hidden Heritage* (Berkeley: Univ. of California Press, 2002); Stanley M. Hordes, *To the End of the Earth* (New York: Columbia Univ. Press, 2005).
3. Koschorke, Ludwig, and Delgado, *History of Christianity,* 6–7.
4. For the Copts, see Febe Armanios and Bogaç Ergene, "A Christian Martyr Under Mamluk Justice," *Muslim World* 96, no. 1 (2006): 115–45. The preacher is quoted from Perlmann, "Notes on Anti-Christian Propaganda," 858–59. Vryonis, *Decline of Medieval Hellenism,* 441. The most systematic study of crypto-Christianity is in Stavro Skendi, "Crypto-Christianity in the Balkan Area Under the Ottomans," *Slavic Review* 26, no. 2 (1967): 227–46; Skendi also describes the *Linovamvakoi.* Compare Noel Malcolm, "Crypto-Christianity and Religious Amphibianism in the Ottoman Balkans," in *Religious Quest and National Identity in the Balkans,* ed.

Celia Hawkesworth, Muriel Heppell, and Harry Norris (Basingstoke, UK: Palgrave Macmillan, 2001), 91–109; and H. T. Norris, *Popular Sufism of Eastern Europe* (New York: Routledge, 2006).

5. Skendi, "Crypto-Christianity in the Balkan Area," 228, 232.

6. Dalrymple, *From the Holy Mountain;* Kathleen Hughes, *The Church in Early Irish Society* (London: Methuen, 1966).

7. Molly Greene, *A Shared World* (Princeton, NJ: Princeton Univ. Press, 2000).

8. John K. Nelson, *A Year in the Life of a Shinto Shrine* (Seattle: Univ. of Washington Press, 1996), 30–32

9. Bede, *Ecclesiastical History*, bk. 1 vol. 30, http://www.ccel.org/ccel/bede/history.v.i.xxix.html.

10. Alex Metcalfe, *Muslims and Christians in Norman Sicily* (London: Routledge-Curzon, 2003).

11. Finbarr Barry Flood, *The Great Mosque of Damascus* (Leiden: E. J. Brill, 2001); Béatrice Caseau, "Sacred Landscapes," in *Interpreting Late Antiquity,* ed. G. W. Bowersock, Peter Brown, and Oleg Grabar (Cambridge, MA: Harvard Univ. Press, 2001), 48.

12. Vryonis, *Decline of Medieval Hellenism,* 197. For Amida, see "The Chronicle of Edessa," http://www.tertullian.org/fathers/chronicle_of_edessa.htm, fn.29.

13. Dalrymple, *From the Holy Mountain,* 78.

14. Vryonis, *Decline of Medieval Hellenism,* 486.

15. Jenkins, *God's Continent,* 270.

16. Mingana, *Timothy's Apology for Christianity.* John of Damascus, *Writings*, vol. 37 of *The Fathers of the Church* (Washington, DC: Catholic Univ. of America Press, 1958), 153–60. Hoyland, *Seeing Islam.*

17. The story of Bahira is widely cited, but see, for instance, O'Leary, *Greek Science.* Moffett, *History of Christianity in Asia,* 1:326. Kenneth Baxter Wolf, "The Earliest Latin Lives of Muhammad," in Gervers and Bikhazi, *Conversion and Continuity,* 89–101; John Victor Tolan, *Saracens* (New York: Columbia Univ. Press, 2002). For Islam as a Jewish messianic movement, see Patricia Crone and Michael Cook, *Hagarism* (Cambridge: Cambridge Univ. Press, 1977). For Dante, see Jenkins, *God's Continent,* 267.

18. For the illusory crucifixion, see Quran 4: 157. Richard Bell, *The Origin of Islam in Its Christian Environment* (London: Macmillan, 1926); Geoffrey

Parrinder, *Jesus in the Qur'ān* (New York: Oxford Univ. Press, 1977); Gustave E. von Grunebaum, *Islam and Medieval Hellenism* (London: Variorum Reprints, 1976); William E. Phipps, *Muhammad and Jesus* (New York: Continuum, 1996); John C. Reeves, ed., *Bible and Qur'ān* (Leiden: Brill, 2004). Brown, *Rise of Western Christendom,* 281, 290.

19. Christoph Luxenberg, *The Syro-Aramaic Reading of the Koran* (Berlin: Hans Schiler, 2007), 104; see also Christoph Luxenberg, *Die syro-aramäische Lesart des Koran,* 2nd ed. (Berlin: Hans Schiler, 2004). Peter von Sivers, "The Islamic Origins Debate Goes Public," *History Compass* 1 (2003): 1–16; Christoph Burgmer, *Streit um den Koran* (Berlin: Schiler Verlag, 2004). Ibn Warraq, ed., *The Origins of the Koran* (Amherst, NY: Prometheus Books, 1998). Luxenberg's comment on Arab schools is from Sandro Magister, "The Virgins and the Grapes," http://chiesa.espresso.repubblica.it/dettaglio .jsp?id=7025&eng=y.

20. Magister, "Virgins and the Grapes." For the meaning of *Quran,* see Luxenberg, *Syro-Aramaic Reading of the Koran,* 104; for the Eucharist, 322–23. For the grapes, see Luxenberg, *Syro-Aramäische Lesart des Koran,* 255–74. For *quran* and *qeryana,* see William A. Graham, "The Earliest Meaning of 'Quran,'" *Die Welt des Islams* 23 (1984): 361–77.

21. François Nau, *Les Arabes chrétiens de Mésopotamie et de Syrie du VIIe au VIIIe siècle* (Paris: Imprimerie Nationale, 1933); J. Spencer Trimingham, *Christianity Among the Arabs in Pre-Islamic Times* (London: Longman, 1979); Elizabeth Key Fowden, *The Barbarian Plain* (Berkeley: Univ. of California Press, 1999). One prolific author in this area is Irfan Shah"d, whose books include *Byzantium and the Semitic Orient Before the Rise of Islam* (London: Variorum Reprints, 1988) and *Byzantium and the Arabs in the Sixth Century,* 2 vols. (Washington, DC: Dumbarton Oaks Research Library and Collection, 1995–2002).

22. McCrindle, *Christian Topography.*

23. For Jabr, see Moffett, *History of Christianity in Asia,* 1:326.

24. Moffett, *History of Christianity in Asia,* 1:279; Axel Moberg, ed., *The Book of the Himyarites* (Lund, Sweden: C. W. K. Gleerup, 1924); Irfan Shahid, *The Martyrs of Najran* (Brussels: Société des Bollandistes, 1971).

25. Griffith, "Christians and Christianity,", 307–15; Nadia Maria El Cheikh, *Byzantium Viewed by the Arabs* (Cambridge, MA: Harvard Univ. Press, 2004).

26. Quran 5: 82–83. "A Bilingual Papyrus of a Protocol," http://www
    .islamic-awareness.org/History/Islam/Papyri/enlp1.html.

27. Meir M. Bar-Asher and Aryeh Kofsky, *The Nusayri-'Alawi Religion* (Leiden:
    E. J. Brill, 2002); Malise Ruthven, *Islam in the World* (New York: Oxford
    Univ. Press, 2006).

28. Kenneth Parry, *Depicting the Word* (New York: E. J. Brill, 1996); Alice-Mary
    Talbot, ed., *Byzantine Defenders of Images* (Washington, DC: Dumbarton
    Oaks Research Library and Collection, 1998); Leslie Brubaker and John
    Haldon, *Byzantium in the Iconoclast Era* (Aldershot, UK: Ashgate, 2001).

29. Oleg Grabar, *The Dome of the Rock* (Cambridge, MA: Belknap Press, 2006).

30. Dalrymple, *From the Holy Mountain,* 168; for seventh-century travelers, see
    Dennis Meehan ed., *Adamnan's De Locis Sanctis* (Dublin: Dublin Institute
    for Advanced Studies, 1958), 98–99; Jerrilynn D. Dodds, *Architecture and
    Ideology in Early Medieval Spain* (University Park: Pennsylvania State Univ.
    Press, 1990), 98.

31. Gülru Necipoglu, *The Age of Sinan* (Princeton, NJ: Princeton Univ. Press,
    2005).

32. For an extended argument about Christian-Muslim continuities, see
    Smith, *Studies in Early Mysticism,* 125–52.

33. Koschorke, Ludwig, and Delgado, *History of Christianity,* 159; Lobo,
    "Voyage to Abyssinia."

34. Sidney H. Griffith, "Disputing with Islam in Syriac," *Hugoye* 3, no. 1 (2000),
    http://syrcom.cua.edu/Hugoye/Vol3No1/HV3N1Griffith.html.

35. Roberto Tottoli, "Muslim Attitudes Towards Prostration (sujūd)," *Studia
    Islamica* 88 (1998): 5–34; Dalrymple, *From the Holy Mountain,* 105.

36. Nadia M. El-Cheikh, "Describing the Other to Get at the Self," *Journal of
    the Economic and Social History of the Orient* 40 (1997): 239–50; Liz James,
    ed., *Women, Men, and Eunuchs* (London and New York: Routledge, 1997).
    For the Mesopotamian case, see Harrak, *Chronicle of Zuqnīn,* 245.

37. For apologetics, see Browne, *Eclipse of Christianity in Asia.* Gabriel Said
    Reynolds, *A Muslim Theologian in the Sectarian Milieu* (Leiden and Boston: E. J.
    Brill, 2004); Dalrymple, *From the Holy Mountain,* 62–63. I owe this information
    about the Balkans to my colleague Tijana Krstic.

38. Dina Le Gall, *A Culture of Sufism* (Albany: State Univ. of New York Press,
    2005).

39. Smith, *Studies in Early Mysticism.*

40. Chryssavgis, *John Climacus.*

41. Smith, *Studies in Early Mysticism.* For wool garments, see Mingana, *Christianity in India,* 35.

42. For Basra, see Mingana, *Christianity in India,* 5. Margaret Smith, *Rabi'a the Mystic and Her Fellow-Saints in Islam* (Cambridge: Cambridge Univ. Press, 1928); Browne, *Eclipse of Christianity in Asia,* 131.

43. Browne, *Eclipse of Christianity in Asia,* 130–31.

44. Browne, *Eclipse of Christianity in Asia,* 130–32; Karen Armstrong, *Islam: A Short History* (New York: Modern Library, 2000), 88; Tarif Khalidi, *The Muslim Jesus* (Cambridge, MA: Harvard Univ. Press, 2001), 42. Jane Dammen McAuliffe, *Qur'ānic Christians* (Cambridge: Cambridge Univ. Press, 1991).

45. Khalidi, *Muslim Jesus.*

46. Valerie J. Hoffman, *Sufism, Mystics, and Saints in Modern Egypt* (Columbia, SC: Univ. of South Carolina Press, 1995); Christopher S. Taylor, *In the Vicinity of the Righteous* (Boston: E. J. Brill, 1999); Richard J. A. McGregor, *Sanctity and Mysticism in Medieval Egypt* (Albany: State Univ. of New York Press, 2004).

47. Mary F. Thurlkill, *Chosen Among Women* (Notre Dame, IN: Univ. of Notre Dame Press, 2008).

48. Vryonis, *Decline of Medieval Hellenism,* 369–77; Irène Mélikoff, *Hadji Bektach: Un mythe et ses avatars* (Leiden: E. J. Brill, 1998).

49. Tord Olsson, *Alevi Identity* (London: RoutledgeCurzon, 1998); Paul J. White and Joost Jongerden, eds., *Turkey's Alevi Enigma* (Leiden: Brill, 2003); H. T. Norris, *Popular Sufism of Eastern Europe* (New York: Routledge, 2006).

50. Vryonis, *Decline of Medieval Hellenism,* 385–87.

51. Micheau, "Copts, Melkites, Nestorians and Jacobites," 402.

52. F. W. Hasluck, *Christianity and Islam Under the Sultans,* 2 vols. (Oxford: Clarendon Press, 1929); Dalrymple, *From the Holy Mountain,* 339–341.

53. Vryonis, *Decline of Medieval Hellenism,* 487–88. The archaeologist is Frederick Jones Bliss, *The Religions of Modern Syria and Palestine* (New York: Charles Scribner's, 1912), 27–28.

54. Dalrymple, *From the Holy Mountain,* 188.

7. HOW FAITHS DIE

1. Mark Twain, *Following the Equator* (New York: AMS Press, 1971).

2. Jenkins, *God's Continent.*

3. Thomas F. Glick, *Islamic and Christian Spain in the Early Middle Ages* (Leiden: E. J. Brill, 2005); Metcalfe, *Muslims and Christians*. For intermarriage, see Gladys Frantz-Murphy, "Conversion in Early Islamic Egypt: The Economic Factor," in Hoyland, *Muslims and Others,* 323–30.

4. Vryonis, *Decline of Medieval Hellenism*.

5. Borsch, *Black Death*.

6. Quoted in Vryonis, *Decline of Medieval Hellenism,* 406.

7. Bat Ye'or, *Decline of Eastern Christianity*.

8. Caseau, "Sacred Landscapes," 21–59.

9. H. A. R. Gibb, ed., *Ibn Battuta, Travels in Asia and Africa 1325–1354* (London: Broadway House, 1929), 147–49. For the Egyptian case, see Evetts, *Churches and Monasteries,* 318.

10. For Kairouan and its historical setting, see Douglas Sladen, *Carthage and Tunis,* 2 vols. (London: Hutchinson & Co., 1906). For Christian attempts to create their own landscape after the Reconquista, see A. Katie Harris, *From Muslim to Christian Granada* (Baltimore: Johns Hopkins Univ. Press, 2007).

11. "One could visit a variety" is from Bethany J. Walker, "Commemorating the Sacred Spaces of the Past," *Near Eastern Archaeology* 67, no. 1 (2004): 26–40. For the earlier creation of the Christian landscape, see John M. Howe, "The Conversion of the Physical World," in Muldoon, *Varieties of Religious Conversion,* 63–80. For the critical role of pilgrimage, see Robert Ousterhout, ed., *The Blessings of Pilgrimage* (Urbana: Univ. of Illinois Press, 1990); R. A. Markus, *The End of Ancient Christianity* (Cambridge: Cambridge Univ. Press, 1991); David Frankfurter, ed., *Pilgrimage and Holy Space in Late Antique Egypt* (Leiden: E. J. Brill, 1998); Otto F. A. Meinardus, *Coptic Saints and Pilgrimages* (Cairo and New York: American Univ. in Cairo Press, 2002); Maribel Dietz, *Wandering Monks, Virgins, and Pilgrims* (University Park: Pennsylvania State Univ. Press, 2005); and Jaœ Elsner and Ian Rutherford, eds., *Pilgrimage in Graeco-Roman and Early Christian Antiquity* (New York: Oxford Univ. Press, 2005). Looking at the destruction of the older sacred geography, many parallels come to mind from Christian Europe, especially in the age of the Reformation; see, for example, Eamon Duffy, *The Stripping of the Altars,* 2nd ed. (New Haven, CT: Yale Univ. Press, 2005).

12. The quotation is from Shaikh Hasan Al Kafrawi, in Jacob Marcus, *The Jew in the Medieval World* (New York: Jewish Publication Society, 1938), 15–19. Bat Ye'or, *Decline of Eastern Christianity*.

13. For Damascus, see Frederick Jones Bliss, *The Religions of Modern Syria and Palestine* (New York: Charles Scribner's, 1912), 29. For Urumia, see Thomas Laurie, *Woman and Her Saviour in Persia* (Boston: Gould and Lincoln, 1863).

14. Samir Khalil Samir and Jørgen S. Nielsen, eds., *Christian Arabic Apologetics During the Abbasid Period, 750–1258* (Leiden: E. J. Brill, 1994); Griffith, *Yahya ibn 'Adi*; Sidney H. Griffith, *The Beginnings of Christian Theology in Arabic* (Burlington, VT: Ashgate, 2002); Sandra Toenies Keating, *Defending the "People of Truth" in the Early Islamic Period* (Leiden: E. J. Brill, 2006); Grypeou, Swanson, and Thomas, *Eastern Christianity.* For Bible translation, see David Thomas, ed., *The Bible in Arab Christianity* (Leiden: E. J. Brill, 2006).

15. Quoted in Browne, *Eclipse of Christianity in Asia,* 48.

16. Brown, *Rise of Western Christendom,* 315.

17. Lapidus, *History of Islamic Societies.*

18. Micheau, "Copts, Melkites, Nestorians and Jacobites," 389.

19. Peter Alvar, quoted in Haines, *Christianity and Islam in Spain,* 118. Thomas E. Burman, *Religious Polemic and the Intellectual History of the Mozarabs, c. 1050–1200* (Leiden: E. J. Brill, 1994); Mar'a Angeles Gallego, "The Languages of Medieval Iberia and Their Religious Dimension," *Medieval Encounters* 9, no. 1 (2003): 107–39.

20. Browne, *Eclipse of Christianity in Asia,* 90.

21. "Islam has blotted out" is from Browne, *Eclipse of Christianity in Asia,* 160. Kublai Khan is quoted from A. C. Moule, *Christians in China Before the Year 1550* (London: Society for Promoting Christian Knowledge, 1930), 156.

22. Browne, *Eclipse of Christianity in Asia,* 184.

23. Vryonis, *Decline of Medieval Hellenism,* 435.

8. THE MYSTERY OF SURVIVAL

1. The quote "in no part" is from Holme, *Christian Churches in North Africa,* 187. Isichei, *History of Christianity in Africa;* Bengt Sundkler and Christopher Steed, *A History of the Church in Africa* (Cambridge: Cambridge Univ. Press, 2000).

2. For the conversion of the Berbers to Islam, see Elizabeth Savage, *A Gateway to Hell, a Gateway to Paradise* (Princeton, NJ: Darwin Press, 1997). Michael Brett, "The Spread of Islam in Egypt and North Africa," in *North Africa: Islam and Modernization,* ed. Michael Brett (London: Frank

Cass, 1973); Joseph Cuoq, *L'église d'Afrique du Nord* (Paris: Le Centurion, 1984); Mohammed Talbi, "Le Christianisme maghrébin," in Gervers and Bikhazi, *Conversion and Continuity*, 313–51.

3. Holme, *Christian Churches in North Africa*. Mark A. Handley, "Disputing the End of African Christianity," in *Vandals, Romans and Berbers*, ed. A. H. Merrills (Aldershot, UK: Ashgate, 2004), 291–310.

4. Holme, *Christian Churches in North Africa*, 253–54.

5. Robert C. Gregg, ed., *The Life of Antony and the Letter to Marcellinus, by Athanasius* (New York: Paulist Press, 1980). E. A. Wallis Budge, *Coptic Martyrdoms* (London: British Museum, 1914); Brown, *Society and the Holy*. For conditions in neighboring Palestine, see Jennifer L. Hevelone-Harper, *Disciples of the Desert* (Baltimore: Johns Hopkins Univ. Press, 2005).

6. Micheau, "Copts, Melkites, Nestorians and Jacobites," 373–403. Edward R. Hardy, Jr., *Christian Egypt, Church and People* (New York: Oxford Univ. Press, 1952); James E. Goehring and Janet A. Timbie, eds., *The World of Early Egyptian Christianity* (Washington, DC: Catholic Univ. of America Press, 2007); and Kamil, *Christianity in the Land of the Pharaohs*.

7. The quote is from Perlmann, "Notes on Anti-Christian Propaganda," 847. Armanios and Ergene, "Christian Martyr Under Mamluk Justice," 115–45. Georges C. Anawati, "The Christian Communities in Egypt in the Middle Ages," in Gervers and Bikhazi, *Conversion and Continuity*, 237–51.

8. Bahaa 'Taher, *Aunt Safiyya and the Monastery* (Berkeley: Univ. of California Press, 1996). Mark Gruber, *Journey Back to Eden* (New York: Orbis, 2002).

9. Yitzhak Hen, *Culture and Religion in Merovingian Gaul, A.D. 481–751* (Leiden: E. J. Brill, 1995); J. M. Wallace-Hadrill, *The Frankish Church* (New York: Oxford Univ. Press, 1983); Chris Wickham and Inge Lyse Hansen, *The Long Eighth Century* (Leiden: E. J. Brill 2000); Julia M. H. Smith, *Europe After Rome* (New York: Oxford Univ. Press, 2005); Barbara Yorke, *The Conversion of Britain* (New York: Pearson/Longman, 2006).

10. Bede, *Life of Cuthbert*, chap. 3, in *Two Lives of Saint Cuthbert*, ed. Bertram Colgrave (New York: Greenwood Press, 1969), 162–65.

11. Leslie Webster and Michelle Brown, *Transformation of the Roman World AD 400–900* (Berkeley: Univ. of California Press, 1997); Smith, *Europe After Rome*.

12. Wickham, *Framing the Early Middle Ages*; Lester K. Little, ed., *Plague and the End of Antiquity* (Cambridge: Cambridge Univ. Press, 2007); William Rosen, *Justinian's Flea* (New York: Viking, 2007).

13. Fernand Braudel, *The Mediterranean and the Mediterranean World in the Age of Philip II* (London: Fontana/Collins, 1975), 1:34–35.

14. The traveler is quoted in Braudel, *The Mediterranean and the Mediterranean World,* 1:40. For the Maronites, see Bat Ye'or, *The Dhimmi* (Madison, NJ: Fairleigh Dickinson Univ. Press, 1985), 62

15. Daniel Power and Naomi Standen, eds., *Frontiers in Question* (Basingstoke, UK: Macmillan, 1999); David Abulafia and Nora Berend, eds., *Medieval Frontiers* (Aldershot, UK: Ashgate, 2002).

16. Tamara Green, *The City of the Moon God* (Leiden: E. J. Brill, 1992).

17. Lewis, *Emergence of Modern Turkey.*

18. Barrett, Kurian, and Johnson, *World Christian Encyclopedia.*

9. ENDINGS AND BEGINNINGS

1. Shusaku Endo, *Silence* (London: Quartet, 1976), 97.

2. Quoted in Bostom, *Legacy of Jihad,* 611 (my emphasis).

3. For John of Córdoba, see Dodds, *Architecture and Ideology,* 90. Solomon is quoted from E. A. Wallis Budge, *Book of the Bee.* For apocalyptic interpretations, see Griffith, "Disputing with Islam in Syriac."

4. R. Payne Smith, *The Third Part of the Ecclesiastical History of John Bishop of Ephesus* (Oxford: Oxford Univ. Press, 1860), http://www.tertullian.org/fathers/ephesus_7_book6.htm.

5. George Minamiki, *The Chinese Rites Controversy* (Chicago: Loyola Univ. Press, 1985); Liam Matthew Brockey, *Journey to the East* (Cambridge, MA: Belknap Press, 2007).

6. Quoted in John Foster, *The Church of the T'ang Dynasty* (London: Society for Promoting Christian Knowledge, 1939), 115.

7. Browne, *Eclipse of Christianity in Asia,* 179, 182.

8. Jenkins, *God's Continent.*

9. Thomas Babington Macaulay, "Ranke's History of the Popes," in *Critical and Historical Essays* (London: Longman, Brown, Green and Longmans, 1854), 128.

Acknowledgments

I am blessed with a number of remarkable colleagues and friends, who have been generous in sharing their knowledge: these include Jonathan Bonk, Christian Brady, Jonathan Brockopp, Roger Finke, Paul Harvey, Gary Knoppers, Tijana Krstic, Gregg Roeber, Gonzalo Rubio, and Janina Safran.

Also freely acknowledged—and very much missed—is my late friend Bill Petersen, one of the great modern scholars of Christian origins and of Eastern Christian history and literature.

In addition, I owe special thanks to Roger Freet, my editor at HarperOne, and to my agent, Elyse Cheney.

As I have said so often in the past, I say again without hesitation that the book could not have been written without the support of my wife, Liz Jenkins.

Index